Gone is the whiteness
of snow—
green returns
in the grass of the fields,
in the canopies of trees,
and the airy grace of spring
is with us again.
Thus time revolves,
the passing hour that steals
the light
brings a message:
immortality for us, is impossible.
Warm winds will be followed by cold.

—Horace's Odes (IV, 7)

Life Stories
The Book of Obituaries

Susan Oleson

United Writers Press
Asheville, N.C.
2022

ISBN: 978-1-952248-22-1 (print)

ISBN: 978-1-952248-23-8 (ebook)

Published by:
United Writers Press
Asheville, NC 28803
www.UnitedWritersPress.com
828-505-1037

Cover photograph courtesy of Fred Laberge.

Printed in the United States of America.

For my beloved daughters
and precious grandchildren—
the highlights of my life story

Contents

Author's Note

Why did I spend years working on a book about obituaries? Because I am fascinated by how people lived their lives. Because common and uncommon truths are revealed through these life stories. And because I believe every life has significance.

Life stories have always captivated me. When meeting someone, I am curious (I prefer this description rather than snoopy) about their backstory. The whole of their life might not qualify as enthralling, but invariably there are portions that are memorable. I enjoy mining these life stories for those hidden gems. This has the allure of a treasure hunt to me. Ordinary people have extraordinary insights that may be similar or different from mine. Either way, there is something to be learned. We recognize each other in our stories. We share the need for love, respect, and meaning.

When I was growing up in New Hampshire, my family subscribed to a daily newspaper. For as long as I can remember, I'd at least scan the local obituaries and photographs. Even when I traveled, I would read the obits from that part of the country. I don't read them just to see if someone I know died. I realize that my reading the obituary does nothing for the deceased or their family. But I know I took the time to note their life and death out of respect for their story.

As I read obituaries, I began to notice that people chose to avoid saying "died." I started a list on a notepad of the other words that people chose to denote death. That led to more lists of out-of-the-ordinary aspects of obituaries. Once I retired, the time available to pursue the project expanded. So did my research. Reading obituaries became nearly a compulsion. I was spending hours a day reading and recording different excerpts that caught my eye. Where do I stop? Obviously, the obituaries keep coming! Common sense had to overcome my empathy.

People may wonder where all these obituaries came from. Legacy.com has hyperlinked listings of obituaries from many newspapers. I would spend hours selecting newspapers from different cities and reading the obits. One "treasure" for my growing collection would be discovered after reading 30-40 obituaries. As these nuggets accumulated, I started grouping them into common themes, then making subgroups. My hardest task was culling obits. I wanted each of these people in my collection, especially if I had seen a photograph with the obituary. Finally I added my own observations and ideas.

When compiling excerpts from obituaries, what struck me was the singularity of a person's life as well as the common threads that weave through many lives. Not many obits note that the deceased will be remembered for their potato salad recipe or hobby of carving avocado pits. But the frequently repeated declarations of love and the importance of family, friends, community, and pets are the universal qualities that we share. I was inspired by the values expressed in these life stories. It was evident that a life does not have to be complicated or sophisticated to be fulfilling. People with ordinary lives were remembered as truly happy and content. In the end, even the successful, as defined by society's standards, valued relationships and life's simple pleasures. I hope you enjoy and benefit from reading these small stories that capture special moments from so many lives.

It sounds odd that reading about dead people would be fulfilling, but it was for me. These people did not experience anything other than what we will all face. Forgive my metaphor, but even though you know the river is streaming toward the waterfall, it doesn't mean you can't enjoy the passing scenery while on the exhilarating ride. You might even dodge the rapids by watching the rafts ahead of you.

After reading thousands of these loving legacies, I believe that nearly all of these people enriched some lives and made the world a better place. Every life has importance and creates a lasting legacy. Each of these people left a hole no one else can fill in quite the same way.

One obituary deeply touched me. It was written by an experienced author and a keen observer of people: "You likely didn't know Barry.

Take a moment to read about his life and the lesson he leaves us in death. Every good soul deserves to be remembered. Wherever life took him, he went with a hopeful spirit even during his final days under hospice care. He died of cancer at 67. He believed heaven would be a beautiful place. He had no living relatives. He never married or had children. The love he received came from the skilled care nursing staffers who cared for him. He suffered from bipolar disorder. It shaped his life, as it does the lives of 5.7 million other Americans who suffer often in undeserved shame. He didn't ask for this obituary. A writer who took an interest in him near the end felt called to tell his story. Everyone's life is worth celebrating. Everyone has something to teach us in death. This includes Barry, who had no family and suffered from mental illness, but who got out of bed every day, no matter the pain, smiling." Barry left us a lesson that bears repeating.

I was surprised at how that obituary so closely mirrors my own beliefs. People deserve to be honored and celebrated in death. Lessons we learn from others inform our perspectives and enrich our life.

Finally, I hope this book is of assistance when the time comes for you to write one of these final love letters. Crafting an obituary is not an easy assignment. These hundreds of examples are intended to encourage you and also to give you permission to do it your way. Obituaries should be as unique as was the deceased. Some of these stories will break your heart or make you cry. Some may frighten you. Some will make you laugh. Obituaries may announce a death, but they attempt to capture a life. And in the end, it is our stories that outlast us.

We are a distinctive blend of relationships, experiences, personalities, and the endless vagaries of life. Each of us adds a unique piece to the mosaic of humanity. We share this planet for a brief moment. There is power in sharing our life story. We are reminded we are not alone. My hope is that you recognize all that we have in common and ponder what gives meaning to your life and why your time on earth matters. This is a book about life. I hope it inspires you.

Disclaimer

I have read thousands of obituaries from around the country in an attempt to illustrate some of the ways people memorialize their loved ones. I have honored each person's privacy by not including surnames. Some specific places are named if deemed essential or innocuous. With a couple of exceptions, I have not quoted any person's full obituary. I have selected only those portions that stood out to me for various reasons—their humanity, uniqueness, simplicity, eloquence, poignancy, quirkiness, or humor. Anything that is bulleted or appears in quotations is from an obituary. Many excerpts were edited for brevity. Lastly, I have intentionally omitted deaths of children.

Life Stories

The Book of Obituaries

"Memento Mori"
Remember Your Death

Life's Little Pleasures

"He lived for 75 years just as he wanted—visiting family and friends, a cup of coffee in his hand, a copy of *The New York Times* under his arm, falling in love with life, eating good food, traveling the world, and flouting convention wherever he went."

— *Chuck's obituary*

Among the lessons to be learned from obituaries is where people found the joy that brightened their lives. Often it was the simple things—friendships, food, nature, pets, and hobbies.

- He loved the sunshine.
- He loved A&W root beer floats.
- He will be remembered for his love of meat and lobster.
- She enjoyed housework.
- He loved to sit in his recliner with his cats purring away and his grand-dog sleeping at his feet.

It's not achievements and honors that are the sources of happiness or define one's time on earth. It is life's passions, some unique, even quirky, but many of them universal, reminding us that we are more alike than different.

> **"He loved computers, outer space, and shirts with pockets."**
>
> — *Don's obituary*

Three pleasures were commonly listed. The third one was sometimes surprising.

- She enjoyed life, family, and makeup.
- He loved dancing, thrift shopping, and Elizabeth Taylor.
- He loved playing tennis, the Miami Dolphins, the color turquoise.
- She loved music, dancing, and she especially loved pigs.
- She loved Vince Gill, Bingo, and gambling.
- He loved law enforcement, Sinatra, and the dog track.
- He enjoyed horseback riding, skiing, and had impeccable taste in ice cream.
- He was a fan of baseball, Broadway, and his bourbon.
- He loved diners, black coffee, and a hot hand of cards.
- She enjoyed the simple pleasures of life like being with her family, thrift shopping, and a dipped cone from Dairy Queen.
- He enjoyed crossword puzzles, tending to his feathered friends, and drawing to his heart's content.
- He loved his family; dogs of all ages, breeds, and temperaments; and bad puns.
- He loved baseball, opera, and retelling old jokes.
- She enjoyed practical jokes, self-deprecating humor, and a good accidental fall.

"She loved calves, kittens, lambs, springtime, buttercups, the outdoors, riding, the smell of sagebrush, rain, gardening, playing golf, and watching her grandkids dance."

— *Eva's obituary*

People find delight in a wide variety of pleasures.

- She loved gardening, sailing, tennis, playing with grandchildren, the 23rd Psalm, traveling, gardening, doing embroidery by a blazing fire, and gardening. She was merciless with men who always talked about themselves.
- Family and friends were always paramount to him, followed closely by gardening, sailing, reading, backyard birding, and his recently treasured double-scooped chocolate ice cream cones.
- He particularly enjoyed old-time country music, indoor soccer, Molson Golden beer, Italian food, and coffee ice cream. He never liked long-sleeve shirts.
- She loved to fall asleep with the sound of running water, so she and her husband purchased a home next to the river. She loved song birds. She especially liked bald eagles, her family dogs, chickens, and ducks!
- He had a passion for country music, kitchen gadgets, growing things, the great outdoors, and strolling hand-in-hand with his wife.
- He loved rip-snorting thunderstorms, delicate lady slippers, juicy blueberry pies, and the haunting cry of loons.

Some obituaries are startling in their details on a life lived well.

- In no particular order, she enjoyed coffee, books, Beckett, hand-rolled cigarettes, Nabokov, dancing, Bonnie Raitt, Kafka, fountain pens, the Grateful Dead, typewriters, Ray Charles, flannel shirts, Flannery O'Connor, guitars, and her two most-beloved dogs, Zen and Pluto.
- He loved fatback, oyster stew, soft scrambled eggs, dim sum, potted meat, popcorn, canned macaroni and cheese, and anything that was dietarily restricted. The more forbidden it was, the better it tasted.

- He loved travel, writing, the Mets, diners, Diet Cokes with no ice, Linzer Tortes, Wiener Schnitzel, and palatschinken. *(That is a crepe-like pancake.)*
- He loved deep fried Southern food smothered in Cane Syrup, fishing at Santee Cooper Lake, Little Debbie Cakes, *Two and a Half Men*, beautiful women, Reese's Cups, and Jim Beam. Not necessarily in that order. He hated vegetables and hypocrites. Not necessarily in that order.

> **"He loved sitting in his New York or London library, enjoying a white wine Kir, reading a favorite periodical, a history or a scholarly journal while listening to classical music."**
>
> — *Richard's obituary*

Some of life's pleasures are sophisticated.

- She loved politics, place cards, seating arrangements, crossword puzzles, cruising, road trips, thank you notes, and her Rolodex.
- He was passionate about photography, vintage Porsche cars, aeronautics, astronomy, computers, fine art, fine food, and fine wine.
- He loved traveling, playing chess, swimming from his boat, his bow ties, black socks, and wingtip shoes (the latter two showing up even at the beach). He loved the evening news, *Nova*, politics, and science. He loved ice cream, chocolate, and a good beer.
- He was a modern day Renaissance man who studied computers and technology before they were popular. He enjoyed many diverse hobbies including golf, computer programming, 3D printing, leather and wood working, gun smithing, welding, ranching, hunting, fishing, and SpaceX.
- She loved many pets, places, and amusements including miniature schnauzers, the memory of childhood summers in Muskoka, silent films, red lipstick, solitude, world music, South Asian clothes, the art of Frida Kahlo and Helen Frankenthaler, and the satisfying look of well-designed rooms.

- He was a connoisseur of classical music, books, trains, British comedies, ice cream, trains, chocolate, rice pudding, and trains.
- She had a fondness for cashmere sweaters, tea from England, Joy perfume, and daisies.
- She loved art, arguments, politics, literature, history, and music. She did not do "fun."
- She was an ardent lover of her family, Yerucham and Israel, the arts, travel, literature, crossword puzzles, and cerebral conversation.

> **"She loved to eat moose nose, Doritos, dill pickles, and dry meat."**
>
> — *Francine's obituary*

People discover joy in the most unusual ways.

- She loved making agutaq by finely grating caribou fat and whipping it by hand to a fluffy, creamy texture. *(Agutaq is an Alaskan ice cream made from whipped fat mixed with berries.)*
- He loved drag racing and was the proud owner of the Alaskan Grizzly, an AA fuel-altered nitro-burning dragster that currently holds the State of Alaska's best speed record.
- He loved to sing in the car and had pork rinds on the seat along with other snacks for the girls. He loved to eat vegetables and had many gardens.
- He loved sweet tea, watermelon, pickle and peanut butter sandwiches, waterfalls, his dog Steve, and monkey movies.

> **"He loved his family, authentic hole-in-the-wall restaurants, his bright vintage car, exotic travel adventures, a classic rock tune, a meal sourced from his garden, and an afternoon boating on the bay."**
>
> *—James's obituary*

These people were complex, or at least had particular or eclectic interests.

- He loved the family house, Bach, calligraphy, miniature writing, award-winning cider making, bread baking, rowing, reading, hiking, and making metal sculptures.
- He loved his big cars: the Ford Galaxy, Chevy Impala, and wood-sided station wagon. His favorite land yacht, however, was his extra-large white Buick Roadmaster. He liked bowling, billiards, cribbage, canasta, and egg foo young and cheesecake.
- He enjoyed communion, speaking Polish, ice cream, and his cigars, a passion the family may not have shared. He enjoyed elaborate practical jokes, over-tipping in restaurants, sushi, and Marx Brothers' movies.
- She loved coffee, sweet tea, fried okra, fried oysters, chocolate, rescuing dogs, cruising on a pontoon boat with her dog, baking pound cakes, the color red, beach music, and above all sitting on her porch by the lake with family and friends watching the water go by.
- She loved chicken pot pie, strawberry shortcake, Stargazer lilies, Andy Griffith, all things pink, and her decades-old Mercedes which she was determined to drive until the wheels fell off.
- She loved her Lumbee Tribal roots, her church, shopping, cayenne pepper, and her Cadillac "Lizzy."
- She liked Elvis, homegrown tomatoes, soup made from scratch, Las Vegas, happy grandchildren, and a gentle rain.

> **"He took pleasure in simple things: a setting sun, a baby's smile, a cloud formation. He was always quick to laugh and engage in a practical joke. He was very humble and never took himself too seriously."**
>
> *— John's obituary*

Some obituary writers were adept at capturing the nuances of a life, offering insights into the personality of the deceased.

- She loved to drink martinis, smoke cigarettes, sing the songs of Noel Coward and George Gershwin, and question people about their lives and beliefs and careers.
- She took care of the Earth; recycling, composting, picking up garbage, growing vegetables, and taking only what she needed. She also avoided pesticides and idling her car.
- She was fond of writing poetry, drinking black coffee, and sending letters to friends and family, always including a Bible verse on the back of the envelope.
- She loved flowers, picnics, the Oregon Coast, crossword puzzles, butterflies, hummingbirds, and was happiest when holding a baby.
- He loved everything fast—cars, motorcycles, and boats.
- He loved driving his red convertible Cadillac in local parades, wearing short shorts and Sorel boots for yard work, rooting for his favorite teams, and sporting his blue hair, matching glasses, and crocs.
- She loved flowers, babies, nature, music, the written word, and had great compassion for animals and the downtrodden.
- He loved a good cigar in one hand and fine scotch in the other.

This man's children wrote his obituary and mourned him with loving humor. Here lived a gourmand who knew what he wanted—and so did his family. He must have been quite a character: "For his signature bacon and tomato sandwich, he procured 100% all-white Bunny Bread from Georgia, Blue Plate mayonnaise from New Orleans, Sauer's black pepper from Virginia, homegrown tomatoes from outside Oxford, and Tennessee's Benton bacon from his bacon-of-the-month subscription. As a point of pride, he purported to remember every meal he had eaten in his 80 years of life. He had a life-long love affair with deviled eggs, Lane cakes, boiled peanuts, Vienna sausages on saltines, his homemade canned fig preserves, pork chops, turnip greens, and buttermilk served in martini glasses garnished with cornbread.

Often we define a successful life by status, wealth, or glory. Then we read an obituary that mentions happiness found in holding a baby, the love of music, or that old Ford Galaxy. What gives joy to your heart? May you learn to appreciate and luxuriate in life's simple pleasures.

The Love Of A Lifetime

> **"Everywhere we went we held hands. It's hard to write with tears in my eyes. I was the luckiest man on earth."**
>
> — *Bernice's obituary*
> *(Written by her husband of 72 years)*

Is there anything more meaningful than having someone with whom to spend your life? The truly fortunate souls are the ones who find and treasure lasting love. The sacred nature of such relationships are at the heart of some obituaries.

> **"He met his wife at the age of 10 and began dating her at 16, the beginning of a lifelong partnership between two strong-willed people with a zest for social involvement, a love of adventure, and a gift for drawing friends into their orbit."**
>
> — *Saul's obituary*

This depth of feeling is inspiring when people meet at such a young age and are able to sustain their love for a lifetime.

- His family moved when he was five and settled across the street from four-year-old Dorothy. They quickly became inseparable friends. His lifelong love for his wife, he liked to tell people, was the source of his warmth and good humor.
- There was a child in his neighborhood whom he met when they were five. They both attended the same high school. She was beautiful and played the field. He was smitten, patient, and waited. He first asked her to marry him on the playground ice rink when

he was in the fourth grade and she was in the third grade. They married and enjoyed a happy life for the next 63 years.

- While skipping Sunday school, he looked in the window of the schoolroom, and a new redhead smiled at him and he smiled back. The wheels were set in motion for them to date for six years and share 52 years of marriage. She was his partner and best friend. His last words were "Love you" in response to her words.
- He met his wife in a sailing race in Woods Hole when he was 11 years old and she was nine. They were married for 56 years, until her death.

> **"She and her husband were incredibly devoted to and in love with each other. They met 83 years ago in the eighth grade and married in 1948. He was by her side when she died."**
>
> *— Martha's obituary*

Who knew the eighth grade was a particularly romantic time?

- She met her husband when they became friends in the eighth grade, by high school they became sweethearts and were chosen by their classmates for the superlative "Most Dependable." They are pictured in their 1957 yearbook leaning back to back supporting each other. Little did they know then that they would spend over 60 years together in loving support of one another.
- She was a firecracker from the start. Energetic and hard-working, intelligent and independent; she was valedictorian of her graduating class. Having met the love of her life in eighth grade, she married him after college.

> **"His wife was the only girl he ever dated; they courted for seven years then were married for 66 years. This love began in high school and ended when she died. He expressed gratitude for the 73 years he had with his high school sweetheart—a beauty queen at Duke University—and the love of his life."**
>
> — *Benjamin's obituary*

The teen years are a time of budding romances, but rarely do young people make choices that weather the tests of time. These couples were fortunate, chose wisely, matured together, or all three.

- Two things caught his attention when he first laid eyes on her in horticulture lab more than 40 years ago: her very long hair and her very short shorts. He made a beeline to her to partner up. "I usually work alone," she said. But he persisted and soon learned that she wasn't just the prettiest girl in class but also one of the smartest. They made the seamless transition from lab partners to life partners for the next 40 years.
- During high school she met the sailor of her dreams and after her graduation married the love of her life. They were married for 71 years.
- He met the girl who would be his wife at the tender age of 14. When they were 20 they eloped and lived an idyllic life for the next 70 years.
- At 16 he met Julia, and they exchanged cards and letters for seven years before they married. His greatest joy was spending time with her, the love of his life, and they cared for each other throughout their 67-year marriage.
- At age 17, he spotted a 16-year-old girl at a dance. "She's the one for me," he recalled thinking of the girl in the purple dress. With his passing he rejoins the love of his life and wife of 64 years. Their exceptional love and partnership was the foundation on which they built their world together. Their vibrant union set the standard for their family and defined two remarkably full lives.
- Walking up the brick walkway of her friend's home at age 16, she heard the piano music of Rachmaninoff through an open

window. She entered the house to meet the pianist, her future husband. They were close to celebrating their 70th wedding anniversary. Each considered the other their soulmate. He described their marriage as two separate oak trees, with separate sturdy roots, whose branches intertwined.

> **"He said he kicked the back of her chair in sociology class to get her attention. She turned around to see who was annoying her; she was attracted to his blue eyes. They spent 70 happy years together."**
>
> *— Joe's obituary*

College romances and the connections that blossom in the early adult years can lead to lasting relationships.

- On her first day in college, she took a seat in a religion class, and another freshman came and sat next to her. They were married for almost 50 years.
- He married the love of his life. After meeting in junior college, they deepened their friendship while corresponding during World War II, and started dating after he returned to the U.S. During their 68 years of marriage, they were equal partners, best friends, and soulmates.
- She graduated from high school in 1946 and met her future husband shortly thereafter. They shared more than 54 years of love and Bingo until he departed this life.
- He met a beautiful coed while sitting on campus. When he took her hand in greeting he held on a long time, and it turned out to be forever. They spent 72 years happily married. She died six months ago, so now they are reunited.
- It was while she was attending Brigham Young University that she met her sweetheart. They were sealed together for time and eternity in the temple.

This lucky man found a true mate and a strong woman: "As a young woman, she worked as a telephone operator and met a charming fisherman from Alaska. When he proposed, Mom responded, 'Yes, as long as we don't live in Alaska.' She adapted well to frontier life in Alaska. Their first home was a one-room tent on the bluff overlooking the Cook Inlet, graduating to a two-room tent the following summer. She cared for both a brown bear cub and a moose calf, retrieved clothes from a clothesline wearing snowshoes, scared moose away with a broom, and killed a chicken hawk with a Winchester 405, the dead chicken still in its claw. During their 67-year marriage, they built a lovely hilltop home on a wooded lake where they raised four children, held three weddings, and buried six dogs."

For the blessed, it is never too late to find true love.

- They shared love and companionship for the last 10 years, before she died at 97. While not always agreeing on politics or interior decorating, they enjoyed a love of conversation, their newspapers, winters in Siesta Key, good food and, most of all, each other's company.
- He met his angel and best friend for the last five years of his life at the retirement home. He carried on his legendary reputation for charming people and proudly causing trouble.
- At 78 he met the love of his life. Their relationship was the stuff of romance novels. They met unexpectedly, but fell in love instantly. They traveled, took in sunsets at the beach, they laughed, they loved, and they had it all.

> **"He worked as a gas station attendant, here he met the love of his life. She worked next door as a waitress, and he would visit often for lunch. She won his heart by always buying him a piece of pie."**
>
> — *Frank's obituary*

Maybe a coincidence brings two people together. Or is it fate? I love the serendipity of these romantic stories.

- He met his wife on a blind date that included driving out into the countryside in the car he had nicknamed the "Miserable Bastard" and shooting at beer cans with a .22 caliber pistol. They married the weekend the Beatles debuted on the Ed Sullivan Show.

- He met his future wife during a Harvard dance mixer at which they were both ditched by their dates. They married at the Plaza Hotel and were happily together for the next 59 years.
- He met the girl of his dreams at age 12 and they married after an 11-day courtship when they met again 20 years later.
- She met her future husband when she was in a displaced persons camp in Germany when he was delivering a letter to her friend. He was her soulmate and she spent the rest of her life in love with him.
- She was married to her soulmate for 70 years. Their love story began at a dance before he left to serve in World War II. They were united in marriage and were as inseparable as a pair of swans ever after.
- She met her second husband, whom she would later call the love of her life, while watching the play *Bye Bye Birdie* at a theater. After hearing his contagious laughter a few seats away, she knew they had to meet. They were married the next year and raised six children.
- She met him on a blind date. They soon married and began a 62-year magic carpet ride.

A highlight of her life took place when she met her husband: "'We fell madly in love when we met in the fall of 1956. I was a young mother staying with friends, and he was a dashing and so attractive pilot who landed at the lake with a couple of hunters for lunch one day. I did my best to get lunch made, and finally he came into the kitchen to help me get food on the table. I was as smitten by him as he was by me.'" The pair married in 1957, and lived passionately together until his death in 2001. She missed him every day."

This man's bad luck ended up being fortuitous: "While driving a propane tank truck, he was tragically trapped when the truck ignited, burning his left leg. He withstood numerous skin grafts over that year, never complaining about the pain he endured. He met his loving wife, who was a nurse assistant while he was hospitalized, and they were married in 1953 following his one-year hospitalization."

> **"He met his wife on a ferry to Fire Island. As a romantic, he always claimed it was love at first sight. His wife, the pragmatist, always maintained he took the last open seat on the boat."**
>
> *— Kenneth's obituary*

Some claim they experience love at first sight, or close to it. They may be right. Not everyone believes this initial and mystical connection is real, but these couples do.

- She met a man in the summer of 1949 and at the end of their first date she turned to him and said, "Harold, you are going to marry me, so you better get used to the idea!" He always said he liked a woman who was decisive, and after several weeks of dating they were engaged and married five weeks later. Married for 62 years, they were lifelong partners in business, the arts, and philanthropy.
- She first met her husband on a college stairwell when she was 18; it was love at first sight. They spent a glorious 67 years together. She was his beloved wife and dearest friend.
- She met her husband when she was 12 years old, recalling that she knew she would marry him.
- In college she met the love of her life. Upon seeing handsome Dave for the first time as she descended the steps of her sorority house, she proclaimed, "I'm going to marry that man." She did, and her husband of 64 years was with her as she died.

These two women sacrificed to marry their special man.

- She met and married the love of her life in 1948. At the end of their first date, her husband told his roommate he had met the woman he was going to marry. The marriage was a choice she made; she turned down a fellowship to study the nature of radical politics in Chile in pursuit of her PhD. They spent the next 65 years together. The essence of their marriage was of unwavering love and respect; a perfect blend of two human beings ideally suited to each other.
- After high school she entered nursing school, but dropped out because she had met her true soulmate and could not be married and be in nursing school.

> **"She is survived by the love of her life, her husband, who adored her. They were engaged to be married three days after they met, and theirs was a marriage of 71 years."**
>
> — *Gloria's obituary*

What is the mysterious alchemy that connects two people for life so soon after meeting?

- His New Year's Eve resolution was to improve his social life. He met his wife on a blind date and they were married six months later. Thus began 26 years of shared joy in a simple life and common values.
- There was a magic between them from the start. They met and within three days were engaged to marry. They lived a life of unparalleled love and devotion. They were a team, living life with a spirit of adventure.
- She was hiking the Appalachian Trail with a friend and, along the way, met a man who was taking the afternoon off from his farm to take a quick hike. They hit it off; three weeks later they were married and were together for 61 years.

> **"He and his wife were inseparable during their 64 years of marriage. They formed the perfect partnership and were happiest when they were together. Most pictures of them later in life show them holding hands."**
>
> — *Walter's obituary*

It's especially touching when the love story is not just a fairytale, but shines every day, to the pleasure and inspiration of others.

- He is survived by the love of his life, his wife, whom his sisters say was God's greatest gift to their brother.
- Dad was born a century ago and married his queen, for whom he did anything and everything.
- He survived the love of his life, who had passed away in their home ten years earlier. His last wish was to have a date with her.
- She is survived by her heartbroken husband, whom she met in 1975. What followed was 45 years of magic. He describes her as

the warmest, gentlest, and most gracious and loving person he ever knew. Her smile lit up every room.

- They are together once again. For nearly 70 years they shared a remarkable bond of love, joy, humor, courage, loyalty, and respect.
- She met the love of her life in 1952 while they were both teaching high school. They enjoyed a 64-year marriage and gardening together. She focused on irises, glads, peonies, and camellias, while he specialized in roses—though she often accused him of over-pruning. They thoroughly enjoyed each other's company and were a true love match, a blessing for them and their children.

Sweet references in several men's obituaries described their true love as the star in his eyes, his hummingbird, his heart's true companion, and his endearing dance partner.

> **"He loved his wife with a beauty and grace that inspires us all. Their home is adorned with little notes everywhere that express his love and affection for her. It is the type of love that brings deep contentment and peacefulness. The understanding and mutual love they shared is everlasting."**
>
> — *Mike's obituary*

These excerpts show that love is not just expressed in words but is evident in deeds.

- He and his wife were married 73 years, still held hands, and were recently overheard saying that they loved each other more now than when they met.
- He loved to dance with his wife of 70 years, his greatest love.
- His devotion to his wife of 73 years was total as well as his constant love and attention to her every want and need.
- He married Margaret and he doted on her. They were both hard workers while living the farm life. They enjoyed each other's company while drinking their daily coffee.

- Her husband will always remember how blessed he was to be able to dote on her, open every door for her, and hold her hand through life.

This is a glorious tribute to the power of romance: "He married the absolute love of his life in 1961. Together they crafted an amazing love story. It was his deep love for her that put the wind in his sails."

> **"They passed away ten hours apart, two weeks shy of their 71st anniversary. They were high school sweethearts. As goes the title of their favorite song, they will now be together 'Always.'"**
>
> *— Sam and Esther's obituary*

Is it a coincidence or no longer having the will to live when spouses die within days of each other? Known as the "Widowhood Effect," people whose spouses have just died have a 66% increased chance of dying themselves within the first three months after their spouse's passing.

- As often happens with long-married partners, the death of one is followed shortly after by the death of the other. George passed away almost four months to the day after his beloved wife of 60 years passed away. There will be a combined memorial celebration.
- His broken heart soldiered on without his wife of 48 years for only 78 hours before failing.
- They met in 1952 and thus began a legendary love story. They were joyously married for 66 years. They lived every day together with a love that was a radiant force to all those lives they touched. He was 93 and she was 87 when they passed away in their home on the same day.
- He was a loving and supporting husband who adored his wife. She preceded him in death by only 26 days. These soulmates lived together for 58 years and left this world together.
- He and his beloved wife were together for 65 years and passed away within the same week. *(Their obituaries were side-by-side in the newspaper.)*

- He lost his loving wife of 73 years just months before he also died. He will best be remembered walking down Park Avenue with the blue-haired love of his life.

Sometimes family and friends witness lasting love stories and are amazed at the successful union of two very different people.

- He met the love of his life who was hoodwinked into thinking he was a charming individual with decorum. Boy was she ever wrong. He embarrassed her daily with his mouth and choice of clothing. To this day we do not understand how he convinced our mother, an exceedingly proper woman and a pillar in her church, to sew and create the colorful costumes and props which he used for his antics. *(She may have been a living saint.)*
- Quite the marksman in his youth, he enjoyed varmint hunting, a pastime his wife found decidedly foreign. Eventually, this too she embraced as one more unique and endearing facet of this never-boring man's persona.

> **"He is survived by his overly-patient and accepting wife who was the love of his life, a fact she gladly accepted sympathy for during their 48 years of marriage."**
>
> *—Terry's obituary*

Especially enjoyable are references to true loves who are also imperfect human beings.

- He loved a full martini, very full and very cold, but most of all, he loved his wife. Their love was deep and profound. Though their fights were legend, passion and deep connection always prevailed.
- Her family takes solace in knowing that she will spend the rest of eternity reunited with her soulmate and lifelong companion, the one individual whom she could not bear to live without, her husband. Somewhere beyond the pearly gates, her family knows that she is once again able to take control of his personal affairs and remind him of every mistake he ever made—something he always knew she would continue in the afterlife.

- He is survived by his loving wife of 57 years, who will now be able to purchase the mink coat which he had always refused her because he believed only minks should wear mink.

Some love stories are just truly remarkable.

- She married when she was only 14 and had a long, loving marriage, just a few months shy of 70 years. She had three children by the time she was 18 and worked beside her husband in the logging business for a number of years. She was an extremely hard worker and never complained, fought through pain and hardships, and always pushed herself to her physical limits. Her entire adult life she helped manage the family business with only an eighth grade education.

- She was a hair stylist who met a handsome young man who packed plaster. After a blissful engagement, they married in 1950. She often milked five or six cows and fed many hogs and chickens while cooking for a work crew and her family of eight.

- When he was 5, he met a little girl named Joyce for the first time, and so their journey together began. They fell in love in the twilight of childhood, and were engaged to be married by the last summer of their teen years. They welcomed their firstborn daughter, and he cried tears of joy in his first moments as a father, and truly came into his own. They were deeply in love and found their greatest joy in the other. They were constant companions in a world of their own, and it is difficult to imagine one without the other. He took his last breaths in the arms of his soulmate and wife.

In real life, there can be no happily ever after. All love holds the seeds of death. Even marriage vows state the eventual "till death do us part."

- At 21, he met a brown-eyed beauty who was a kindred winter spirit. They were constant companions and closest confidants. Their love for each other was deep and true and obvious to those around them. They married in 2018 on a mountainside in Alaska. He snow machined to the altar, and the bride's father skied her down the snowy aisle. A year later, he died in an avalanche.

- He married the love of his life. They were in love; they were soulmates. They shared common values, work ethics, and many happy memories. During their 43 years together, times were not always easy, but they persevered. They spent the last five years, five months enduring an unsolvable illness, but their combined strength of mind and body gave them the will to carry on. He died in her arms, taking a piece of her heart with him.
- He married the love of his life, and they were devoted to each other. Over the years, they shared thousands of laughs; hundreds of dances; dozens of beach trips, golf courses, and horse shows; and one inexorable cancer diagnosis.

> **"Together Eileen and I fulfilled a lot of our dreams.**
> **The Latin expression *'dimidium anima mea'* says it best—**
> **Eileen was the 'one half of my very existence.'"**
>
> — *Brian's obituary*

These accounts of a lifetime of shared love are uplifting to read. True love does exist in this world—not for everyone, but for the fortunate few. This realistic tribute to a loving couple's life that was neither simple nor trouble-free was an inspirational part of the obituary: "He married the love of his life. Together more than 45 years, they exemplified true love when things couldn't have been any better, and true love when things couldn't have been any worse."

All The Loves Of A Lifetime

"Who am I? I can define myself only by referring to my existential relationships. I am my mother and father's third son, I am my siblings' brother, I am Alice's husband, I am my children's father, my nephews' and nieces' uncle, my grandchildren's grandfather. I am the grateful friend for all those wonderful people whose warmth and loving friendships I've cherished. Without these relationships, I did not and do not exist. The more we grasp the enormity of these relationships, and the more we love them, the more we exist."

— Charles's obituary

The preceding obituary excerpt is a particularly apt beginning to this chapter. Relationships give meaning to our life. They sustain our spirit. We are shaped by each of our human connections, even as they vary in depth and intensity throughout our lives. When we are gone, memories of these interactions will endure, giving significance to our life. Therein lies a person's immortality.

"She shared her love for her family in many ways, from the gentle stroke of a hand in hers, to the many squishy-cheeked kisses, knitted slippers, telling of stories, baking of cream puffs, and a fond walk with loved ones through her garden to pick juicy raspberries."

— Durgica's obituary

Obituaries usually emphasize the importance of family to the deceased. Parents, spouses, children, grandchildren, siblings, and so on—both living and dead—position the person within their family tree. Even simple statements express the significance of these connections: "Family gatherings were sweet noise to his ears."

- She outshined June Cleaver in taking care of her family.
- He was known as one of the great strategic minds on Wall Street, but will be remembered for his deep love of family.
- He wasn't perfect, but he made our family perfect.
- He kept everyone laughing over the years, and he also kept us together.
- His family and farm were his pride and joy. Over three generations grew up in his home. He raised five sons, welcomed delightful, lovely daughters-in law, and lots of grandchildren and great-grandchildren.

I have no idea how these families managed.

- When he and his wife decided to have children, they agreed to accept whatever God gave them, and God gave them 12 children.
- She and her husband were united in marriage and to that union 14 children were born, whom she homeschooled.
- He and his wife enjoyed being foster parents to more than 50 babies.

Some obituaries include a jaw-dropping number of family members.

- She is survived by eight sons and five daughters, 58 grandchildren, 91 great-grandchildren, and two great-great-grandchildren.
- He was married for 59 years and together they raised 10 children on the family farm. He is survived by all 10 children, 29 grandchildren, 29 great-grandchildren, and two great-great-grandchildren.

This man had the "advantage" of having had three wives: "He was predeceased by his two wives and is survived by his third wife, six daughters, 48 grandchildren, 95 great-grandchildren, 31 great-great-grandchildren."

This woman's "advantage" was living to be 116 years old! "Her eight daughters and four sons gave her 68 grandchildren, 125 great-grandchildren, and at least 120 great-great-grandchildren."

She was blessed with energy and stamina: "In April of 1942 she and her husband introduced their first child, and their family grew to 19 children. Most people couldn't fathom raising a family that size, but with a lot of patience and love, she just did what she needed to do with a smile and that twinkle in her eye. She grew acres of vegetables, fruits, and flowers creating a paradise as she loved nature of every kind. She made the most delicious meals, bread, fruitcakes, and jams and everything was homemade. She fed the whole family and often had company on Sunday. She died at 95 years old."

Nontraditional families are worthy of including in an obituary.

- She is survived by her honorary parents, foster mother, one cousin, and her loving honorary and foster siblings and their families.
- She is survived by her boyfriend of 22 years.
- She is survived by her common-law husband's children.
- Six years ago, she was able to be reunited with her oldest daughter and enjoyed these last few years of spending time with her.

I found this statement is shocking: "He was one of nine siblings born to his parents. At birth, he was adopted by another family to carry on their name."

> "At 20 years old, she was married and was promptly wheeled down Main Street in a wheelbarrow with a flat tire, and their wild ride began."
>
> — *Melody's obituary*

The descriptions of a spouse's love are charming.

- She enjoyed a wonderful marriage with her husband; they were deeply compatible, inseparable, and each other's best friend.
- She was her husband's greatest supporter, and he was her greatest admirer.
- He eagerly followed his wife on many amazing adventures. He thought she was perfect.

- His wife was his best friend, his lover, and often his "Mother." He married her 60 years ago for the warm welcoming arms of her family. Stability.
- He was extremely proud of his wife of 72 years whom he adored and still called his lover while holding hands in their last days together.
- His last words were "I remember it all" right before he gestured towards his loving wife and uttered "Amazing."

> **"For sixty years they filled their house with German shepherds, cats, countless dinner parties, and an immense amount of love and laughter."**
>
> — *Maury's obituary*

Some descriptions of marriages are lighthearted.

- His longest career was with his wife of more than 50 years, and they both considered that a most notable accomplishment.
- The story goes that dad couldn't take his eyes off a girl, and in 1956 they were married. They had started building their home that summer, and with only two rooms completed they moved in on one of the coldest winters on record. To no one's surprise, the following year their daughter was born.
- When she met her husband, she refused his invitation to dance. He asked her to give him three good reasons why not. She chose to give him only two. They were married and remained husband and wife for 68 years.
- He married his wife in 1977 when she worked for him. He liked to tell people he was the boss until they married, then she was the boss.

> **"She often set tongues wagging with her flamboyant life. She frequently married and divorced—at least nine times. Her relationships lasted from one month to 17 years. That marriage was to a dancer, who was an indeterminate number of years younger than her."**
>
> — *Sabah's obituary*

These people loved their spouses.

- He was blessed with three marriages during his lifetime.
- After a couple of lovely marriages that blessed him with his two children, he married the love of his own third act.
- His third wife brought out his softer side.
- She was preceded in death by her first husband, with whom she had 12 children. In the last three years of her life she enjoyed spending every inseparable moment with the person who made her soul happy: her joy, her second husband.
- He married Clarissa and had a daughter. They divorced, and he married Eva, and they had five children. They later divorced, and he married Kathy, who later passed away, and he never married again.

> **"First and last she was a mother who loved nothing more than holding a child in her lap with gentle ease, a joyful smile on her face."**
>
> — *June's obituary*

When I gave birth to my first child, I looked out the hospital window and thought the world was now a different place. And it was. When I had my second child, I wondered if there could possibly be enough love for this baby too. And there was. This shared sentiment is apparent in obituaries of mothers who leave behind children they treasured.

- She was a loving and caring mother to four rowdy boys, and the laughter and activity of her children was her greatest source of happiness.
- She probably didn't plan to have eight children, but she made each of us feel like the most special.

- She had always thought motherhood would never be for her. She couldn't have been more wrong; through word and deed she gifted her children the same extraordinary qualities that defined her own personality.
- She was a loving wife and mother to six children. She also cared for more than 200 children over 25 years as a foster mother.

This mother wrote to her children on her last Mother's Day: "I have treasured every moment I have spent with you two and can honestly say there is nothing I love more in the world. You both are light when there is darkness, happiness when there is sadness, strength when there is weakness, and THE purpose when I question. I am so grateful for you both. You are, and always have been, pure joy. Thank you for making me a Mom, and for your souls choosing me. It's the greatest gift life has ever given me."

These sons showed deep love and respect for their mother: "Two of her sons built her casket, and her third son took the last year off work to care for her."

After 51 years, this mother was reunited with her son: "Because of the stigma of being an unwed mother in the early 60s, she was pressured into giving him up for adoption. Jonathan often refers to their story of re-intersection by saying, 'The story is very much akin to a *Hallmark after School* movie wherein one should have an abundance of tissues at hand.' He not only gave her the love only a child can give, but also a wonderful family to fill her final years with much joy. From many streams may mighty rivers flow."

These children remember their mother fondly: "She and her husband had four kids in just over five years (good Catholic girl). She was your typical Depression-era parent (she was cheap). She made most of her children's clothes, stylish or not, and sent them to school with peanut butter sandwiches EVERY DAY for lunch. She cut her children's hair even though she could never cut bangs straight, and made 'Rotten Apple Pie' for dessert if the fruit was going bad. She was known within her family and friends for an expertly timed 'Well, shit' when the occasion called for it."

> **"He loved his sons with his heart and soul for the people they are and the men they will become. They were not only the greatest gifts in his life, but also his most precious gift to the world he leaves behind."**
>
> — *Dave's obituary*

Not to be outdone, fathers expressed the love they had for their sons and daughters.

- To each of his six children he was an example of unconditional love.
- He leaves behind his daughter, whom albeit less sociable, is every bit as weird as he was, and also has the family nose.
- He married his main squeeze almost 50 years ago, and they had two girls. He taught them to fish, to select a quality hammer, to love nature, and to just be thankful. He took great pride in stocking their tool boxes.
- He is survived by his husband and his quadruplets.
- When his children were young he built stilts, put together potato light bulbs, and made the best kites. *(Potatoes make electricity when copper and zinc nails are inserted into them.)*
- His sons cherished, and his wife tolerated, the annual rainy fortnight in the Adirondack Mountains, where he could see patches of blue sky and rays of sunshine when no one else could. He instilled in his sons an unshakable love of nature, the outdoors, and dogs.

These fathers are remembered with love and laughter, surely a reflection of their parenting.

- Dad and Mom raised eight children and somehow all the kids survived to adulthood. We didn't have a lot of money, but it was more than made up for in love and togetherness. Dad was in all our memories growing up, leading our mountain and beach camping adventures. These were some of the happiest family years. The family attended church, arriving by camper or station wagon and taking up an entire pew. A child may have been left behind once or twice.

- He has left his daughters to figure out what the heck to do with 10,000 Christmas ornaments, all those seashells, dozens of terra cotta planters, and way too many dimmer switches for better lighting. Six devastated grandchildren are all worried who will wear the life-size skeleton next Halloween and the twinkling Rudolph head at Christmas.

Difficult relationships with children, sometimes a part of life, are shared.

- He loved his children. He strived to have a better relationship with them.
- He had two sons and though they were not actively in his life, he loved them and wished things had been different.
- After being absent from the lives of his two daughters for nearly 30 years, he was able to reunite with them. He knew his not being there while they were growing up caused them great harm. He was able to share a meal with them, and this may have been his proudest moment.

The nostalgic memories these children had of their father's little acts of love are touching: "He was always there for his children. Whether it was helping with their paper routes, taking them to sporting events, camping, or fishing, the stories are numerous. He always built an ice rink in the backyard for his sons to play hockey as they grew up. He never skated, but he was always out there with his homemade hot mop, made from plumbing pipe and old canvas. He ran a hose out the bathroom window connected to the hot water faucet. During sporting events he could be heard yelling encouragements at the top of his lungs to his kids."

> "His grandchildren were his greatest pride. He often said that he couldn't imagine what he could have ever done to deserve such blessings."
>
> — *Michael's obituary*

When my daughters made me a grandmother, I thought I had discovered a world of love as yet unexplored. I know other grandparents feel the same emotion. Is it the sheer joy of loving them without having ultimate responsibility for them? Are they an improved version of you?

- What gave her the most joy over the past few decades was the time spent with her grandchildren. If it wasn't making waffles, it was watching pig shows, riding horses on rocky trails, walking around the farm, rocking, cuddling, and reading favorite stories.
- When his grandchildren began to arrive he was truly in his element. His joy in each of them was palpable, and that was before he learned magic. No one will forget during a family luncheon when Granddaddy complained to his grandchildren he had a stomach ache, gathered them around him, and then cured his problem by slowly removing, one by one, a dozen or more brightly colored silk handkerchiefs from his mouth.
- Each of his grandchildren said they had a special relationship with him and, no question, each of them is correct. He spoiled each of them in their own way.
- He had a permanent smile whenever his grandchildren were in his presence. A visit to his house was met with love and happiness, positive energy, and good humor.
- While many grandparents believe their grandchildren are the smartest, kindest, and best looking, he knew it for a fact.

> **"He took his job as grandfather so seriously he changed his license plate to 'IMGRAMPS.'"**
>
> — *William's obituary*

Some fortunate grandparents earn special names given to them by their grandchildren: Sassy, The Graminator, Grandma Cookie, Grandy, Noodles, Grandma Coo Coo, Poppy, Popsie, Papoo, Granddude, Jobu, Grandpa Pizza, Grandma Gorgeous, and Grammy Taxi. One grandfather was called Grandpa Kitty—his wife was Kitty.

- She was referred to as Big due to her larger-than-life personality that outsized her diminutive stature.
- He was called Grandpa Pinball. Only the best grandpas have a pinball machine in their living room.
- She was known as Story to her grandchildren due to her love of reading.

Grandparents too had special names for their grandchildren including My Grands and the Joysters. Grandchildren were described as the smartest, kindest, and best looking; remarkable in every way; the light in her eyes and the music in her heart; her true pride and joy; delightful apples of her eye; and even as delicious.

> **"He was a generously loving grandfather who invented wildly adventurous bedtime stories which invariably ended with, 'and the next day, it rained.' (Which he maintained should be his epitaph.)"**
>
> *— Harold's obituary*

Many grandparents loved doting on their grandchildren: "He spent countless hours supervising, antagonizing, and playing with his grandchildren."

Specific activities that grandparents shared with their grandchildren formed memories so dear they are included in their obituary.

- Paw-Paw slicing up an apple picked from a backyard tree for his grandkids was a perfect fit for his Sunday afternoon.
- He will be remembered by his grandchildren as the legend that ate ice cream for breakfast on warm Maine mornings.
- Her greatest joy in life was her grandchildren. She loved nothing more than taking them to video arcades or McDonald's for breakfast.
- Her grandchildren have fond memories of her homemade cookies, pies, soups, fresh carrots and raspberries picked from the garden, her laughter, and the covert $20 bill that was given with the condition "Don't tell your mom."
- The supreme pride and joy of his life was his grandson whom he absolutely adored with all of his being. He spent hundreds of hours attending Little League games, fishing off the wharf, planning excursions, listening with interest to every minute detail of his life, and beaming with pride at his accomplishments. The bond between the two of them was precious and rare.

- He loved his grandchildren very much and never missed an opportunity during their birthday celebrations to use his surgeon's skills and precision to make the first cuts of their cake as he said, "One for you, one for me."
- He was a beloved Papaw who gladly spoiled his grandchildren, smiled proudly at their laughter and excitement, and was always equipped to make an ice cream sundae for the whole crew before bed, with a cherry on top.
- He was a devoted family man and spent many hours cuddling with grandkids on the couch and giving them rides on his riding mower or golf cart.
- He was a good-humored grandfather who spent many nights building forts and sleeping in them with his grandchildren. As their fun-loving babysitter, he kept them well supplied with junk food, inappropriate television, and lottery tickets.
- She loved making things extra special for her grandchildren and would spend hours curling the girls' hair, sewing costumes, and showing them her favorite Shirley Temple movies.

How grandchildren enriched the lives of their grandparents was also included in obituaries.

- Spending special times with the grandchildren and great-grandchildren brought out the playful, imaginative, quick wit that we all now miss so much.
- A high point in his life was the 2018 birth of twin granddaughters. When he looked at their smiling faces, he said, "Who could ask for anything more?"
- As each grandchild was born, a twinkle was added to her heart and eye. She was the total and complete grandmother, a persistent presence, mentoring the parents and advocating for the kids.

Years ago, people often had children at a younger age. They were fortunate to live long enough to love and enjoy their great-grandchildren: "He and his wife had two rowdy, but beautiful great-grandsons."

"She was known as TFS (The Favorite Sister) to her 13 siblings."

— *Randy's obituary*

Siblings share a history that only they can understand fully.

- The youngest of four children and the only girl, she was adored, cherished, and loved by her older brothers. They were very protective of her even if she was being a pain.
- He was very protective of his younger siblings. During the last seven years, he cared for his brother as Alzheimer's became their companion. His brother passed away just nine days after he did. They were the best of lifelong buddies from the crib until the time of their death. Neither would have wanted to continue without the other.
- She and her sister had a special bond and were like two peas in a pod. A favorite pastime was having a picnic in the mountains. They always kept emergency picnic supplies on hand: pimento cheese sandwiches, chips, Vienna sausage, Little Debbie oatmeal cream cookies.

Some obituaries mention aunts, uncles, nieces and nephews. "She is survived by too many nieces and nephews to name, but not to love."

- She was loved and adored by 7 nieces and nephews, 15 great-nieces and nephews, 30 great-great nieces and nephews, and a great-great-great nephew.
- He excelled at the role of uncle. He acted rich with his nieces and nephews, even though he wasn't. He took them on trips and picked them up when their cars broke down. He praised them, gave them a place to stay when times were tough, and reassured them when they doubted themselves. He never bragged and never yelled. He listened more than he advised.
- He was awarded the Lifetime Achievement Award as the Greatest Uncle in the World by his 80 plus nieces and nephews. He loved spending time with them and treated them as his own children.

> **"Some people collect books, coins, or seashells. She collected friends. Their lives, and hers, were so much the richer for it."**
>
> — *Sally's obituary*

Friends have always been important to me. I treasure the regular contact I enjoy with a friend since the second grade. (Believe me, that was several decades ago.) My friends are smart, hilarious, interesting, accepting, generous, and kind. They enrich my life in countless ways.

- He had more friends than anyone has the right to have, and every one of them thought of him as their best friend, because he was.
- One of her greatest attributes was her ability to establish and nourish long lasting friendships. She reached out to people from all walks of life to be her friends. When she became seriously ill, it was her friends who selflessly and faithfully came to her aid for five years.
- He wanted nothing and needed nothing. His currency was human connection, and he collected lifelong friends.
- He treasured lifelong friendships and was instrumental in starting the Saturday Coffee Club which has been meeting for more than 40 years.
- She made many lifelong friends, particularly a group of girlfriends referred to as the Magnificent Eight, who remained friends for more than 65 years.

> **"He was active in his church and his community. He showed up, participated, led, and supported organizations, efforts, and causes of many kinds."**
>
> *— Norman's obituary*

Love for one's church and community can be an integral part of a person's life story.

- He was a longstanding member of the non-profit organization, Angel Flight, logging more than 120 flights, bringing patients from all over New England to their cancer and other medical treatments free of charge. As a cancer survivor, he quietly paid it forward and truly found it to be his passion to help where he could.
- She was an inveterate volunteer, attentive to the needs of those on the margins, especially in her decades of work in soup kitchens and delivering meals to shut-ins.
- Silently and privately, he unselfishly volunteered every weekend for five years helping pick up and distribute supermarket food donations to those less fortunate families. He never missed a weekend, even when it was 40 degrees below zero. Along the way, he became affectionately known as The Muffin Man, and children of the families he served looked forward to a treat from him.
- She joined the church when she was 10 years old and remained faithful to God and that church her entire life —86 more years. She played the church organ for 66 years, directed the choir for 38 years, and led the women's group for 40 years.

> **"The greatest loves in her life were her canine companions. There was never a time when she did not have a dog or two."**
>
> — *Elsa's obituary*

Even as a pet owner, I was surprised at how often pets are included in obituaries, usually by name. The importance of these relationships in the life of the deceased is obvious.

- His special four-legged companions will always haunt the rooms of their home, trying to follow his endless scent trail.
- He reluctantly leaves his pet Schnauzer Buddy, but he will be interred with the ashes of former canine companions Bogie, Beamer, Grover, and Benzie.
- In addition to his family, he loved animals, especially Boxer dogs and likely has Butch, Luke, Willie, and Duke by his side or in his lap, which is what he and all of them preferred.

Some pets provide emotional support during the dying process.

- Her faithful Labradoodle stood a resolute vigil beside her bed during her last two weeks.
- His therapy kitty Cleo was with him until the end.
- He is survived by Kobuk, a much-loved Malamute, who rested his head on the bed during his master's final days.
- He is leaving behind his beloved Saint Bernard and Great Pyrenees. They never left his side throughout his extended journey with cancer.

One obituary of a much-decorated veteran sadly listed no people in his life: "His true love in the final years of his life was his little off-white Labradoodle named Ranger. During his bout with cancer, Ranger was always by his side and gave him much comfort and strength to fight. Ranger was his love and his life in these final years and was such a true, trusted, and loving companion to the bitter end."

Some people preferred animals other than a cat or dog.

- He loved all animals especially his buffalo, llama, cats, and precious golden retrievers.

- She loved animals and had a number of pets over the years ranging from Peep the chicken to Seymour the duck.
- She loved animals and after her retirement she enjoyed spending time with her goats.
- He was an animal lover his entire life and will be sorely missed by his two cats Freddie the Freeloader and Lily von Stupp, his scurry of squirrels, and his flocks of pigeons and song birds.
- His best friend in the animal world was Willie, a Double Yellow-head Amazon parrot.

Sometimes the listed order of the survivors makes you wonder.

- He was a loving father to his canine companion and five sons.
- He leaves behind his cat Stubby and his brothers and sisters.
- He is survived by his longtime companion, his dog Chu-Chu, and also his fiancée.

When all is said and done, we are given a brief moment in time together. Why not make the most of the opportunities we have to give and receive love? This man seems to have done it all. He was an internationally successful businessman who was predeceased by the love of his life. He lived to be 100 years old: "He was cherished by his daughters, revered by his sons-in-law, adored by his grandchildren, treasured by his friends, trusted by his business partners, and respected by everyone who knew him—proof positive of a life well lived."

Roles In A Life

"He was widely known, deeply loved, always the life of the party, a saint, a sinner, and cherished child of God."

— John's obituary

People are complicated. They interact through various roles with scores of other people throughout their lives. Based on these personal relationships, other people see different aspects of the person, but only from their perspective. These many facets of an individual make it nearly impossible for anyone to wholly understand another person.

Relationships, however complex, make people happier, keep them healthier, and give meaning to their lives. These roles extend beyond family and friends into a wider sphere of the groups and communities to which one belongs. People are remembered differently by the innumerable identities they have in life: the riders one sees regularly at the bus stop, baristas at the coffee shop, cashiers at the neighborhood grocery, the children's teachers, and so on. The fabric of our lives is woven by the threads of many relationships. Trying to capture the fullness of a life in an obituary is nearly impossible since one person's life intersects with so many other lives.

The writers of these obituaries attempted to convey the fullness of the life. For example, this writer included the loves of the deceased's life with other significant roles: "She was married to the love of her life; she was a supportive sister, magnificent mother, magical grandmother, natural leader, excellent bridge player, respectable golfer, and an avid quilter." *(I loved the "magical grandmother" designation.)*

One four-line obituary included only the name of the person, the date he died, and his roles in life: "Loving spouse, brother, dad, papa, orthodontist, professor, and friend." *(Simplicity.)*

Some obits, within practical constraints, include the wide impact of a life by listing several roles of the deceased: "He filled many roles for his family, friends, children, grandchildren and great-grandchildren: jester, role model, father figure, bad example, and inspiration."

Roles that a person had were reflections of how they chose to live. The descriptions of this woman's roles were not unusual: "She was many things to many people: wife, mother, daughter, sister, and teacher, but to all, she was a friend." However, reading the roles in this other woman's obituary, one envisions a drastically different woman: "She was an axe thrower, rock climber, and world traveler."

> **"He held many titles in his life: husband, son, brother, father, uncle, father-in-law, grandfather, doctor, surgeon, partner, mentor, friend, neighbor, fishing buddy, proofreader, fixer-of-things, gift giver, and coach."**
>
> — *Neil's obituary*

These excerpts describing the deceased begin with their personal relationships followed by how they chose to connect with the world: their work, hobbies, skills, and interests. One can infer these are in order of priority.

- He was Pop, Himself, Red, and Amos as well as a lifelong Presbyterian, Eagle Scout, self-taught chef, highly regarded martini maker, boat captain, voracious reader, nature lover, and beloved raconteur.
- In addition to being a husband, father, and grandfather, he was a teacher, land surveyor, carpenter, amateur architect, builder, deacon, soldier, world traveler, and lover of nature.
- He was a fiercely proud Dad, a tender loving Papa, a doting Grandpa, a vigilant assessor of the legality of hay bales, the greatest Disney tour guide ever to have lived, and no race car driver will ever compare to him for us.

- She was the unrecognized force behind her sons' academic and career accomplishments and the very obvious center of her husband's joy.
- He was a beloved colleague, novelist, columnist, reviewer, raconteur, financier, art historian, and unabashed chronicler and critic of the foibles of humanity.
- She was the undisputed boss in a house full of men: coach, advisor, demanding critic, and staunch defender of her husband, her three sons, and eventually their families; and surrogate mother, chef, counselor, cheerleader, scolder, and shoulder-to-cry on for any and all friends, neighbors, co-workers, teammates, or others who—for a short time or forever—entered her family's circle.

This list of roles even included the length of time this man served in these capacities: "For 44 years he was a devoted husband to his beloved wife; for 75 years, he was the gently teasing and adoring older brother to his sister; and for 30 years, the wise-cracking political lampooner to his sister's husband; and he was a loving and supportive father as well as an incredibly proud Pop-Pop to his two grandsons."

This man's description was detailed and humorous: "He was a great many things—a rascal of a son, perhaps also a rascal of a husband, an animated and loving father, a brother, a highly over-educated construction worker, an unbelievably dedicated educator, a rough and tumble hockey player, a teller of colorful jokes, a taker of long road trips with not enough stops, an appreciator of music, especially rock and roll, a rescue dog lover, a proud Cornish gent, and at his core he was an empath."

The order of these roles was curious: "She was a fascinating daughter, wondrous gardener, admired dancer, teacher, designer, pianist, potter, writer, producer, and loving wife."

This fellow was tough to sum up: "He was many things to many people: a pilot, an operator, a cowboy, a drinking buddy, an entrepreneur, a hard-ass, a loved one, a friend, and neighbor."

Of course, what is included in the obituary depends on the perspective of the person writing it. This obituary focused on what this woman meant to her sons: "She was a teacher, a tender hugger, a Lego master, a partner in crime, and a master prankster."

This excerpt shared what this man meant exclusively to one person, the writer of the obituary. "He was my soulmate, lover, best friend, travel companion, personal chef, and magnificent other, we had it all." *(It struck me as odd to wholly claim a person and leave out the rest of the world.)*

> **"He was a kidder, food enthusiast, big thinker, voracious reader, golf addict, music lover, and a dyed-in-the-wool romantic."**
>
> *— James's obituary*

Some obituary writers define a person in terms of what they loved and how they lived rather than their personal connections.

- She was an avid reader, party thrower, cook, crossword puzzle solver, world traveler, piano player, social justice activist, and a lover of all the fine arts New York City has to offer.
- She was a traveler to 89 countries, renovator of buildings, world-class bargain hunter, knitter of baby sweaters, bungee jumper, risk taker, teacher, avid birder, bicyclist, activist, pacifist, community organizer, and cancer survivor.
- He was a gourmet cook, marathon runner, rower, dressage rider, classical pianist, freelance photographer, book editor, and children's book author.
- He was a political thinker, a wordsmith, a dairy co-op manager, an artist, a quipper, a jokester, a lover, a mandolin player, a formidable Scrabble player, a furniture designer, a carpenter, and an optimist. Above all, he was a dedicated communist activist from the age of 15, committed to the cause of social justice.

Observant writers have added color to the various facets of the person: a voracious reader, an enthusiastic mariner, a fanatical sports fan, a dedicated angler, a skilled painter, a cowboy cook, a noted scholar, an elegant athlete, a prize-winning architect, a dance-loving matriarch, a gifted trombonist, a staunch Socialist, an avid angler, a haphazard but enthusiastic gardener, and a merciless bridge and Boggle player.

> **"He was a pioneering ecologist, poet of consilience, pupil of esoteric gastropods and sentimental parrots, romantic New Yorker, and defender of wildlife."**
>
> — *Gerald's obituary*

Some people's roles in life are complicated, or maybe the writers had a dictionary close at hand.

- He was a gentleman, an instigator, an outrageous disciplinarian, a sesquipedalian (he would tell you to look it up), an intellectual, a Humanist, a good and challenging listener. He was also embarrassing in a wonderful way.
- She was a tiny but formidable woman who was an educator, bibliophile, culture vulture, 70-year subscriber to *The New York Times*, and a diehard Democrat. She believed in excellence, and had little time or patience for fools, charlatans, and liars. We are glad she lived to see the defeat of Donald Trump.
- He was a lawyer's lawyer, an insatiable enthusiast, an amateur linguist, an irrepressible gastronome, and an avid traveler.
- She was a forthright arts lover, lifelong educator and learner, avid reader, technophile, gourmand, dedicated friend to many, Francophile, politically passionate, and did we forget to mention forthright?

This man led a multi-faceted life: "He was a lifelong enthusiastic learner; a lover of many art forms including classical music, woodworking, playing the dulcimer; an avid supporter of public radio; a Master Gardener; a collector of nature who appreciated the beauty of Japanese maples, azaleas, and rhododendrons down to the tiniest seed; an avid traveler and storyteller; a lover of wine, food, and friendship; an accomplished sailor and scuba diver; a skier; a beekeeper; a genealogist; a lover of Greek culture; a mentor to youth; and known as The Stork, a deliverer of 10,000 babies."

> **"She was a 96-year-old loving wife of 50 years, widow, free spirit, member of MENSA, computer programmer, *bon vivant*, and mismatched-earring bohemian."**
>
> — *Gloria's obituary*

Sometimes a cleverly written list of roles ends with a surprising observation.

- He was a world traveler, gardener, skier, nature lover, meticulous dresser, and a whistler.
- She was a tart-tongued newspaper reporter, a deft headline writer, an accordion player, and her oxtail stew was sublime.
- He was a loving husband and father, a land surveyor, soccer coach, Boy Scout leader, math whiz, construction master, dedicated Papa, and a man of many beans.
- She was an anthropologist, feminist, social justice warrior, worldwide traveler, and lover of loons.
- She was a beautiful artist, long time volunteer, Mexican food connoisseur, and ornery friend.
- She was a dedicated letter writer, an accomplished poet, and in the arms of her beloved husband, an exceptional dancer.
- He was a devoted husband and father, a career Navy officer, a skilled surgeon, an amateur boatman, a reluctant handyman, a farmer's market connoisseur, an avid cyclist, and a lover of all things teddy bear—his spirit animal.
- She was a lifelong student, sharp historian, wonderful debater, singer of 1000 songs, hilarious storyteller, engaging conversationalist, and successful moose hunter.
- He was a father, partner, brother, friend, uncle, competitor, mentor, traveler, carnivore, consumer of large amounts of food, and a terrible singer.
- He was a husband, father, brother, Vietnam veteran, bargain hunter, artist, fried chicken connoisseur, card shark, and maker of the best blue cheese dressing ever.

This was part of a short obituary in *The New York Times*. Because it seems he was an ordinary man, it was quite unusual to find it in this newspaper that usually includes paid obituaries largely for the accomplished and wealthy: "He was a good son, husband, and father, an HVAC technician, fisherman, kite surfer, and more." *(Good for him.)*

This woman was one busy individual! "She was a wife, mother, grandmother, great-grandmother, friend, waitress, dancer, bartender, hair dresser, business owner, farmer, water aerobics instructor, and bridge player."

The order in which these roles were listed was striking: "He was a hugger, story teller, basketball player, runner, college tennis player, Ping Pong player, drummer, and a successful banker."

This obituary was written with so much love. It captured the wonder of this woman, tragically: "She was a school psychologist and fierce advocate for all kids, but being a mom was her most special role and she relished everything about it. She was a First Team All-American at painting nails, providing the safest and warmest hugs, tickling backs, doing hair, and lathering on cherry almond Mom lotion. She was a world-class secret keeper, proofreader, banana chocolate chip muffin maker, and without question, the best gift giver. She passed away while giving birth to her sixth child, doing what she loved most, being a mom."

In the end, the roles you played in other lives form the foundation for memories of you. Consider your impact on the people you encounter. Do your ripples through the world spread happiness and love? What impressions are you making? How will you be described and remembered?

Pursuits And Passions

> "She was happiest reflecting on nature, hearing the call of a bird, and commenting on the return of butterflies and frogs in spring."
>
> — *Mary's obituary*

Pursuits and passions have the power to enrich lives. These pastimes, which enrich lives, were embraced to such a degree they merited inclusion in an obituary.

> "She enjoyed cooking, gardening, and camping, and spent many quiet, early mornings in her bountiful garden, meticulously weeding and caring for her plants."
>
> — *Norma's obituary*

Various hobbies are related to nature, the most frequently mentioned being gardening. British psychiatrist Sue Stuart-Smith said, "When we sow a seed, we plant a narrative of future possibility." Maybe involvement with the inevitable process of nature—growing and dying—is what one embraces. We may feel a part of a larger world.

- "I'm addicted to pulling weeds," he would chuckle. He spent many happy hours working in garden beds and enjoying the beauty of nurture and nature.
- She was a Master Gardener who could coax even the most recalcitrant seeds into busy tomato or cucumber plants, or a sprawling field of vegetables and herbs.
- She loved her annual summer tradition of growing and selling corn, becoming known locally as the Corn Lady.
- Her last earthly pleasure was looking at the blooming anemones and hellebores in her splendid garden.

> **"As a man of great faith, he loved the outdoor chapel behind his home, walking or cross country skiing the streamside trail through the woods."**
>
> — *Coley's obituary*

People love being outdoors, finding peace in natural surroundings.

- She felt closest to God watching the egrets and planting black-eyed Susans in the dirt outside her mountain home. Nature was her sanctuary.
- He enjoyed recreational gold mining and had many adventures in the pursuit of the elusive nuggets contained in many Alaskan streams and rivers.
- Hat and backpack at the ready, she was dazzled by the beauty, power, and softness of nature, which she captured in numerous photographs while hiking, skiing, and snowshoeing well into her 80s.
- His favorite place to be was on the back porch, with a bourbon, listening to talk radio, and enjoying nature.

> **"He loved all animals, but especially wolves, crows, blue jays, and sharks, as well foxes, owls, hawks, and falcons, but he particularly adored chipmunks."**
>
> — *Mark's obituary*

People enjoy hobbies that relate to animals, so excerpts such as these were included in the stories of life: "He treasured his goat Vanessa." "She had a special fondness for giraffes." "He had a special love of Springer Spaniels." "He loved watching belugas in Alaska."

- Over the years she raised horses, chickens, ducks, pigs, sheep, donkeys, cats, dogs, and a hedgehog. She rescued a baby Great Horned Owl, raising it to adulthood, even teaching it to fly, before releasing it into the wild.
- She drove all over North America, which included annual trips to Yellowstone, to see her beloved wolves.
- She enjoyed showing her blue-ribbon miniature horses.
- He was an avid bird watcher, accumulating a lifetime list of 4,000 species.

There were humorous observations.

- She had a love of animals including the squirrels that lived on the fire escape of her fifth-floor walk-up. They were welcomed into her home—of course, with certain restrictions.
- Everyone knew he was a cat man! Humorous anecdotes abound of him and his cats. He arrived in Vermont with Pussy Galore and Sgt. Pepper and there were many kitties that followed.

Here's an unusual entry: "He had a particular love of Great Danes and adopted four older rescue Danes and helped them through their end-of-life stage. His local Dane community held a Moon Howl in his remembrance, a ceremony very fitting for him, and one which he would have viewed as an honor." (*I suppose a Moon Howl is self-explanatory.*)

Some observations showed what people considered a priority: "The love of his life may not have been wives or children, but fishing. It was his passion."

- She loved to fly fish and holds the record for the largest brown trout caught in Montana. She traveled the world with the Women Fly Fishers, an inveterate group of like-minded anglers.
- He loved hunting wherever and whatever he could, and fishing anywhere he was allowed to wet a line.
- He was active in Safari Club International, has taken 20 of the big game species in North America, and has killed animals listed in record books.
- Many people love to travel. Their obituaries often include their life list of countries visited, a point of pride, in their final itinerary.
- He wore out seven campers much to his wife's chagrin. Their 45 years together proved to be filled with good companionship and many adventures.
- Her love of travel started with a subscription to *National Geographic* magazine as a child. An avid and adventurous traveler, she had visited 114 countries according to the rules set up by the Traveler's Century Club. Her first adventure trip was to Ukraine and her last trip was a gorilla trek to Uganda.

- As an adventure traveler, he climbed Mt. Whitney, Mt. Kilimanjaro, and Mt. Fuji and trekked through Nepal to Mt. Everest base camp with National Geographic Expedition's host Peter Hillary.

> **"An adventuresome and intrepid person, at difference stages of his life he was an accomplished wrestler, skier, squash player, pilot, world traveler, and bridge player. His lifelong passion, however, was for sailing."**
>
> — *David's obituary*

Athletic pursuits can be more than just a game.

- His 30-plus years as a volunteer soccer coach afforded hundreds of children and parents exposure to his unique personality. Half a dozen or so of these folks might speak of him fondly if pressed.
- He was an avid golfer. He loved the game, its traditions, and the camaraderie with his golfing partners. Many have played better, but few have loved the game more.
- She organized a women's ice hockey team alternatively called the Ms Sticks and Mother Puckers. The average age of the team's roster was 50+.
- She was a trophy winner in Special Olympics bowling and swimming programs and enjoyed a lifetime of loving moments with her family and friends.
- When he wasn't with his wife, kids, or grandkids, he was probably throwing a game-winning pitch, sinking a hole-in-one, or bowling another strike.

People can be fanatical about sports.

- He was an avid New England Patriots fan and did not accept their losses calmly or silently.
- The only time her family ever heard her utter curse words was during Auburn football games.
- As a professional armchair consultant to the NBA, she was nicknamed Hoop Mama Two. Ball handling and dribbling were her biggest weaknesses.

> **"Her appreciation for art enriched her free time and fueled her passion to create places of peace and acceptance."**
>
> — *Marie's obituary*

Some hobbies are evidence of the endless creativity of the human mind.

- Dozens of babies in and beyond her home town have been warmed by her botanically accurate knitted hats resembling grapes, berries, lemons, tomatoes, and more. They were complete with stems and leaves.
- She was most happy creating metal neckties as jewelry.
- He was an expert at the design and construction of cardboard box mazes.
- Her husband wore a white dress shirt each work day, so every summer she would buy bolts of white cotton gabardine and make him a year's worth of dress shirts.
- She loved to draw and paint flowers and made homemade valentine cards for us kids using lace, ribbon, and velvet fabric, a real treasure.
- She loved sewing and made hundreds of quilts to comfort babies with AIDS.
- She hooked rugs she designed herself. She and a group of women met weekly for years, calling themselves the "Happy Hookers."

Bridge, Sudoku, crossword puzzles and other cerebral challenges often make their way into obituaries. Those fortunate people who complete *The New York Times* crossword puzzle in pen each week are sure to have it included as a point of pride.

- He was a force to be reckoned with at pinochle, cribbage, and Scrabble. He enjoyed his weekly poker games for 60 years, each time journaling his winnings.
- She was an avid bingo player and started hosting games at her home to bring family and friends over for a dinner and a visit. It was loud, full of laughter and silliness, but, oh so much fun. She liked to show us that we could have a good time without alcohol or drugs.

> **"She was a gifted jazz vocalist and an accomplished professional musician, performing and composing throughout her life."**
>
> *— Dorothy's obituary*

A love of music is a powerful force, whether making it or listening to it.

- She loved classical music and would paint for hours while enjoying her own little world in her heart and soul.
- He was an accomplished bagpipe player who was proud to wear his Scottish kilt.
- He had a passion for hard rock music and the bass guitar. Spending time jammin' with his band brought him much happiness.
- He always had his toe tapping to old time music, especially the fiddlers.
- He was a wannabe ukulele and guitar player.
- She loved the clarity and perfect pitch of hand bells.
- She easily popped champagne with family and friends to celebrate the incredible joy she felt for life, always eager to play a tune on her treasured organ.

For many cooks and bakers, the kitchen inspires more than a meal; it is their refuge.

- She will be remembered for her adoration of baking and sharing her cinnamon rolls, banana bread, pies, and brownies with the communities, churches, and people she treasured.
- For 50 years, he made pickles that he freely gave to anyone who would return the jar.
- He enjoyed cooking burgoo. *(Burgoo is a meat and vegetable stew similar to Mulligan stew.)*
- As a pie-baker extraordinaire, she set the standard for the perfect homemade crust.
- He was known for sharing his pecan fudge clusters to the delight of many. It was a tedious recipe he learned from his mother at the age of 12 and he used her "Magic Spoon" for every batch.

> **"He was a passionate collector, combing flea markets and online auctions daily in such diverse areas as Chinese bronzes, American prehistoric pottery, Frank Lloyd Wright furniture, quartz crystals, and early daguerreotypes."**
>
> — *Daniel's obituary*

Collecting one thing or another is a popular hobby: stamps, coins, rocks, baseball cards, or shot glasses. Some hobbyists focus on the unusual: Buddhist art, Native American artifacts, antique Scottish shotguns, British antiques, Hawaiian shirts, Elvis memorabilia, and World War II watches. Psychologists say collectors find more than an object; they find satisfaction and peace.

- As a hobby, he studied medicine and pharmacology his entire adult life, collecting medical memorabilia along the way. His collection of medical pens alone grew into the thousands.
- Due to her affection for her horse named Pig, she amassed an extensive collection of equine and porcine décor—pictures, figurines, and especially Christmas ornaments.
- He collected old Colts and Springfields.
- He was a renowned collector of baseball memorabilia, and selected pieces now reside in the Smithsonian Museum.
- She proudly displayed her collection of tobacco signs and antique toasters in her crowded kitchen.
- He was a collector of John Deere memorabilia including life-size and toy tractors. He really enjoyed the new John Deere puzzle he received every Christmas.
- She enjoyed collecting whirligigs which were proudly displayed along the top of the fence in her yard for the wind to animate them best.
- Her collection of Santa Clauses numbered more than 700.
- She was a lifelong cat lover and also a collector of everything cats, from faucet handles to clocks to light switch plates, earning her the reputation of living in a veritable cat museum.
- She was a very accomplished shell collector, and imparted this interest to her sons, who still suffer from "Shell Stoop."

> **"He and his wife visited covered bridges over the past 30 years. He enjoyed photographing and documenting them from a draftsmen's perspective."**
>
> — *Rollin's obituary*

This wide variety of hobbies reflects the diverse nature of humanity.

- He had many interests: he was an avid gambler, going on many junkets around the world. He and his wife trained and became blackjack dealers when the casino came to town.
- He was a marksman and he shot competitively in bench-rest rifle and pistol on the national level.
- He was an avid putt-putt player.
- His favorite pastime was taking his truck out to play in the snow.
- She restored small statues and other ceramic items. "Momma Smurf's" claim to fame was they all left her care with eyelashes.
- His hobbies usually revolved around rural activities such rodeos, threshing demonstrations, and vintage machinery shows.
- She was known for the bear statue in her front yard, which she dressed up for many occasions.
- For many years she taught workshops in the art of Ukrainian Easter eggs and enjoyed traditional Ukrainian cross stitch.
- With her son, she had been memorizing the books of the Bible and had memorized up to Amos before she passed away.

Hobbies usually make a person more interesting. Meaning no disrespect, I'm not sure I'd have enjoyed a long conversation with these people. *(Please note that most of these unusual hobbyists are men.)*

- He loved figuring out mathematical functions on his smart phone.
- He was a map enthusiast.
- His passions included trains, and he knew everything about them. He also liked a great cassoulet.
- She enjoyed looking for and processing rebates and coupons.
- His favorite area of discussion was taxes, which he could inject into any conversation.

- He developed a love for poison dart frogs, even building a temperature-controlled room for them in his home.
- He mastered crab grass eradication, and squirrels were his ultimate nemesis.
- He read each new issue of the *Harbor Freight Tool* catalog cover to cover.
- He produced an expansive body of avocado seed carvings.

> **"His passion was animals, especially horses. He was a horse whisperer if there ever was one. It just came naturally to him; he had a sense about animals."**
>
> — *Raymond's obituary*

Some pursuits are defined not just as a hobby, but as the center of a life.

- He would keep track of the weather around the country on the computer for his relatives. He loved Google Earth and Google Maps.
- His main passion was woodworking, and he was best known for his complex scroll saw projects.
- His true passion was that of being a picker, a person who goes to garage sales and estate sales and looks for those special one-of-a-kind items to buy and then either to keep for personal enjoyment or sell for a profit. He would tell customers that his markup was only 10%. Some actually believed that.
- She enjoyed planting and caring for her gladiolas, planting as many as 7,000 some summers.
- Whether she was taming Spanish mustangs while living in a rural community, or advocating for organic gardening in the early 70s, she could be counted on to show energy and conviction in all she did.
- She had a passion to have a place where "Big girls" could go to be comfortable, not be judged, and learn to love and accept themselves.
- His passions included relishing every moment of toiling over his plants in his greenhouse that he built with pride, and mowing his lawn that would always be greener than our envy.

- He spent the last two decades cultivating American chestnut trees in hopes of restoring these majestic giants to prominence in the American forest.
- He loved working on anything that had a motor.
- He had a lifelong passion for raising and racing homing pigeons. He loved his birds.

I found this excerpt poignant: "While in high school she was a regular on Dick Clark's *American Bandstand*. Throughout her life she had a passion for dancing. Although weak, on the day before she died, she danced the cha-cha with her husband in their kitchen."

> **"She loved her summers at the pond where you would find her enjoying the call of the loons and the laughter of family with her companion Cuddles purring on her lap."**
>
> — *Ann's obituary*

Obituaries also share simple joys.

- He loved snow removal.
- He enjoyed using his metal detector.
- She spent hours picking berries.
- He was happiest when tinkering.
- He just loved being in his garage.
- He enjoyed visiting family every Sunday, keeping his truck washed and cleaned, and going to the movies.
- She liked to travel, work on word puzzles, and spend time with her crazy cat.
- He especially loved taking his sweetheart dancing and only did the Two-Step.

These people enjoyed varied interests. Perhaps they were more complex or just harder to amuse.

- He had a wide range of interests from medicine to high speed rails to history, literature, music, and the arts. He loved fly fishing; could recite poems from Rumi and Rimbaud; was fascinated by the connection between China, the Silk Road, and the Etruscans; and enjoyed the music of Mozart, Mahler, and Beethoven. He was also a frequent (and often unconventional) contributor to the opinion page of the local newspaper.

- He was a primo pizza expert, seasonal flower displayer, professional photographer, and nothing beat a Porsche on a California Highway. But his heart exposed itself as a dachshund aficionado extraordinaire.
- His interests were wide and each one pursued thoroughly. He was an excellent marksman, an avid hunter, and a lifelong Mason. He learned to sail, scuba dive, operate a ham radio, program a computer, play classical guitar, and grow the best tomatoes.

The final words of these obituaries caught me off guard.

- He enjoyed riding his Goldwing motorcycle, music, and knitting.
- He collected pirate knives, motorcycles and classic cars, and made quilts and pillows.
- He enjoyed fishing, hunting, and drinking every day.

Early Life Stories

> "At the age of 13, she came north to Alaska on a ferry with blacked-out windows, evading the U-boats prowling the area during World War II. Her first winter was spent in an army tent. The next few years saw the family ensconced in a little cabin. She snowshoed and skied through snow and moose to get to the old eight-grade schoolhouse. Hers was to be a fascinating life."
>
> — *Marion's obituary*

A moment in time, even if it occurred long ago, can shape a person's life. Those significant events become memories that endure and are passed from one generation to the next. These unusual life experiences enrich an obituary.

- Tiny, as she was known to all, was born in Alaska, the eighth of 10 children. She grew up on her parents' riverboats that ran freight on interior rivers. It was hard work, but a beautiful life.
- Growing up, she did the cooking and would help her mother take out the rowboat and run a trap line consisting mostly of foxes, weasels, and other small animals.
- As a boy, he would grab his .22 rifle on the way to school and hunt for dinner after school on the way home.
- Her parents, believing they were doing the right thing by her, had her admitted to the state school when she was young. She was proud to share her story so that others could learn from her experiences.
- He spent many summers at his aunt's farm, which was also a summer camp for the boys of political activists and intellectuals of the day. There he gobbled 20 ears of corn in a single sitting,

learned to butcher a chicken, and astounded family and farmhands alike by wiring the barn for electricity.

- His widowed mother raised him and his brother in her boarding house with a 24-hour bridge game playing out in the kitchen and a dozen World War II vets as big brothers.
- Eighty years ago, at the age of 12, he was the youngest angler to receive a gold button for catching a sailfish more than eight feet long.

Details of his birth must have held special meaning. He became an esteemed environmental scientist: "He was born on his parents' seed wheat farm on a polder in the Netherlands." *(A polder is low-lying land reclaimed from the sea and protected by dikes.)*

You can hear the nostalgia in this memory: "As a child he and his brother put up a basketball goal in a vacant lot next to their house and played deep into the night under the glow of a streetlight. It was a boyhood enriched by Scouts and centered at the church."

> **"Her first job was at the age of eight, when she cleaned houses. Her first paycheck was for 85 cents. She cashed her check and bought her siblings color books, crayons, and candy. She was so excited to be able to do this for her siblings."**
>
> — *Mildred's obituary*

Memories of hardship and poverty are recurring themes in obituaries.

- He was born in 1932 and lived above the family's chicken coop.
- He was raised in the Bronx where he was a member of the 1948 high school city championship basketball team. His introduction to basketball came as a child when, because he did not have access to a ball, he repeatedly shot his own hat through a playground hoop.
- He rose from humble beginnings, an awkward reality that underscored his entire life. Aware from an early age that responsibility for himself was his own, he worked at shining shoes and selling newspapers and socks. As a safety crossing

guard he earned his crayons and pencils, paper, and schoolbooks. In the school cafeteria line—on the other side—he earned lunch.

- She was born on the edge of a Georgia swamp and shared her childhood with seven siblings and countless kinfolk, all of whom contributed to a rural fabric she treasured and never truly left. She described her family as poor by the standards of most, but having as much as anyone else they knew, enjoying abundant fresh food, and surrounded by loving family and friends.
- The youngest, born into a bustling family and being a late-in-life child of the Depression, his shoes were never large enough. Eventually, those feet of humble beginnings grew to a 12 quadruple E and it would have been hard for anyone to fill those shoes.
- He was the sixth child of his mother; his father had been killed in a train wreck before he was born. Later, his mother remarried, and they had three more children. The large family lived through the Great Depression in a one-room house. They were a poor but loving family.
- Her family lived on a ranch-homestead in Montana, about 30 miles from town. Their log house had kerosene lamps and an outhouse, but no running water or telephone. She rode a horse with her older siblings to attend first grade in a one-room school.
- She learned to drive the big farm truck in the Kansas hay field while her dad and brothers picked up hay bales. She was a petite nine-year-old requiring a block of wood under her foot and a box to sit on so she could see over the steering wheel.

> **"Famously known throughout her life for being voted 'Best All-around Camper' at Camp Birchwood in Vermont, she died at 89."**
>
> — *Gloria's obituary*

Writers often share some witticisms that are probably part of family stories. Life is filled with laughter. Why not an obituary?

- During his childhood and early years, he was a frequent disturber of the serenity found in the mountains, fields, golf courses, and ski slopes.
- He created interesting and mostly-legal memories with his school buddies, and told the tale of releasing bowling balls from the top of the hill on 27th Street with some friends just to observe what path the balls might take.
- She attended the local Catholic school where she was the favorite of the nuns for her sweet disposition. Then she went to high school, where she always reminded us that Truman Capote was her classmate.

This excerpt is from one was of the most extraordinary obituaries I have read. Its eloquence is in the details: "Young Charley was attentive to honor and duty. He once bloodied the nose of a bully who had jumped his cousin. Gentle Ruby (his mother) made Charley apologize. Irascible Bill (his father) was proud, prouder still when Charley won the 1942 National Marble Championship. The victory became a newsreel feature and pictorial in *Parade* magazine. Marbles introduced Charley to lifelong sports virtuosity. Instinctively, he has been a team player. He led, and he also followed."

> **"She graduated from high school as valedictorian in 1955 and was the first female school bus driver in the county while in high school."**
>
> — *Ellen's obituary*

Strong memories are formed during the volatile and impressionable years of high school. Romantic crushes, struggles for popularity, peer pressure, and social, athletic, and academic competition are the stuff of teenage angst. If you were class valedictorian, as it seems many people were, this accolade is included in your obituary, even after 80 years: "He graduated from high school in 1938 as class valedictorian."

> **"In the fifth grade she was asked to play high-school-level basketball and was the MVP of her team. She died at 82."**
>
> *— Ruth's obituary*

If it wasn't academic accolades people recalled, it was athletic prowess.

- During his senior year in high school he tied for the state championship in pole vaulting. *(He died at 94 years of age.)*
- He was an accomplished football player in high school and made the All-State team in 1952 following a winless season.
- She graduated from high school in 1932, having won the award for the best athlete in the school for three years in a row, a record that stands to this day.
- His proudest achievement, and something he steadfastly maintained until the end, was that he was one of the all-time highest scorers, per games played, in the 1949-1950 season.

> **"She was a brilliant public speaker, winning the 1949 high school public-speaking competition, much to the dismay of the second-place finisher, her brother Brian, the future Prime Minister of Canada."**
>
> *— Olive's obituary*

Social standing and popularity in high school remained important decades later.

- She graduated from high school in 1931, where she was the first May Day Queen.
- She graduated from high school in 1945, where she was a cheerleader and voted the cutest senior.
- He graduated from high school in 1950, where he was voted Best Dancer and Best Singer, two of his many talents which he shared throughout his life.
- She graduated from high school in 1952, and she helped to establish the school's colors, original mascot, and the school song.

> **"She was so proud of being given the Zaner-Blosser Handwriting award in school in 1948, which she displayed in her home."**
>
> — *Sarah's obituary*

Inclusion of these school memories make me hope they were not the highlight of a person's life.

- She graduated from Mrs. Hunter's kindergarten class in 1939.
- While growing up, she attended a one-room schoolhouse where she had perfect attendance. She died at 101 years old.
- In 1938 she was Cinderella in the second grade school play, and in the fourth grade she was a Junior Rose Festival Princess.
- He played saxophone in his high school band. He died at 96.
- He was elected a class officer by his peers in 1946, and even dated the school's prom queen his senior year.
- His claim to early fame was a stunning rendition of Elvis Presley in his high school's talent show in 1957.
- Among her fondest memories was her role as head majorette in the high school marching band. She later reminisced: "I remember believing my high school was the center of the universe."

A few people excel at everything.

- He graduated from high school in 1945 as the class valedictorian. He was also an outstanding athlete who lettered in football, basketball, and baseball.
- During high school she acted in all school plays, played the cello, participated in sports and dance, modeled housecoats in Manhattan, and sang in the All-State chorus. She graduated as valedictorian in 1938.

People who changed the trajectory of the dearly departed's life are remembered in obits.

- After leaving Communist Bulgaria in 1959, he arrived in Beirut, Lebanon. After learning English from an American high school teacher in Beirut, he was accepted to college on a full scholarship but couldn't afford his living expenses. He thought he would not be able to pursue his education when an anonymous benefactor altered his life. He later learned that his English teacher of minimal means made his education possible. This act of generosity and kindness is one he never forgot. He provided educational opportunities for more than 350 individuals of Armenian descent.

- As a young boy he loved working with his dad at their family-owned newspaper store. Always eager to learn, he received a full scholarship to a prestigious high school. After graduation, a loyal and affluent customer saw him working at the family shop and asked why he was not in college. After learning that his family could not afford the tuition, she offered to pay for any college of his choosing. He went on to graduate from Columbia University and then medical school.

Success in college is an important part of a legacy.

- She graduated from college and received a double major and double master's degree by the age of 19. She was able to skip some grades and do extra studies, working overtime on schoolwork and jobs to get through quickly during the time of World War II.
- She graduated from college with honors in 1939, when only four percent of women earned a college degree.
- A highlight of her college career was the opportunity to meet First Lady Eleanor Roosevelt and lead her on a campus tour.

This man may have been the brunt of family jokes: "He was the first in his family to attend college. He graduated from Harvard Law School where he majored in commas and semi-colons, and supported himself at the expense of his poker buddies."

Some people are the cream of the crop!

- He graduated from medical school with distinction, academically first in the class, earning eight of the ten awards given at graduation.
- He was valedictorian at his high school, graduated in the top of his class from the US Air Force Academy where President Nixon presented him with his diploma, and graduated with honors from medical school.

Who could top this man? "He was incomparably charismatic and indefatigably competitive. During college, he played on the football, baseball, basketball, and golf teams and was the university-wide handball champion. He was part of the legendary squad to defeat #1 ranked Army, still considered to be the greatest upset in college football history."

> **"He taught himself the workings of pinball machines and jukeboxes, and was honored by the Wurlitzer Company as a top repairman at the age of 12."**
>
> *— Mariano's obituary*

People who were truly exceptional, if not child geniuses or musical prodigies, leave memories worth bragging about.

- She was the youngest graduate of Columbia University at that time. She was 14.
- At the age of 15 he entered college, one of nine students chosen internationally for their remarkable levels of intelligence. He was officially categorized a genius very early in life.
- She learned to read at age 3 and started school at age 4. She was the valedictorian of her senior class and the first in her family to go to college. She worked at the Oak Ridge National Laboratory during World War II to earn her college tuition.
- Growing up, he was an avid reader and computer genius. At 12 he could already type 110 words per minute and he made his own miniature computer the size of a small wallet.
- His love of science started as a child, leading a group of neighborhood kids in various real-life experiments that allowed them to hone their problem-solving skills. They performed chemistry experiments in his lab inside his family's chicken coop. They developed an interest in things that go "boom" well beyond simple black gunpowder. The chickens did not appreciate the experiments for sure.

- He was a child prodigy and the youngest oboe soloist with the Pittsburgh Symphony.
- Her gifts were recognized early with a childhood scholarship to study music. She played the Haydn Concerto in D Major with the Juilliard Orchestra at 9 years old, and at 16 she played at Carnegie Hall.

This man had a remarkable childhood: "He was born in Poland in 1924. When World War II broke out, his family fled, but he and his mother were eventually arrested by Soviet police and sent to a Russian labor camp. After being released in 1941, he and his mother spent the remainder of the war in Tajikistan. After the war, they sailed to the United States and were reunited with other family members who had successfully escaped at the beginning of the war. When he was 24 years old, he entered Yale's PhD program and received a doctorate and then taught Russian as a Yale professor. He was the only tenured professor without a high school diploma or bachelor's degree."

First jobs hold a special spot in people's memory banks.

- At 14, he had a nine-mile paper route and got his first camera, thus developing a lifelong love for photography.
- As a teenager he worked in his dad's business. It was hard physical work for 56 hours a week for 15 cents an hour. That job made him strong.
- During high school she worked as a secretary at a prisoner-of-war camp.
- He felt he was destined to be a funeral director from an early age when he saw a funeral being conducted outside his classroom window. He served as an embalmer and funeral director for 61 years.

> **"Shortly after she was born, she and her family were thrust into the events of World War II when they were forcibly relocated from their home to an internment camp in Idaho. Having been interned at a very young age, her outlook on life and the world was influenced by this experience and it had the lasting effects on her family. As such, she was a lifelong advocate for civil rights and equality, which guided her perspective and passion towards making a difference."**
>
> — *Betty's obituary*

Experiences of war are imprinted on the minds of children and may become part of their family's legacy.

- In his youth he was a political renegade. He worked tirelessly towards liberating Albania from communism and personally spearheaded the emancipation of Kosovo, among the most consequential figures involved in its historic fight for independence. He was a champion for the rights of refugees and a courageous and selfless man.
- He and his younger sister came to the U.S. in 1941 after a two-year stay with a foster family in Sweden and an arduous journey across Siberia on the "Kindertransport." *(This organized rescue effort brought nearly 10,000 children from Nazi-controlled areas of Europe to Great Britain between 1938 and 1940.)*

Memories of hardships and successes are integral parts of any life story. Including them in an obituary underscores their significance and makes for fascinating reading: "She was 14 when the Soviet Union attacked her homeland of Finland in 1939. The war brought many hardships including a period of separation from family as a child evacuee in Sweden, safe from the bombing raids over Helsinki. She had little food during many months of teenage years and no winter coat for several years. Her mother told her to sprint everywhere to keep warm, so when she walked, it was super fast! At age 91 she still easily could cover two miles."

Military Service

"He was a well-dressed three-time war vet. He served tours
in South Korea, Vietnam, the Battle of Heartbreak Ridge,
and the conflict of Grenada. He was a military intelligence
commander and served under General Westmoreland."

— *Richard's obituary*

Obituaries lift up military service as a profound experience in the life
of the deceased. When people endure these rigors together, they form
lifelong friendships and, for good or bad, hold tight to the military life
forever.

- His most cherished military memories were that of a Captain
  in the 5th Division of the Army Infantry in Vietnam. He has
  corresponded with and maintained his friendship with many of
  his much-respected warrior friends.
- Those he led were devoted to him. He was the epitome of the
  combat infantry soldier. He loved his men and they worshipped
  him. He flew out to missions to be among the ground-
  pounders, talking to them, absorbing the burdens they carried
  and the arduousness of the mission. He had that extraordinary
  leadership characteristic that made you want to please him.
  When the mission was accomplished, nothing felt better than to
  have him look at you, and smile, and say "Drive on!"

> **"He always emphasized that his experiences during WWII, including being a prisoner of war, imbued him with a deep and abiding faith in the grace of God."**
>
> — *Edward's obituary*

The culture of respect, order, and ultimate dedication defines the military culture, impacting the rest of a service member's life.

- Many an evening heard him recite old war stories over the flickering light of a campfire, alone or with others. He would often recite the Gettysburg Address while walking down a trail. He loved that memorable speech.
- Among the incredibly numerous and significant events in his life, those formative years serving in Korea left the most indelible mark.
- Between graduating from Princeton and enrolling in Yale Law School, he had the enlightening and democratizing experience of enlisting in the Air Force.
- Like many of his generation, he rarely spoke of the war and what they went through. Only in his later years did he reveal stories of missions he'd carry with him forever.
- He credits the Marine Corps with putting him on the right path and giving him the focus he needed as a tough kid growing up.
- His experiences in the Pacific aiding wounded and traumatized soldiers inspired him to become a minister.
- This great man served in the U.S. Navy, of which he was deeply proud. This experience shaped him and his hope for humanity.
- After his Army career, he went to college on the G.I. Bill and graduated. He believed the G.I. Bill changed his life: "I loved the service: it did more for me than I ever did for it."
- His service in post-war Germany helped shape his life's outlook, and changed the lives of countless people. His work was to comb through files, documents, and photos amid utter devastation to help survivors stitch their identities back together.

> **"He endured both the pride and punishment of the war,
> carrying with him five bullet wounds, 25-35 shrapnel wounds,
> and first- and second-degree burns received during combat
> after two tours of duty in the Republic of Vietnam."**
>
> *— Robert's obituary*

Many veterans rightly believe their service is a badge of honor.

- A decorated U.S. Marine in Company G, 2nd Battalion, 21st Marines, Third Division, he participated in combat at the Battle of Iwo Jima. He educated others about his experiences and his pride in being a Marine.
- As a WWII veteran and part of the Greatest Generation, he began his service as a gunner on a B-24 bomber. He is credited with completing 50-plus combat missions with the 474th Fighter Group. He loved his country and was proud of the flag when he died at 96.
- He volunteered for service in the United States Navy at the ripe old age of 17 and immediately realized he didn't much enjoy being bossed around. He only stuck it out for one war. Before his discharge, however, the government awarded numerous ribbons and medals for various honorable acts.

World War I spanned July, 28, 1914, to November 11, 1918. I noted only one mention of World War I in my obituary research: "He served as a tugboat captain during World War I in the European theatre." *(Most heroes who fought in what was considered "The War to End All Wars" are already deceased.)*

"Immediately after graduating from high school, he joined the U. S. Navy. During his service he participated in the then-secret mustard gas testing and suffered severe blistering of his skin. Later he was a plank owner on the attack cargo ship, USS Leo. During the assault on Iwo Jima on February 19, 1945, he was wounded by shrapnel from an attack by a Japanese Zero plane. He was never without his USS Leo cap on his head."

— *Robert's obituary*

The Greatest Generation helped win World War II (WWII). Many enlisted in the armed forces at a very young age, often disrupting their education.

- His college education was interrupted in 1943. He served in the Army as a sergeant in the Pacific Theater where he was badly burned in a munitions dump explosion and nearly died.

- He quit school in the 10th grade and joined the Navy. He ran the arresting gear to catch the planes when they returned from a run, on the USS Shangri-La aircraft carrier. He was in "Operation Crossroads" when the "A bombs" were dropped on the Bikini Atoll.

- At age 19 he landed on Normandy on the second morning of D-Day and also fought bravely in the Battle of the Bulge in the Rhineland and Central Europe. He was a recipient of many Purple Hearts.

- He entered the Navy at 17, exchanging the quiet of his parents' berry farm for battle in Okinawa. He joined the service in the fall, and spent Christmas that year traveling to the Pacific front. "My parents felt it was the patriotic thing to do." Serving on a troop transport ship, he traveled nearly 50,000 miles, taking soldiers to combat in Asia and bringing back the wounded.

- In 1944 he enrolled in college but only got to stay for 19 days when he was called to active duty in the U.S. Army Air Corps. He served in the Pacific Theater as a radio operator and gunner on B-17 Bombers. He was stationed in Okinawa and was later assigned to General Douglas MacArthur's personal aircraft "Bataan." He was a proud patriot.

This writer injected some humor: "He enlisted in the Navy at 17. Never having learned how to swim, he walked across the bottom of the pool when he took the swim test, undeterred that this technique might not work so well in the Pacific Ocean. He applied his love for electronics to the brand new technology of radar, becoming the go-to authority for his 'Universal Maintenance Adjustment' a.k.a. a sharp whack on the side of any recalcitrant device."

Two obituaries in *The New York Times* on the same day caught my eye. One was only 15 lines long, 9 lines of which are: "He helped to liberate the Dachau Concentration Camp on April 29, 1945, by driving a tank through its front gate. He served as a technical sergeant for the 23rd Tank Battalion of the 12th Armored Division." *(He was 20 years old. I imagine whatever else he did in the next 75 years paled in comparison to this monumental feat.)*

A major portion of the second man's obituary in *The Times* was a longer description of the 92-year-old's military service. This obituary, published at considerable cost, demonstrates the impact this experience had on him: "He enlisted at the age of 17 and was assigned to the 9th Army's 95th Battalion, Company C, as a medic, trained especially in the treatment of those wounded by chemical gas in warfare. He served with distinction in the clash at Hurtgen Forest and at the Battle of the Bulge. He and his Company aided in the liberation of detainees from the Bergen-Belsen concentration camp and from the Theresienstadt death camp. Since he spoke German, he was able to communicate with the survivors and their families, who later regularly wrote to him and telephoned to thank him for his service."

As George Patton said, "It is foolish and wrong to mourn the men who died. Rather we should thank God that such men lived." These veterans believed the honor of serving with this legendary General was momentous enough to include in their obituaries.

- He entered the military, where he served in General George Patton's 3rd Army, receiving multiple mortar shell injuries. In 2018 he was awarded the French Legion of Honor for his service to France.

- He served in the Ardennes Forest with the 87th Infantry "Golden Acorn" Division, part of General George Patton's 3rd Army. His unit passed into Belgium in January 1945 and spent the coldest winter of the last century in the trenches. He was wounded in Germany at the Siegfried Line during the Battle of the Bulge in February 1945.

> **"He served in the U.S. Army Medical Corps during World War II, captured at the Battle of the Bulge, forced onto the Seven Day Death March, and remained a POW until the war ended."**
>
> *— Robert's obituary*

Some veterans endured unimaginable horrors, and their bravery is difficult to fathom.

- While aboard the USS Curtiss, he survived a kamikaze attack that killed 35.
- He served his country as a gunner on a Navy bomber where he survived not one, but two plane crashes, and several days on a life raft.
- On June 6, 1944, he was on the first troop transport ship to arrive at Omaha Beach.
- He volunteered for the U.S. Army Air Corp, working first as a mechanic and then as a B-24 pilot. He served overseas in Italy and was shot down twice. The second time he was captured and spent 14 months in German Stalag Luft 3 and then in Nuremberg prisoner of war camps before being liberated by the U.S. Army in May 1944. He was a good man.
- He enlisted and was sent to Europe in the early 1940s. He trained as a booby trap explosive detonator and survived the frontline foxholes. He was among the troops that liberated France during the war and the Nordhausen concentration camp at the end of the war.
- He marched from India to China and helped set up a hospital laboratory in Shanghai.

> **"He was a B-25 pilot and was shot down twice. He flew 65 bombing missions over North Africa before being sent home due to this high number of missions. His bravery in war earned him a private audience with the Pope."**
>
> — *McDaniel's obituary*

Wartime pilots took particular pride in their service. Their obituaries lauded their flying duties and hours, which rightfully earned them commendations.

- He was a Navy air ace during WWII who shot down nine Japanese planes while flying propeller-driven fighters. He was credited with his first "kill" when he shot down a Japanese dive bomber. The next year he downed three torpedo bombers and became an ace when he shot down a Zero fighter off the Palau Island chain in 1944, and shot down four more Zeros that same year. He later became a member of the Navy's Blue Angels. *(A flying ace is a military aviator with at least five kills.)*
- He was a B-17 pilot in WWII and flew 66 missions before being shot down in Germany. He was a prisoner of war for 11 months.
- He was a ferry pilot in WWII with the Army Air Corps, flying every type of plane the Army had in its inventory, including the B-17 "Memphis Belle." In 2018, he was honored at the 75th anniversary ceremony celebrating the restoration of the "Memphis Belle." He was the last known surviving pilot to have flown the Belle on a 10-day bond drive after the end of WWII.
- He logged more than 600 airtime combat hours flying over "The Hump." *(This is the name given to the eastern end of the Himalayan Mountains over which Allied pilots flew transport aircraft to resupply forces based in China.)*
- He served in the U.S. Army Air Corps as a pilot with the 446th 8th Air Division and flew 260 combat hours over Europe in a B-24 named the "Rubber Check."

Some military service is unique.

- He was a member of the U.S. Marine Corps Honor Guard that accompanied President Franklin Delano Roosevelt's body during the farewell parade in Washington, D.C.
- He was a soldier in the U.S. Army and served for several years as a spy in Munich during the 1950s. Posing as an art student, he ventured forth ostensibly to sketch picturesque buildings and settings. He would then draw the East German military installations and sites whose parameters and specifications he had memorized for the benefit of Army intelligence. He also processed intelligence reports from defectors during the Hungarian uprising.

During WWII, 350,000 women proudly served in the U.S. Armed Forces, at home and abroad.

- She enlisted in the Navy and was VERY proud to be a veteran.
- A proud veteran, after 101 years, may she rest in peace.
- She was a captain in the Army Nurse Corps, serving as a nurse in the African Theater and in Berlin, Germany, during the War of Occupation and the Berlin Air Lift.
- Following the bombing of Pearl Harbor, she enlisted in the Army Nurse Corps and served in England for two years. She then landed on Omaha Beach following the 9th Army through Northern France, the Rhineland, Ardennes, Belgium, Holland, and on to Germany. She had always said, "Our Country needed us; it was as simple as that."

The oldest known Marine died in early 2021 at 107 years of age, having enlisted in 1943 as a female Marine reservist: "They put me behind a typewriter instead of flying an airplane. Still, I loved the hats we were wearing. It was fun when I got the first complete Marine outfit. I loved it very much."

"She was a plane spotter on Village Hill."

— Liz's obituary

Some women served in civilian support of the war effort.

- She served in the Civilian Observer Corps and she watched for bombers from a tower in downtown Cleveland for the U.S. Air Force.
- She worked for a propeller company as a vibration analyst and an engineering aide until the war ended in 1945.
- During the 1940s, she worked at Sylvania making tubes that were used in bombs during WWII.
- She was a dutiful Army wife, supporting her late husband throughout his 28-year career as an officer. We often take for granted the sacrifices of the military dependents—the people who keep the home fires burning while their loved ones deploy. At times she was a single mom for a brood of six children. What a strong woman she was. She and others like her deserve medals. She was of The Greatest Generation.

These women played remarkable roles.

- A 1939 graduate of Wellesley College, she was a "computer," performing complex calculations at the MIT Radiation Lab.
- She was always a brilliant student, having completed high school at 15. After graduating from college, she worked at Oak Ridge, Tennessee, as staff support for the Manhattan Project, the top-secret development of the atomic bomb that ended WWII.

Sadly, the contributions of women were not always appreciated.

- She worked as a shipfitter, helping the U.S. cause, while experiencing discrimination both as a Jew and a woman. She left a legacy of fighting for justice.
- Commissioned as a Lieutenant in the Navy, she was in one of the early classes of WAVES training at Smith College, choosing celestial navigation as her course of study. After training, she taught navigation to pilots. After the war, using a slide rule, she was a human computer on the team that designed and built the Piasecki H-21 Workhorse/Shawnee helicopter, nicknamed the

"Flying Banana." She applied to graduate school in Engineering and was accepted, only to be denied admission when it was discovered that she was a woman!

> **"She was a 'Rosie the Riveter' at Tinker Field building C47s."**
>
> — *Hattie's obituary*

Industry recruited women workers. Remember the U.S. government's "Rosie the Riveter" propaganda campaign? The strong, bandana-clad Rosie became the iconic image of working women during WWII.

- She served as part of the legendary Rosie the Riveter brigade where she repaired and assembled airplanes.
- She worked grinding burrs off crankshaft casings from 1942 to 1945. She was a member of the American Rosie the Riveter Association.
- She worked as a riveter for the Brooklyn Navy Yard.

> **"He joined the U.S. Army in 1942 and experienced segregation by being attached to the 999th Field Artillery Battalion (all-black unit). He was part of the D-Day invasion."**
>
> — *Ulysses's obituary*

Veterans' unusual experiences in service to their country were worthy of inclusion in their obituaries.

- He served in the U.S. Army with distinction. Landing in Normandy shortly after D-Day, he was the first G.I. to cross into Luxemburg during the Battle of the Bulge.
- He enlisted in the Army serving as a Japanese language officer and cryptanalyst in the Signal Intelligence Service, reading foreign codes and ciphers. Their work was known to have shortened the war. In what he always regarded his proudest achievement, he translated a message from the Japanese Ambassador to Germany recounting German preparations in North France to repel the expected invasion, which proved

invaluable to Allied planners in England. He received a War Department Citation for his service.

- He parachuted into France on D-Day and into Holland during Operation Market Garden. He was in Belgium during the Battle of the Bulge and participated in all the battles of WWII in which the 101st Airborne "Screaming Eagles" were involved.

- He served as a combat photographer in WWII with the 11th Airborne Division in the Pacific Theater of Operations where he received a Bronze Star for Valor. As one of the first American Soldiers to enter Tokyo after the Japanese surrender, he documented the capture of Premier Tojo, Tokyo Rose, and the Butcher of Warsaw. He remained in Japan with the Army and directed the filming of the Tokyo War Crimes Tribunal.

> **"He served as a gunner in the 25th Division "Wolfhounds" G Company 27th Infantry Regiment, earning three Bronze Stars for valor under fire."**
>
> *— Raymond's obituary*

Obituaries include service in the Korean Conflict, which began on June 25, 1950, when North Korea invaded South Korea, and ended on July 27, 1953.

- He served in the Army as an experimental engineer on secret government projects for the military during the Korean War.

- After basic training, he joined the U.S. Army in an elite paratrooper unit. He selected jumping out of airplanes to avoid active combat.

- In 1952 he was drafted into the Army and sent to fight in Korea. He was assigned to Company D 279th Infantry as a heavy machine gun operator and saw more than his share of action.

This excerpt is interesting: "He served our nation as a Captain in the U.S. Army Medical Corps and as a surgeon at the famed 8055th Mobile Army Surgical Hospital in Korea, which became the basis for the movie and television series *M*A*S*H*. He served as the inspiration for the fictional character Hawkeye Pierce."

> **"He was a member of the elite 'Wolf Hound' unit when he was awarded his first Bronze Star in Vietnam by General Westmoreland. "**
>
> — *Dale's obituary*

The Vietnam War began November 1, 1955, and ended with the fall of Saigon on April 30, 1975. More than 58,000 Americans were killed. Opposition to the war bitterly divided the country. Sometimes the struggle raged within an individual: "Despite his opposition to the war, he went to Vietnam in 1968. He proudly served, first as a combat medic, and later as a surgical assistant in a field hospital."

- For his 17th birthday he got a red 1966 Mustang; for his 18th birthday he was in the U.S. Army practicing how to stay in a helicopter; for his 19th birthday he had been in Vietnam three months flying around as a Door Gunner assigned to the Spartans of the 145th Combat Aviation Battalion. Manning an M-60 was life-changing and attitude-changing for him, as for many others.
- He enlisted in the U.S. Army in 1964, proudly serving with the 101st Strike Force "Widow Makers," earning three Bronze Star Medals. He was most proud to be a part of the Ranger brotherhood.
- He was captured in South Vietnam in the Tet Offensive of 1968 and spent more than five years as an American POW of the communists, under often brutal and harsh conditions.
- He was drafted to serve his country as an infantry soldier with the First Air Cavalry. He served approximately nine months when he suffered a "Million Dollar Wound" on Christmas Eve. He spent Christmas day in a hospital in clean, white sheets with pretty nurses.
- Upon graduation from MIT, he was assigned to the 389th Tactical Fighter Squadron to fly F-4s. In 1966, he was deployed with his squadron and flew more than 220 combat missions, with more than 2,900 flying hours.

Here's a particularly poignant story: "He enlisted in the Air Force just days after turning 17, following the example of five of his older brothers who had served in WWII. His Douglas A-1E Skyraider was shot down over the Ho Chi Minh Trail in Laos in 1967. He had flown combat missions almost daily before his death and was posthumously awarded many medals for bravery. He was declared dead in 1974, and his remains were identified in 2019. His son, also a pilot, flew the Boeing 737 bearing his coffin. He was greeted by an Air Force Honor Guard at a solemn homecoming." *(A Skyraider is an American single-seat attack aircraft.)*

> **"He was in Vietnam three times and tread through concentrations of Agent Orange, which led to his being rated 100% Combat Disabled, and ultimately to his metastatic lung cancer, which even a 'Marine's Marine,' could not overcome."**
>
> *—Jan's obituary*

Many soldiers suffered lasting physical and mental effects from their courageous service in Vietnam.

- Serving his country, he flew over 70 helicopter trips in and out of the jungle, surrounded by war and Agent Orange. He didn't talk much about those times and in that era, when our boys came home they were made to feel less than welcome. We changed that for him as we became his source of home, love, and comfort.
- He was diagnosed with multiple myeloma that the VA believed was triggered by Agent Orange during his time in Vietnam.
- His downfall in life he learned in the military, beginning at age 17. He was introduced to alcohol which affected his whole working career. He tried to beat the addiction with treatment at military facilities, but that led to a new addiction, pain pills and his eventual passing.
- He was proud of his service in the U.S. Army; they were and will always be his "Brothers forever." He suffered, as do many vets, from the effects of Agent Orange used during the Vietnam War.

> **"He died in combat operations while serving his county in Afghanistan. He loved the Army and his soldiers. Being a Ranger was the fulfillment of a dream."**
>
> *— Kyle's obituary*

The most recent veterans served in Iraq and Afghanistan. This powerful obituary speaks for the many who serve with honor. They have our gratitude and compassion: "She passed away due to a long battle with PTSD and depression/bipolar disorder. She was a disabled veteran and a U.S. Army E-4 Corporal veteran, serving as a Cargo Specialist in Iraq. She was a hard worker and pushed herself too hard. She was a loving mother of five, whose world revolved around her children. She was 33."

> **"He served in Vietnam and the war defined who he was for the rest of his life. May his soul be freed from the demons that haunted him for so long. The war is finally over."**
>
> *— John's obituary*

Military service, especially involving combat, leaves an indelible scar. Reading obituaries of hundreds of veterans was a sad, educational, and humbling experience. Be sure to thank a veteran for their service: "At a young age and with a sense of duty and commitment to his country, he joined the U.S. Marine Corps, 25th Marines, Bravo Company, and would go on to fight in the Battle of Iwo Jima as a Flamethrower with the 1st Battalion. He was one of the few who served in his battalion to come home and was always proud of the sacrifice that he and his brothers made in the service of their country."

Earning A Living, Making A Life

> "She was a trailblazer in the macho world of auto racing, where she was not considered a woman, but rather a driver. Her explosive speed in 1960 on the hard-packed sands of Daytona Beach earned her a place in the record books. She died at 101."
>
> — *Vicki's obituary*

Our life's work at least partially defines us. "What do you do?" is a universal question. Most obituaries include descriptions of work lives, some in excruciating detail, as though it were a death resume. Some obituaries sum up the work of a lifetime in a few words: truck driver, farmer, disabled coal miner, barber, school bus driver, mason, attorney, heavy equipment operator, lab technician, cashier, or Wal-Mart employee.

> "He enjoyed a 45-year career as a gas pump technician."
>
> — *Donald's obituary*

These obituary writers get right to the point, including length of service.

- She sold Avon for nearly 40 years.
- He was a salesman for Wonder Bread for 38 years.
- He was a cosmetologist until he retired at 93.
- She worked for decades as an oven operator in the bakery department of a cracker company.

> "He operated an auto garage, always smelled of gas and oil, and never said no to anyone in need of auto repair. Although he was often paid in Molson Ice, this was when he was most happy."
>
> — *David's obituary*

A person's pride in their work and the satisfaction they derived from their job can be captured in a few words, if they are descriptive enough. As reflected in one obituary: "The trick in life is to do what you like, and then get paid for it."

- He worked as a tollbooth attendant and was well liked by many of the commuters who traveled through his booth. He lived a pretty simple life that he enjoyed very much.
- He enjoyed being a miner, above ground or underground.
- He loved driving trucks, and was proud to say he had driven almost five million miles accident free.
- He was proud of his 50-year career as a reporter. He wrote a commentary shortly before he died that included the following, "We journalists are not the enemy of the people we ARE the people."
- The two great loves of his life were his wife and the railroad life. He was happiest when he was driving a train. He never wanted to be a conductor because he would have to give up his beloved locomotive.
- He spent his entire working life doing what he loved, driving tractor and running farm equipment, until the age of 95.

> "He was the top-rated Private Eye for over six decades in New York."
>
> — *Joseph's obituary*

Being admired for what you contribute is gratifying. These obituaries show that the work of the deceased was valued by others: skilled backhoe operator, talented surgeon, respected physicist, esteemed professor, a living legend in the stage lighting industry.

- He was known as "Mr. Wizard" in motorsports circles for his work in ignition and wiring systems, which can be viewed in multiple museums.
- He was a world-renowned weaver whose designs were identified by his use of natural yarns.
- His true passion was in towing. He was a legendary tow-truck driver.
- He was blessed with a talent for working with his hands and went into the field of pipefitting. He left his mark in the construction of many landmarks.
- She was a superstar in the optical industry, specializing in designer eyewear and accessories.
- He was an expert in personality disorders, particularly studying psychopaths.

> **"He was a breakfast host where he was told their coffee urns had never been cleaner. Whatever he did, he took pride in doing it well."**
>
> — *Richard's obituary*

These accolades are testament to the fact there is dignity in all work done with pride.

- He worked for 25 years as "the best damn steel pipe buyer in the free world."
- She had a career as the world's best diner waitress.
- She was meticulous in her work as a janitor and cleaning lady. In a message to her friends and family she wrote: "I was very thankful to have been so richly gifted in my life. I loved to keep busy and keep working."
- She worked for UPS early in her career and won an award for "best packing of a truck."
- He worked as a potato shed supervisor most of his life, and his boss considered him a genius.

> **"She was a pioneering AIDS doctor and the creator of housing and health care for prostitutes and drug addicts."**
>
> *—Joyce's obituary*

These people engaged in work that was significant because of its positive impact on others.

- He was a renowned oncologist who was committed to compassionate care and communication with patients and loved ones. He was 38.
- She spent her entire career as a physician assistant providing hope and improving the quality of life for patients with amyotrophic lateral sclerosis.
- He was an internationally renowned pediatrician and pioneer in addressing child abuse and neglect.
- He rose to international academic fame for his groundbreaking work in non-verbal communication. His research explored understanding how we are understood and how we influence others without words.
- Throughout her decades-long legal career she dedicated herself to justice and fairness for all that she represented.
- As a science teacher for more than 40 years, she touched the lives of many students and helped them become the fullest versions of themselves.
- He was a master neuro-linguistic programmer and worked with drug addicted teens.
- She was a nurse for more than six decades who devoted her life to Korean orphans and children with special needs.

The writers' pride for their loved one shines brightly.

- Whether he worked packing crackers, seeding lawns, dairy farming, or detailing cars, he approached every job with care, dependability, attention to details, and a commitment to make it perfect. Work was his passion. Faithful and determined, he worked hard until the final day of his life that he was conscious.

- He was skilled at auto body repair and welding and owned and operated an auto body repair shop for more than 30 years until his retirement. He enjoyed being his own boss and was able to support his family with his business. He resided at the family home above the shop until his death. He loved his business and home and was proud to have built the place with his own two hands.

> **"He owned a machine shop and invented the electric self-compensating chain sharpener. He also invented the hydraulic cattle squeeze chute."**
>
> *— Lowell's obituary*

Some people have unusual jobs: obesity expert, vaudeville acrobat, master doll maker, porcelain artist, horse appraiser, handwriting analyst, and a bouncer at the Red Garter. There are certainly innumerable ways to earn a living.

- He enjoyed flying his plane as frost patrol for potato farmers.
- He worked at an airplane graveyard.
- She worked as an inker for animations like Woody Woodpecker.
- He was a crop duster and caught snakes for extra money.
- He was among the last to work on the steam engines. He retired after 49 years and 9 months of working on the railroad.
- She was the head cook on the Alaskan Oil Field Platforms for many years.
- He had a career as a distinguished bass baritone in the opera world. His specialty was the "buffo" realm. *(A bass singer of comic opera roles.)*
- He was a conductor and engineer on the Yukon Route Narrow Gauge Train in Skagway, Alaska.
- He was a master bookbinder. Many of the books he restored and bound can be found in colleges and museums, a 1614 Latin Bible at the Vatican, and a set of 40 books in Westminster Abbey.

- He trained under professional growers and became, after legalization, a master grower of cannabis in his own right.
- He was founder of the Association for Pet Loss Bereavement, helping people worldwide overcome the loss of beloved pets.
- She was a forensic sculptor who helped law enforcement identify missing or murdered people by deftly reconstructing their faces. Over her 40-year career she sculpted about 300 faces and produced an estimated 70 percent identification rate.

> **"He was a New York State Bingo Control Investigator."**
>
> — *Stanley's obituary*

You probably never knew anyone in these lines of work.

- He was a director of lavishly lurid horror films.
- He drove a Zamboni. *(A machine used to resurface ice for skating.)*
- He was a gold miner by trade.
- He worked as a marine worm digger for more than 50 years.
- He retired after 43 years as a stagehand and sound man on the Las Vegas Strip.
- He served the country as a NASA Astronaut Recovery Team doctor.
- He was president of the Lamp and Shade Institute of America.
- She produced over 1,000 comedy shows at hospitals, nursing homes, and homeless shelters.
- He was a cemetery manager and finally a Certified Crematory Operator.

Meaning no disrespect, I chuckled at these references.

- He retired from the apparel industry after making significant contributions, including bringing men's fashion underwear to the USA.
- During the last two decades of her life she devoted herself to publicizing her husband's 1962 creation of the "Interrobang," a punctuation mark combining a question mark with an exclamation mark.

- His first assignment after college was assistant product manager for Cool Whip and he was subsequently promoted to be product manager for Jell-O.

Some obituaries inject humor into a straightforward job description. One man had an optimistic view of what a job might provide: "I had three requirements for seeking a great job; 1 - All glory, 2 - Top pay, 3 - No work."

- He forged a career in Arctic anthropology, proving his bold claim: "There's always room at the top."
- She was a bookkeeper, working for 45 years alongside her husband in their accounting practice. The plaque on her wall read: "Do you want the man in charge, or the woman who knows what is going on?"
- He was employed for 43 years in the trucking industry. His job descriptions and responsibilities varied, but according to dependable sources, his duties always required carrying a clipboard.
- He was considered to be a poultry expert. If you ever had to choose "Chickenman2" as a username or password—it's because he had already taken "Chickenman1."

> **"She explored many professions, including crab fisherwoman, houseboat deckhand, furniture builder, and entrepreneur. But her expertise in spreading joy, laughter, and kindness was as a bartender."**
>
> — *Mary's obituary*

These people worked at two or more jobs during their careers.

- He was a library administrator and a gambler.
- He was a taxi driver, a foreman on the docks, a self-taught master of computer programming, and then he managed a hedge fund.
- In her early life, she was a ship welder during World War II. She met her husband when she worked as a carhop. She loved to rodeo and was a rodeo secretary. She owned her own bar and was a bartender for several decades.

- As well as being a Teamster for 40 years, he was a truck driver, mechanic, roofer, and electrician. He also won an award for his cake making.
- He embarked on a political consulting career, but times changed and he sought a less stressful life and spent 24 years as a meat cutter.
- She was an Alaskan lodge owner, bush pilot, and licensed hunting guide.
- He was employed as a yogi, polarity therapist, and holistic care practitioner.
- She was a baker before starting her professional piloting career.
- Although he graduated from UC Berkeley with a degree in physics, he bought his own boat and fished.

This man surely held the record: "He led an extraordinary life. While he worked, he had more than 90 jobs. He was manager of a flea market, a door-to-door vacuum cleaner salesman, an executive at the Board of Trade in Chicago, a security guard at a rehabilitation center for celebrities, and many more unusual and interesting jobs."

> **"She was a brilliant geneticist who is known for her pioneering work in the use of forward genetics. Her lab discovered a previously unknown role for cilia in receiving signals from a protein called Hedgehog."**
>
> *— Kathryn's obituary*

Some careers can be summed up in a few words. Others can't. Extraordinary people with extraordinary careers made extraordinary contributions to the world. What they did is difficult to understand. Just be thankful there are such brilliant people.

- At age 3 he taught himself to read using *Motor Trend* magazine as his primer. Some years later he began disassembling his mother's appliances to see how they worked. He spent his entire career in computer innovation and architecture, and was issued 36 patents.
- She was a research physicist in a field known as condensed matter.

- He was a chemical engineer who developed world-renowned expertise in the use of nitric acid in the mining industry to eliminate waste and protect the environment.
- He was an evolutionary ecologist who researched mammal sociality and introduced the theory of human extinction.
- He had a long and distinguished career in weak interaction physics.

These two obituaries describe people who didn't think like the rest of us.

- Considered a classical geometer and magical genius, his boundless curiosity produced contributions to number theory, game theory, coding theory, group theory, knot theory, topology, probability theory, algebra analysis, combinatorics, and more. He discovered an entity in the realm of mathematical symmetry that inhabits 24-dimensional space and discovered surreal numbers.
- He was an internationally known mathematician recognized for his work in Diophantine and commutative geometry. He became known for Szpiro's conjecture, which gave rise to the famous abc conjecture. *(Yes, the very famous abc conjecture!)*

> **"Among his many accomplishments as a neuroscientist, he discovered opiate receptors in the brain and coined the word 'endorphin.' This led toward a better understanding of the biological basis of drug addiction and pain, and the role of the endogenous opioid system on ingestive behavior."**
>
> *—Eric's obituary*

Helen Keller said, "The world is moved along, not only by the mighty shoves of its heroes, but also by the aggregate of tiny pushes of each honest worker." Most of us have benefited from the labor of those who went before us. People we never knew improved our lives.

- She was an attorney who dedicated her life to advocating for unaccompanied immigrant children from all over the world, developing an entirely new model for fighting for their rights.

Thousands of children are safe and reunited with their families because of her work.

- His pioneering work focused on the understanding that reading is most effectively evaluated and addressed as a multisensory experience. He provided millions of struggling students around the world the opportunity to become proficient readers.

- He became an early champion of methadone for the management of intractable opiate addiction and ran one of the best clinics in New York in the 1970s, helping hundreds of people, including the incarcerated.

- She found her niche and followed her passion for nursing, working in the community as a home and public health nurse. She worked in New York City, providing home health to both the excessively wealthy and unreasonably poor, and she offered HIV testing in gay bars and brothels.

- He is mostly known for his many years as a Major Crimes detective specializing in sex crimes. He was a keen investigator and a staunch advocate for the victim. He knew his duty was to give the victim justice and closure.

- He worked as a research biologist and discovered a red algae that has been used by many people for relief of cold sores and shingles.

- For more than 30 years she worked tirelessly on behalf of patients with facial differences and their families. She was gracious and caring and understood how the lives of those with facial differences are improved through comprehensive care.

- She was a physician who worked in support of humanitarian causes with Mother Teresa in the slums of Calcutta, in the refugee camps on the Thai border during the time of the Khmer Rouge genocide, and in France with an organization supporting the needs of people with intellectual disabilities.

- As an attorney, he practiced law for more than 40 years, and was active in the early civil right cases involving the City of Montgomery, and the Rosa Parks and Tuskegee Syphilis cases.

- He was a machinist who crusaded against corrupt labor leaders and introduced labor reforms to entrenched labor unions. He helped draft federal legislation that granted rank-and-file workers guarantees of free speech, assembly, fair hiring, and other civil liberties.

"He was a surgeon who held the record for the fastest appendectomy by an intern in a Naval Hospital, and the patient survived. He also was known for 18-minute bloodless hysterectomies."

— William's obituary

Obituaries extol the pioneering work of the deceased in their fields.

- He excelled in the field of merchandising, marketing, and strategy development. He conceptualized the McDonald's Happy Meal, in use since 1977.
- She worked as one of the nation's most prominent rights advocates for sex workers, devoting her life to the cause of decriminalizing prostitution and destigmatizing its practitioners. She organized an annual Hookers' Ball, a fundraising event that celebrated sex workers and drew politicians, police officers, and movie stars.
- He was a much decorated 35-year journalist and photographer who covered the first moon landing, the Iranian hostage crisis, the launch of the first Space Shuttle mission, and the events of September 11, 2001.

"She was a doctor who conducted early work in senescence (aging of cells) and held a patent on a biomarker of cellular senescence; one of today's most dynamic fields of scientific research. She left an imprint on many a young woman in science and was an inspiration and role model."

— Monica's obituary

Women's obituaries include pioneering accomplishments, achieved despite roadblocks sometimes related to sexism. This woman was extraordinary, but at that time, had trouble landing a job: "She was the only woman in the Yale Law School Class of 1941. Chosen to be on the Editorial Board of the *Yale Law Journal*, she was nevertheless turned down by over 40 firms before being hired."

- She broke the sound barrier in an Air Force F-15.
- She was a physician and pioneer in prenatal cytogenetics.
- She was one of a handful of underground coal miners.
- She was one of the first women neuroanesthesiologists and improved outcomes for countless patients.
- She was a fervent defender of teachers' First Amendment rights and a focus of a landmark case that went all the way to the Supreme Court.
- She had a "can do" attitude and was a pioneer for women's rights. She was the first woman on a remote Alaskan pipeline construction project where she earned the respect of her male counterparts with her work ethic.
- She was raised by staunch socialist émigrés from Tsarist Russia and was a 20-year veteran of the NYPD, a pioneer in her time. She died at 95.
- She went to work for I. M. Pei in 1964 and was one of only three women architects. Her life's work contributed to the ever-changing New York City skyline, where she designed nearly 50 buildings.

This woman did not participate in the traditional workforce nor did she break through any glass ceilings. But there is no doubt she was a hard worker, deserving of accolades: "Every spring, she covered the kitchen floor with newspapers and took her Rototiller apart, cleaning and oiling it, and replacing the worn parts. She built and repaired fencing. She raised an enormous garden and canned or preserved almost everything her family ate. She raised cattle, pigs, and chickens; milked as many as 14 cows by hand morning and night; she sold cream; had 500 laying hens; and had an egg route."

This career could be the plot of a fascinating novel: "In 1961, while raising her four children, she obtained a job at NASA becoming one of the first women to install advanced electronics on the Apollo rockets being built at the facility. Then she was one of seven women to enter the police academy in 1968. Of those, only five women would finish, with her being the first African American woman. As a woman of color, acceptance was not always a given. In 1972 she went undercover and was instrumental in breaking up one of the largest drug organizations during that time. She retired as a lieutenant in the New Orleans Police Department and died at 86."

Our work is a profound part of our life, worth being affirmed at our passing. We not only support our family, but also contribute to the world. And the lucky ones enjoy every moment.

Facing Life's Challenges

> **"She gracefully managed a simple life, full of ups and downs, with courage and calm."**
>
> — *Vivian's obituary*

A life journey is filled with anxieties, blessings, surprises, disappointments, fears, hopes, heartbreak and more. Any measure of a life involves how a person endured the pain and savored the joy.

While each person plays the leading role in their own story, they are not the sole author of its script. Randomness and chance also play an important part. It is so easy for a life to go one way rather than another. One man's obituary summed this up: "His childhood was difficult, his service in Vietnam traumatic, his addiction to alcohol overcome, his life lived in service, and his death after a short but hard fight against cancer." Obituaries prove that the road is almost never easy.

> **"The past two years he traded in his battle with Heartbreak Hill in the Boston Marathon to face his own cancer, which he did with grace, humor, and an 'I hate cancer!' attitude. The battle waged, the outcome is now clear, he sets off on what he calls his next great adventure."**
>
> — *Leo's obituary*

People usually succumb to disease or illness, so these are generally mentioned in obituaries. Most people are remembered as having faced these challenges in a hopeful manner, with courage and even good cheer, even if a wheelchair was needed: "She walked through life with a fierce independence and later persisted rolling through life, taking the limits she had and finding a way to make the rough road she traveled a full and fun one."

- Even in the face of her continuous medical issues, she remained courageous, loving, strong, funny, grateful, and hopeful.
- She cared for her sick mother for 14 years until she herself had a tragic stroke that left her with the use of only her right side. After intense therapy, she rallied to regain her strength only to have a recurrence 20 years later, which left her wheelchair bound. She had a vivacious spirit and was a force to be reckoned with.
- Although he had endured various medical indignities in recent years, he remained to the end a vigorous lover of life.
- She had courageously battled Stage 4 cancer for 11 years and throughout it all she faced each challenge, setback, and treatment with determination and hope. The disease may have taken her body, but her spirit remained strong until the end.

Some people possess an inner strength that enables them to face whatever difficulties they encounter. They adjust their lives accordingly and forge a different path to happiness.

- In spite of years of medical issues, she continued to show her strength with a smile on her face and an appreciation for small pleasures: the warmth of the sun on her face, a good song, or a holiday party.
- Her independence accounted for her inner strength and she was admired by all who knew her. It is also what allowed her to fight breast cancer for 23 years, even when it became Stage IV, metastasizing to her brain. She was adamant that she would beat it when doctors said it was impossible—beat it she did for 14 more years.
- At 20, he broke his neck in a tragic diving accident which resulted in him being a quadriplegic. He lived 30 years as a medical miracle and proudly raised two children. He cherished his time with family and friends. For years he would plow driveways in a modified truck and lived for snowy nights. He never let being in a wheelchair slow him down. Despite the cards he was dealt, you could always count on him for a smile or to lend an ear.

- Her struggle with Parkinson's disease didn't stop her from enjoying her love of biking. As her balance deteriorated and it became harder for her to ride her regular bike, she switched to an adult-sized tricycle and rode the one-mile dirt road where she lived virtually every day.

The resilience shown by these people is awe-inspiring.

- His life took a dramatic turn when he was diagnosed with a motor-neuron degenerative disease which robbed him of his strength and independence. The long-distance runner and body surfer was forced to turn to family and friends for support in meeting his basic needs. But he refused to let the disease define who he was; he never became bitter or blamed others. When it came time to compile material about his life, using a voice augmentation device, he dictated to his son, one letter at a time.
- Despite having cerebral palsy and epilepsy, he enjoyed many pursuits. He had a photographic memory and a passion for studying volcanoes, baseball, and presidents. He enjoyed daily visits to the library to conduct research.
- After her cancer treatment ended in 2017, she started roller derby training. She loved the derby and threw herself into it with the same drive and cheerful stubbornness that she approached everything she loved. Shortly after she passed her skill test, she discovered the cancer had returned and spread to her lungs and bones. She fought for every minute and showed all of us how to carry such burdens, with grit, grace, and love.

At age 55, six weeks after retiring, this man had a massive stroke that changed his world. He lost his ability to speak: "But he refused to stop communicating. Whether through a kind smile, sound effects, and his very own personal version of sign language, he continued to connect, inspire, and endear those around him. He never quit lifting his thumb in the air with a big half smile, charming every waitress, nurse, or stranger he met."

"He battled health issues of almost cartoonish proportions; you name it, and he had it. If it was supposed to work, it didn't. It is a rare gift to navigate the hardships in this life and still retain such a sunny outlook, but he found humor even in times of despair."

— Jerry's obituary

Some people have a gift of turning a dreadful situation into something worthwhile, even wonderful.

- He had several medical disorders, one of which was a rare, very painful disease which left him bedbound for four years. Through the years, he thoroughly researched medical literature and studies in order to optimize his chances to survive and raise his two sons. For many years he was the first point of contact for dozens of people from around the world who sought help for their painful condition, helping prevent at least six people from committing suicide.

- At the age of 24, she suffered a serious stroke. For the rest of her life, she worked hard to overcome the mobility, dexterity, vision, and hearing effects of the stroke. Her determination, perseverance, positive attitude, and accomplishments earned her recognition, including on the floor of the U.S. Senate. She was a tireless advocate and diligent public servant providing service and supporting independence for individuals with disabilities, like her. Post-stroke, she earned a master's degree in U.S. History and took up stand-up comedy, among other pursuits.

The love of family sometimes shines brightly: "He couldn't walk or talk. He could not do many things other people take for granted every day. And when some people looked at him, that's what they saw; the things he couldn't do. But that's not what we saw, and that's not who he was. He could smile. He could frown and cry and even give a dirty look by raising that eyebrow. He would express his love with a look, with a smile, with a squeeze of his hands and the twinkles of his eyes."

I was touched by the respect I heard in this obituary: "He suffered a traumatic brain injury which closed the doors to his business in 2007. Then in 2010 he ended up with throat cancer that left him unable to speak any longer. Well, that didn't stop him from getting his message across or getting your attention; he did that quite well. He was also the guide for getting in and out of the driveway. He would stop traffic so you could back out or park. He wasn't on anyone's payroll, but he sure had a lot of important jobs!"

This was a remarkable woman: "She had a quiet inner toughness and resolve. She was hit by a car as a child and survived; in 1988 she was diagnosed with breast cancer and survived. At age 80, she was struck head on by a 30,000-pound dump truck while traveling home. She was cut out of her vehicle and flown to the hospital with multiple injuries. She spent three weeks in ICU and more than two months receiving in-patient medical treatment. While she was hospitalized, her husband died suddenly. She survived to leave the hospitals and rehab facilities, and amazingly returned to safe driving and living independently. She broke her pelvis in 2017, returned to walking and living in her house, and was still able to have a rewarding life. After her late-life diagnosis of vascular dementia, she was even able to battle her way out of the hospital one more time to pass away at home with family as she desired."

> **"He passed away peacefully after the black cloud of Alzheimer's robbed him of his memories and zest for life."**
>
> *— Ronald's obituary*

There is obvious anguish in obituaries that include the loss of a loved one's mental capacity. Many death notices of older people cite dementia, or specifically Alzheimer's disease, as a late-in-life struggle for both the deceased and their families.

- After the onset of dementia, she did not understand her dilemma, but accepted the circumstances with extraordinary grace and love.
- She overcame the challenges of lupus, breast cancer, congestive heart failure, two aortic valve replacements, and two hip replacements; it was Alzheimer's that finally overwhelmed this fine lady.

- She and her husband are together again with all their friends and loved ones, and now she can remember ALL of their names.
- She suffered from dementia and her fierce independence was taken from her, yet throughout her long battle, she found many reasons to smile and hands to hold.

These survivors knew the heartbreak of loss, but were able to find the silver lining: "All who knew and loved her chose not to think of her as the victim of an incurable brain disease. Rather we think of her as a wife, mother, gifted graphic artist, and a loyal friend whose quiet warmth made the world a kinder place. She was only 67 and had faced Alzheimer's for six years; what a life it stole. The only blessing of the disease is that it brought family, friends, and neighbors together in love and care."

> **"Born in Poland, she was a "Hidden Child" during the Holocaust and grew up with a false identity. Her childhood years were a profile of bravery and resilience. Notwithstanding the hardships she endured, she celebrated life cherishing family and friends. "**
>
> *— Rita's obituary*

When tripped up by life's heartbreak, some people are able to recover their footing. These unusual trials were significant enough to influence the person's remaining years. These excerpts provide perspective as to what we might regard as challenging.

- Her life was shaped by a tragic accident in which she lost her father and all her siblings when she was only 12 years old.
- His life was one of many challenges and hurts so troubling to his psyche. His biological parents were unable to care for him, and he was adopted into a family at a very young age along with his sister. That adoption didn't work, and he was returned— without his sister—to the "system." He was again adopted at five years old. Fetal Alcohol Spectrum Disorder negatively affected him in so many ways his entire life. He struggled mightily to make good decisions, to have impulse control, and was prone to chemical dependency. *(He died of a drug overdose at 31.)*

- She accidently drank lye as a toddler and would spend most of her childhood in hospitals where they reconstructed her throat over the years. She suffered a learning disability because of the 40 surgeries, and the effects of anesthesia, known as ether. She was strong willed. She struggled and fought and endured and was able to earn an 8th grade diploma. She then stayed home and helped her mom and dad in the household.

- He was the fourth of five orphans who were cast adrift in 1964 after their parents were killed by a drunk driver. He and his brothers and sisters created a life raft of support that carried them through their lives.

- He was the oldest of 12 children having a humble beginning and learning to work hard at a very young age. Education was a luxury he was not afforded. As a child he grew up in a Mexican desert village with no running water or electricity. His days consisted of burning needles off cacti to feed cattle, transporting water, and cutting mesquite for firewood.

- In 1921, she moved with her mother and sister to New York City when she was three. Her single mother had to work long hours and was unable to care for them, so she placed the girls in an orphanage where they resided through secondary school. As a result, she was fiercely independent, feisty, opinionated, and unapologetic about all of that.

- Her father worked on the oil rigs for many years so they were always moving. As they travelled by car, she was allowed her favorite doll and blanket, her bible, and clothes.

- A child of the Great Depression, she spent many hours in the "meat" lines to receive either lamb or horse meat.

- She was reunited at age 18 with her father and three sisters after many difficult years in foster care and she has been close to them ever since. A book about her and her three sisters was written by her stepmother, describing their struggles to survive abuse, addiction, and poverty.

- As a person with undetected autism, he remained a lifelong misfit and his family life centered on cats.

This story was fascinating. I can't help but wonder what layers of her life were not revealed: "She had a difficult childhood, running away at 16 to enroll herself in school. At 17 she married a defense attorney, at 28 she married the owner of a cab company, and then she married again. She moved east and married someone in the beverage industry, and then she married a man with whom she shared 28 happy years in New York, Paris, Switzerland, and the Bahamas. In her later years, she rested comfortably in her beautiful home, protected and surrounded by her family. She died bravely, though she had had to live not without fear."

Unpredictable events that fall from thin air can change the course of a life: "When he was a child, his oldest brother drowned in the river. He discovered the body after his mother sent him to the river to call his brother home for dinner. To the day she passed away, he said he could always picture his mom holding her son's head in her lap and sobbing, as if it were just happening."

> **"She survived the Holocaust, but lost her parents and her only brother. Despite her unbearable suffering in the concentration camps, she chose to face her future with hope and love."**
>
> *— Ruth's obituary*

Particularly moving are the obituaries that share the toll taken on children by war.

- She lived through the Nazi occupation of Holland and the murder of her father by the Gestapo, a member of the Dutch resistance. Her experiences of the war shaped the woman she would become, her intense moral character, support of the underdog, and sense of right.
- Born in Syria, his childhood was marred by conflict. His three-year-old younger brother died in his arms after being struck by a military vehicle.
- She was born in 1939 in Germany. As a small girl she was exposed to the violence and bloodshed of World War II. She was haunted by memories of being rushed to the bomb shelter in her mother's arms.
- She was born the 12th of 13 children in Spain. Her family fled the fascist tyranny of Generalissimo Franco after their father,

a prominent attorney, spoke out against the regime. He was dragged out of the family home in the middle of the night and summarily executed in 1936, just before she was born. The family became refugees of the Spanish Civil War.

This story raised many questions: "She began this world with another name. In the 1930s it was unthinkable for a child to be born to a single mother. Her mother contacted the Tennessee Children's Home, now notorious for selling babies, which found a couple who was willing to purchase her child. Her new parents were chosen; they had already adopted one high-profile Memphis baby. She had a rich but strict childhood."

This excerpt from an obituary could certainly provide the plot for a fascinating novel: "She survived the Holocaust and lived a full life well into her 90s. She was born in Poland, one of seven children, before the Holocaust struck Europe. After her father's death, the family was deported to the Mendzec ghetto. She survived several concentration camps and was liberated from Auschwitz-Birkenau and was part of a theater troupe that performed in other camps. She caught the eye of another survivor and they arrived in the United States in 1952. She created a home filled with music amidst other Holocaust survivors."

"Determination never had such a warm and pleasant face."

— *Marybeth's obituary*

These people had the capacity to make something good from their early hardships.

- She and her older brother grew up in Montana and were in the newly built high school for two months when the 1935 earthquake struck. As a result, they went to school for two years in railroad coaches. At the outbreak of World War II she was interned in a Japanese prisoner of war camp for 41 months. The stay at the camp shaped her personality to be full of thrift and gratitude.

- Of Japanese descent, she and her family were incarcerated from 1942 to 1945 at the Minidoka War Relocation Center in Idaho. Undaunted by this experience, she graduated from college and medical school.
- Fleeing anti-Semitism in Europe in 1931, her family took an arduous journey to Argentina and led a life of subsistence farming. She said she was not bitter because of her deprivation, but she was grateful for the sacrifices others had made for her.
- As a child, the meager circumstances of her family necessitated frequent moves between mining camps in the mountain towns of Colorado. However, she enjoyed life with her family, whether living in a small house, a clapboard shanty, or a tent.
- She was the fourth child in a family of ten children. During World War II her family was interned. She never spoke badly about the internment, but talked about all the friends she made in "camp."

There should be some kind of endurance award for this man: "He faced and overcame many obstacles in his life. Starting with polio at age 2, he survived multiple car accidents, two heart attacks, major orthopedic issues resulting in four joint replacements, chronic migraines, and very recently, a quintuple cardiac bypass. He also suffered from depression all his life and won a difficult battle with addiction. Despite being a successful businessman, he also had severe dyslexia. He did not live a single day without pain of some kind. In spite of all this, or maybe because of it, he was always concerned and caring for others."

> **"Challenged in recent years by house fires, suicides, ill-health, and divorce, she remained buoyant with laughter and faith that even these misfortunes expressed a greater glorious plan. Her sketchy early exposure to religion had matured."**
>
> — *Roxanne's obituary*

Over the years life can, and usually will, take unexpected and even unwanted detours. It is uplifting to read how some people weathered these storms, survived, and even thrived.

- She was a fighter, a strong soul who endured more than her fair share of loss over the years, never letting it overshadow her affection for others or her zest for life. She spent over a decade battling cancer with committed determination and managed to find humor in her circumstances through the toughest of moments, routinely defusing even the most dire situations with her infectious laugh. She allowed no illnesses to define her experience and she weathered the storm with dignity and grace. Her attention and positive spirit were always trained on the well-being of those around her.

- About a year ago, Patty expressed a preference to be called Patrick. She did so with the recognition of the cons of pronouns and the habit-hewn limitations of those who loved him most. Our words may have slipped from time to time, but our hearts remained grounded in acceptance and love. We remember the kindness of Patty and we cherish the bravery of Patrick, who lived according to the advice of Kermit the Frog, "Always be yourself."

- There were some turbulent years that resulted in the estrangement of their adopted sons and ultimately a divorce after 30 years of marriage. In 2019, she and one son were reunited and able to reconcile with each other. He struggled with addiction and was in end-stage kidney disease. Her son died in September and she died two months later. This was a time of reconnecting and healing for the whole family.

- As a civilian again at 20 years old after serving in Vietnam, he gravitated toward things fast and wild for a while before finding love, beginning a family, and trying to settle in and make it all work, until the wheels fell off. With his own resilience and some guidance, he was redirected and started again, but never really found his groove. He never lost his optimism and had confidence in God.

> **"She had an indomitable spirit that bounced back from every adversity with a steadfast determination; whatever wave life sent her way, she rode it."**
>
> — *Sheila's obituary*

My selection for the ultimate listing of challenges was this persevering centenarian's life story:

"She spent a year bedridden with rheumatic fever when she was 12 years old and always credited her mother for nursing her back to health from a disease that was fatal for many others. She lived through the Great Depression and experienced the toll it took on her family when they lost their farm to the bank for a matter of a few hundred dollars of debt. Her husband was killed in an explosion in 1977, so she moved and helped build her own house three miles from town and helped raise tons of grandchildren and rescued stray cats. Her resilient spirit was tested in 1995, when she lost both her second husband and a son, and then again in 1999 when another son was killed in a helicopter crash. To the end, she was stubborn and fiercely independent. She died at 103 years, and when she returns to earth again, we are sure it will be as a cat."

The Gift Of Longevity

What are some personality traits and habits that contribute to a long life? Obituaries of those who died later in life included numerous factors: remaining physically active, seeking new experiences, pursuing life goals, enjoying stable relationships, cultivating gratitude and optimism, connecting socially with others, continuing to learn, and being open, resilient, and independent. Being interesting and interested were common themes in these obituaries.

Two women's deaths were memorialized on the same day in the same newspaper. They had much in common. Each died at age 96. Each had a 60-year marriage, worked outside the home, had large families and good friends, enjoyed many hobbies, and remained deeply involved in the community. Also, they each were excellent and active chess players. What can we learn from them? As one lady's obituary stated: "She lived an extremely active, positive, and determined 96 years of life." Deep personal relationships and meaningful activities won't guarantee a long life, but they do make it a more fulfilling experience.

> **"She skied around the Mendenhall Lake at age 90, a world record in terms of blending enjoyment, effort, and inspiration to the people and pets she passed."**
>
> — *Connie's obituary*

Many older people stayed physically active throughout their life.

- In his retirement, he added powerlifting to his weekly workout regime and inspired his grandchildren, workout buddies, and strangers alike.
- When he was in his 70s he and his wife hiked the 73 miles of Hadrian's Wall, from the west coast to the east coast of Britain, with three of their hardiest cohorts.
- He enjoyed biking, and on his 80th birthday, he rode 80 miles.
- Always the athlete, he was still playing flag football with teenagers into his 80s.
- He enjoyed walking two hours a day, and at the age of 87 he took up Pilates.
- At 65 years old she decided to embark on a two-week backpacking train trip through Europe with her grandson and granddaughter.
- She began curling at the age of 17 and continued to curl into her 80s.
- An avid athlete her whole life, she played center forward in field hockey and excelled as a long-distance ocean swimmer and competitive tennis player. After she took up golf later in life, she twice scored a hole-in-one at age 80.
- A scuba diver for over 40 years, he never gave up his passion for the deep, and his last dive at 100+ feet was at the age of 91.
- He was a gifted athlete and became a world-class Frisbee golfer in his later years.
- He was physically active well into his 80s. He swam, played tennis, and roller bladed, although he had no idea how to stop. When he had a heart attack on the tennis court, he still insisted on serving, and was upset when the game was cancelled.
- He made many friends at the gym who looked forward to his constant smile and his bright yellow workout shoes. He died at 92.

- His energy and dedication to improving his physical health led him to start running 5Ks with his grandson at age 77. He celebrated his 85th birthday skydiving. He received a national award which recognizes seniors who inspire and encourage others to maintain an active and healthy lifestyle.

I admired this man's take on aging and life: "He discovered golf after his new knees prevented him from playing tennis, yet many wonder what he enjoyed more—teeing up or searching for lost balls in the rhododendron and creeks. He wasn't fazed by a high stroke count, but was exhilarated to finish a round with more balls than when he began."

> **"Despite knowing the inevitable challenges of a 96-year-long adventure on planet Earth, he brought cheer and strength, dignity and honesty to every struggle. And by example he taught us that giving up is not an option."**
>
> — *Sam's obituary*

Some people remained active, but accepted the limitations of aging and its inevitable impact on their physical abilities.

- He did 1000 crunches a day until the age of 95, when he made some slight modifications.
- She golfed well into her 90s, and even when she gave up skiing, she lived vicariously through the ski trips of her family.
- He played high-level club tennis for many years and only gave up when his knees became too rickety in his late 80s. In his later years of his devotion to the sport, he liked to play what he referred to as Cinderella tennis. "I'm just hoping to make it to the ball."
- In her 89th year, her son took her out to golf. She said, "Honey, this is my last round. I just can't keep up with those 70-year-old girls."

> **"Six months before she died at 99, though she could barely see, scarcely hear, and hardly walk, she was determined to cast her ballot and be counted."**
>
> *— Alice's obituary*

Civic involvement was often celebrated. Despite the fact people were not going to live long enough to reap the rewards of their efforts, they remained committed to their communities and involved in national issues.

- She opposed the war in Vietnam. As one would expect, she embraced the civil rights movement and federal action to enforce racial and religious civil rights. A child of the 20s and 30s, and a woman who knew her own mind, she also embraced the feminist movement, supported passage of the ERA, and most recently, at the age of 94, proudly participated in the 2017 Women's March.

- On her 80th birthday, she campaigned door-to-door for Barack Obama.

- She was a faithful voter and worked for the polls for many years, believing fiercely in the power of the ballot box. And though she was raised and lived her life within conservative enclaves, she was convinced that both the government and the church should be kind and supportive of all. Eager to promote this ideal through her vote, she cast her ballot for the last time in the presidential election when she was 99 years old.

- He continued to find ways to take care of the mountains around him. He volunteered until he was nearly 90 years old by helping to build and maintain trails as well as instilling a love of the outdoors in the next generation.

"She loved rocking and comforting distressed infants at the Neonatal Intensive Care Unit and qualified her first Portuguese Waterdog as a therapy dog for the pediatric ward."

— *Shannon's obituary*

Those who suffer from loneliness are more likely to develop dementia, depression, heart disease, and other health issues. Volunteer opportunities provide human contact and a reason to get up in the morning: "Volunteering was a source of great pride to her and even long after she became a senior citizen, she would volunteer at the senior center. She referred to 'her seniors' as though she was of a different generation, and it is true she remained young at heart."

- He lived in an assisted living facility where he spent many hours reading to the residents and calling bingo.
- In her later years, her special interest was in support of a coalition against domestic and sexual assault. She enabled a local organization to acquire her former home which now serves as a transitional shelter for women and children.
- He helped with the organization of Warriors and Quiet Waters to bring wounded warriors from Iraq and Afghanistan to Montana for fly fishing and rehabilitation.
- In his retirement, he and his wife helped teach the second graders cribbage to help improve students' math skills.
- She served as a tutor to Somali Bantu refugees.

Heartily engaged in life, this man was lucky to live to old age: "He was a frequent contributor to newspaper opinion pages and always proudly signed his real name. He took great delight in the occasional unsigned hate mail he received in plain white envelopes with no return address from what he disdainfully described as 'spineless cowards whose convictions aren't strong enough or valid enough for them to claim, much less about which I need not be concerned. They're lower than whale (poop) at the bottom of the ocean.' The banes of his existence were Right to Life Fanatics, Religious Zealots, Autodidactic Pomposities, and Neo-prohibitionists."

> **"Even in his advanced age, he retained his amazing memory, sense of humor, and keen interest in just about anything: people, history, politics, literature, and music."**
>
> — *Roman's obituary*

Lifelong learning, whether through a formal program or on one's own, plays an important role in helping compensate for cognitive and emotional decline. Obits listed ways that people remained curious and continued to grow in later years: "He was intrigued by almost every aspect of our complicated world."

- After retirement he returned to college to study computer sciences and was inducted into the Honor Society.
- As a lifelong learner, she had always seen the latest movie, read the latest book, and had her finger on the pulse of current events and pop culture.
- He had an early cell phone the size of a small briefcase lodged between the front seats of his car. Even at 95, he was video chatting with his children and grandchildren on his "Grand-pad."
- After raising her four children, she went on to graduate from college and law school. She had a thriving appellate practice in her 80s, and then went on to become a writer and published poet.
- She embraced her retirement with great vigor, becoming an avid and knowledgeable birder. She traveled to many countries for birding such as Belize, Costa Rica, and even the Galapagos.
- He conducted his own dinosaur-hunting forays in Patagonia, where he eventually discovered a new species that was named in his honor.
- Even at 98 years old, he always had a question and thought Google was the greatest!
- He never tired of learning. On his 90th birthday he left his morning Rotary meeting early to attend continuing education classes in order to renew his engineering license.

Hats off to this man: "A lifelong learner, he was dedicated to growing as a person, a husband, a father, and a grandfather. And this continued throughout his life: at the age of 40 he learned to ride horses; at 50 he learned to water ski; at the age of 60 he learned to pilot an airplane solo; at 70 he learned to golf; and at 80 he learned how to use a personal computer. He was an avid woodworker and voracious reader. He was fiercely independent, and made it a point to clean his own gutters well into his 90s. He never stopped learning, listening, and living."

This gentleman, who died at 94, exemplified the essence of a life well lived: "He was internationally known as an innovative heart surgeon and was also considered a Renaissance Man. He had the ability to remember facts and details about art, history, literature, and geography. In addition to holding patents on many medical devices, he received numerous honorary doctorate degrees in medicine, archeology, anthropology, and literature. He was known for telling stories and had a tremendous joke repertoire, which he insisted were all very good. In his spare time, wrote poetry and painted depictions of blood oxygenators, hearts, landscapes, and flowers."

> **"After retirement, he continued to bring joy to the world by performing as a clown for orphaned children in Vietnam, Haiti, and refugee camps in Syria."**
>
> — *Gerard's obituary*

After retiring, some people aren't ready to take a more leisurely approach to life. They use this time as an opportunity to reinvent themselves, writing additional chapters in their life scripts.

- He took on a successful second career as a Welfare Fraud Investigator for the Inspector General for the state at age 80.
- After retirement, he began his second career at the hardware store, a profession that allowed him to indulge in two of his better skills—sharpening things and collecting flashlights.

- He closed his art gallery in the wake of 9/11 and moved to Thailand where he built his home and found his husband.
- After retirement she was a full-time visiting scholar at New York University and was promoted to Adjunct Associate Professor at 78, retiring from this position at 94. At 80, she began weekly piano lessons and became an avid bridge player.
- Later in life, he found his true passion, Tai Chi, and was able to become an instructor. He embraced Tai Chi as a way to practice patience and inner calm.
- At the ripe young age of 88, his flair for the dramatic inspired him to join an acting class. He gave spirited performances and enjoyed the camaraderie of his fellow actors.
- At 68 years old, he launched a whale-watching business which he operated for 12 years.
- In her mid-50s, she started a very successful 20-year modeling career and was for many years the only senior female model on the West Coast. She moved to Paris and was noticed in the street by an agent and began modeling again, working regularly for French magazines until the age of 96.
- He started a "second act" as a costume performer. His favorite and longest lasting gig was as Santa Claus.
- Upon retirement, he took back up with his fiddle and began teaching music for the next eight years. Teaching fiddle to his students gave him the most pleasure and fulfillment.
- She taught law and worked *pro bono* into her mid-90s. At a college commencement in 2019, when she was 100 years old, she was given an award for her trailblazing civil rights and fair housing work.

"She'd be the first to admit a strange thing happened on the way to aging. Instead of becoming more set in her ways, she became more open. More voices were welcomed and heard. At 89 she wanted to show her support and attended a Gay Pride parade. Her love was not conditional. Her family came in every size and shape, culture and color, belief and non-belief, and she embraced them all."

— *Marybeth's obituary*

The key to a happy and fulfilling time late in life is a person's attitude. People who died at advanced ages were described as independent, strong willed, optimistic, resilient, and possessing a sense of humor. These traits enhanced whatever years a person had: "She always amazed her family with her positive attitude, her fascination with the world around her, and her care for others. 'Lucky ME,' she said. Indeed a charmed life for 98 years."

- Even near the end she maintained her spunky attitude. When physical therapy paid off enough for her to walk to the end of the hall, she proudly said, "I kicked butt!"
- She lived with flair; she acted in Community Theater into her late 80s, made jewelry, painted, and sang until her death. She delighted in painting her nails different colors all at once.
- She died at the age of 94. She found joy in every day. She would be sad to miss spring.
- He loved his Saturday lunches with his ROMEO (Retired Old Men Eating Out) buddies, a weekly highlight at the country club.
- He went cliff jumping in his 50s, earned his pilot's license in his 60s, drove a Formula race car and taught himself to play the ukulele in his 70s, and threw the first pitch at a Major League baseball game in his 80s. He had a voracious appetite for life.
- After retirement she built a house, planted flowers, cleaned three acres, and killed every snake and lizard in sight, drove a tractor into the lake, and perfected her cycling moves in that same lake supported by her trusty life belt.
- She always said she lived life with a spirit of adventure. When she was 88 years of age, she drove from Florida to New York to outrun a hurricane.

- She was known as the woman with striking blue hair on Park Avenue. She had a free spirit and indomitable will, and lived life to the fullest and according to her own beliefs until she died at 93.
- She died in her cherished home at 96; she was fiercely independent and was known as the Mayor of Cedar Avenue.
- He was able to maintain his independence to the end at 90 years old; even driving himself to the hospital. He leaves behind an empty bar stool at his favorite restaurant on Sunday nights.
- He purchased his last car at the age of 92 and drove until the age of 96, letting his driver's license expire at 100.

These widows were not finished with life.

- After her husband died when she was 81, she moved and created a new life for herself. She was independent and vibrant, with a keen intelligence and sense of humor. She had a terrific style, was kind, charitable, wonderful company, and a generous friend.
- After her husband died she remained happily unmarried. She was interminably inquisitive, an avid reader, enjoyed keeping up with current medical news, new age spiritual studies, and was known as a lively, intelligent, and interesting conversationalist.
- After her husband died in 1993, she remained fiercely independent. She made her last unaccompanied trip to Paris at 95.
- She was married again on her 80th birthday. Fifty years had passed since they first met, but both immediately recognized each other. They were inseparable from that night on and they experienced tremendous joy and adventure until her husband's death.

This obituary honored a great person: "She lived life (for 99 years) with unrelenting optimism, even as her vision and hearing declined and she faced increasingly difficult orthopedic issues. She sought the best in everyone and in every situation. She inspired others with her friendship and kindness, her determination, and her love and generous spirit. Her contagious laugh and quick, yet gentle, wit were essential parts of her being."

"A life-long gardener, she planted and tended her most recent vegetable gardens through months of chemo and eventually even while home in hospice care. An avid reader, she still enjoyed a trashy romance novel."

— *Patricia's obituary*

Engaging in hobbies enriched many a life: "God granted her the gift of longevity. She was also blessed to find her passions and participate in the activities that brought her the most enjoyment. Among her personal items was a note she had written: 'These are the things I like: quilting, crocheting, cooking, antiques, traveling, ballgames, and my computer.'"

- In addition to writing mystery stories, she was an accomplished musician having played the cello, harp, classical guitar, and piano at various times in her life. She was a water color painter, a horseback rider, and an avid gardener. She took her last horseback ride at the age of 82.
- He pursued his lifelong passion for model railroading.
- Never without binoculars and a nature guide, she was an avid birder, often heading to wildlife refuges during the spring migration.
- For many years after her retirement, she knitted hats for needy children. It started as a way to use her leftover yarn, but when people heard what she was doing, they donated more and more yarn. Over the years she made and donated over 1,500 hand-knitted hats to children around the world. In the end she never ran out of yarn.
- He enjoyed restoring Massey Harris tractors and traveling to many tractor shows and parades.
- During his retirement years, he raised and donated many dozens of Lenten Roses, gave away hundreds of pounds of beautiful tomatoes, and built and donated hundreds of bluebird houses.

> **"She began running marathons at age 64 when she stopped smoking, eventually being recognized as the oldest person—81 years and 101 days old—to complete a marathon on every continent. During a race on a glacier in Antarctica she fended off the meanest birds on Earth, predatory dive-bombing skuas. She ran her 81st and final marathon in New York City at age 91 and died at 92."**
>
> — *Margaret's obituary*

Dr. Oliver Sacks believed that old age is, "A time of leisure and freedom, freed from the factitious urgencies of earlier days, free to explore whatever I wish, and to bind the thoughts and feelings of a lifetime together." These people confirmed it.

- Over the years, he and his wife had purchased older homes and upgraded them. Just once he wanted to live in a brand new home so they bought a lot, hired a contractor, and had a house built to his specifications from the ground up.
- In his late 60s, he fulfilled his lifelong desire to own and ride motorcycles.
- He discovered a new talent late in life. At the age of 81 he began to draw as a way to pass the time as his wife underwent chemo treatments.
- At his 70th birthday he purchased a pair of men's black figure skates and pursued his lifelong dream of gliding on the ice by enrolling at the Boston Skating Club.
- He was an architect and spent his later years designing tree houses in Maui.
- He had been taking music classes for the past five years learning to play bodhrán, an Irish drum.
- She loved polka dancing and later in her life she took up roller-skating.
- After retirement from the ministry, he went on to become a farmer raising cows and peaches.
- She began carving and scrimshawing ivory.
- After he retired, he began woodcarving and specialized in crafting ducks with feathers.

Trained as an analyst and researcher, this man's obituary was appropriate: "His singing, writing, piano playing, laughing, and listening to music have kept him going far beyond the actuarial table for an insulin-dependent diabetic for more than 80 percent of his 92 years."

> **"She and her husband bought an old farmhouse, and for the next 25 years they enjoyed their country life with him growing their food and her pickling, freezing, and cooking the produce. They felt that these retirement years were the happiest times of their lives."**
>
> *— Lucille's obituary*

Basking in nature and pursuing artistic passions were enjoyed by many.

- He loved to tend and watch life grow from delicate seeds and saplings to their majestic glory.
- He lived his final years as a Buddhist in a solar-powered house he designed on an old pineapple plantation surrounded by a rain forest on the northeast coast of Maui.
- He pursued his hobbies of gardening, bird carving, and sitting on the porch watching the loons. He was especially protective of the loons and several chicks fledged from the nesting rafts he designed and built.
- He pursued an array of artistic explorations from painting and printmaking to hula dancing and quilting.
- In retirement, he did some woodworking and became a proficient oil painter, completing 80 pieces of art. He produced three volumes of his memoirs and wrote poetry extensively.
- He was fascinated by monumental sculpture and completed several large sculptures in steel.
- He wrote a novel about climate change and the fate of polar bears, and also raised a national champion longhaired dachshund.
- After retirement, he and his wife moved to their farm and enjoyed raising and showing Paso Fino horses for 20 years.
- He took up creating yard art pieces made of horse shoes as a hobby and turned it into an income source in retirement, often setting up at craft fairs and community events to sell his art.

> **"She celebrated her 82nd birthday in the Antarctic and accomplished her goal of visiting all seven continents."**
>
> — *Bobby's obituary*

Travel is a gift to the mind and soul. Once retired, more people have the time and, hopefully, financial resources to make that dream come true: "Travel for her was an intimate exploration and warm personal experience with people and cultures."

- She was adventurous and ageless. At the age of 75, she braved snowmobiling to Canada with her grandson.
- When she was 70 she went to Egypt with a group of college students. This was a trip of a lifetime for her and a source of wonderful memories.
- After her retirement, she began her travels with post-graduate studies in London and Paris. Those experiences whetted her appetite for more travel. Over the years she and her husband took extensive trips to Europe and Asia, a highlight being a hike to the top of Mt. Fuji in Japan and Ben Nevis in Scotland.
- In retirement, he and his wife lived on their catamaran six months a year, sailing from Trinidad to the Dominican Republic and throughout the Caribbean.
- He and his late wife had spent the past 27-plus years as full-time RVers, traveling all over the United States.
- He and his wife set sail in 1990 for what would become a five-year journey around the world. They had family join them at different intervals so they could share the experience. In all, they visited 42 countries.
- Fulfilling a promise he made to his wife, they quit their jobs, flew to Europe, bought a Volvo, and traveled and camped around the continent for six months, including two weeks spent in the Soviet Union.
- Her travels ranged from a cruise to Antarctica to riding a camel on the Great Wall of China to camping in Glacier National Park.

> **"She died peacefully at 101 years of age. She danced her way through life and left smiles wherever she went."**
>
> — *Sylvia's obituary*

Fewer than one in 5,000 Americans reach the century mark. Actress Betty White, perhaps the nation's most famous nonagenarian, recently said, "Old age is all up here," gesturing to her head. This centenarian may have discovered a simple formula for making it to this milestone: "Throughout his 100 years he worked hard, played hard, and most of all, he loved easily."

- As his 100th birthday approached, he decided to celebrate with a trip to his much-loved Venice. Despite his friends' concerns about him being a one-legged man with limited vision and hearing, he managed to plan and make this trip alone, without plunging into the Grand Canal.
- He worked as an attorney for 83 years, making him the oldest living attorney in New York State, until he died at 108.
- Her 103 years were filled with much love and service to her community. She enjoyed travel, had an adventurous spirit, and shared her love of the beach with her offspring—even swimming in the ocean with them at 90 years old!
- He was reluctant to leave after 108 amazing years on the planet. He often said: "I want to know what's going to happen next."
- She went to heaven just before her 102 birthday, where her parents were waiting to polka with her. Her life journey began in an 18th century farmhouse during the Spanish Flu epidemic and ended during the COVID-19 pandemic.
- Lured by Asian art, she made many trips abroad both alone and with her daughter. In her 80s and 90s she attended college classes, enjoying the lively discussion and making many younger friends. She died at 108.
- She loved Moxie and M&Ms and her beloved dog. She claimed her longevity was because of drinking Ballantine Ale; she died at 105. *(Moxie was the official soft drink of Maine, and the oldest continually produced soft drink in the U.S.)*

- She was well known for her hair piled high with a matching colored bow to coordinate each outfit. She loved spending time with her family, music, whale watching, and relaxing in her home. She died at 105.
- At 103 she was the second oldest person in her family with her Aunt Sophie living to 107. We attribute our mother's longevity to good genes, a contented spirit, avoidance of medicine, and continued interest in learning. She first used a computer at age 80. Family members would call to see if she was okay when they hadn't received their daily email from her.
- He drove his own car to his 103rd birthday luncheon.

No matter how many trips loved ones have made around the sun, people still yearn for more: "What's sad is that she is gone, and the life she enjoyed before she took ill couldn't have gone on just a while longer."

> **"She filled whatever room she was in with boundless energy, passion, and caring, and taught her family how to live life to the fullest."**
>
> — *Dorothy's obituary*

What wonderfully rich lives these people made for themselves, leaving the world a better place. Their stories are inspirational.

- She had a personality larger than life, full of a sense of awe and adventure, extending courtesy to all, with a great sense of humor, and a sharp mind to the very end. She was the epitome of love, grace, intelligence, and loyalty.
- She died just days shy of her 96th birthday. She had an adventurous loving spirit. She spoke five languages fluently, enjoyed world travel, hiking, theater, photography, playing bridge, and singing.
- At age 87, she sewed herself a new dress for her granddaughter's wedding. She loved to cook and preserve food by canning, pickling, and making jams. She was a kind, wise, personable, helpful, interesting, and interested woman.

- She was a woman of strong faith, and that faith sustained her in every way. She loved people and animals and saw the good in the world. She was a wonderful friend, a very helpful woman, a great spoiler of grandchildren and great-grandchildren, a spirited adventurer, and a very strong woman. She met life with grace and her passing at 91 with dignity and the love of God.
- He continued to exercise vigorously until his death at 90. He also continued to operate a computer skillfully, drive his car safely, and text emojis expressively. He maintained a lifelong interest in Libertarianism, brain science, and cosmology, and later studied western philosophy. He remained "sharp as a tack and neat as a pin" to the end.

Here is a worthwhile lesson. To add years to your life, add life to your years: "She stayed active and interested in everything around her even in her 80s and 90s. She was involved in book clubs, bridge clubs, tutored children in local schools, and was active in her church. She had countless friends who visited her. Perhaps it was her wonderful smile that drew people to her; to the last month of her life it was joyous, infectious, and easily given."

Gone and Not Forgotten

"She was a beloved theatrical agent (not an oxymoron in this case). She was as smart as a whip, sharp as a tack, pretty as a picture, and fresh as paint. And she could cook too."

— *Suzy's obituary*

The loved ones we lose are never far from our hearts and minds. They are with us in the memories that move us to both smiles and tears. Even the most innocent objects from the past can come alive, sparking a memory. Several months after my mother died, I found a stash of her peppermint LifeSavers. The depth of my ensuing grief shocked me.

In obituaries, people named seemingly innocuous items because they are forever connected to their beloved: flip-flops, dental floss, cherry ChapStick, red eyeglasses, dragonflies, bluebirds, salmon-colored petunias, pickled hot peppers, butterflies, crispy livermush, sequin-adorned clothing and hats, lipstick, ravens, a Gin Rickey in a Styrofoam cup, homemade kiwi ice cream. A maxim proposes we die when the last person says our name. Maybe we live on in memories such as these.

This woman's survivors will forever find memories around every corner: "We will remember her for her unorthodox golf swing, bridge club beach trips, putting on her "face," best ever chocolate pie, bright lipstick, high heels, NC State basketball, dying Easter eggs, coral geraniums, shopping, charades, green beans, Christmas, her many yellow and coral outfits, boating, boiled custard, Talbots, beach hats, peach cobbler and more. She also hated snakes and thunderstorms. But her devotion to us and her absolute love for all of us is what we will remember the most."

> **"He was happiest with his toes in the sand and his face to the sun."**
>
> — *Bob's obituary*

After someone dies, we miss the gestures, words, stories, and experiences we shared with them. These memories are sweet and simple reminders.

- He gathered weather apps like a squirrel gathers nuts. He gardened like a champ and skied like a bum. He paid vet bills for strangers and took calculus for fun.
- He was known and loved for his profound intellect, sharp wit, arcane vocabulary, and love of chocolate cake.
- She had a very outgoing personality and the voice to go with it; if she was around, you knew she was there.
- He will be remembered for his wicked sense of humor, fast cars, love of single malt scotch on two pieces of ice, and near instant recall of song lyrics and bawdy limericks from his childhood.
- She could easily be coaxed to dance and make funny faces.

> **"He could recite all the emperors of Rome and all of the kings and queens of England from 1066, if one happened to ask, and then recite a poem from any such reign for kicks."**
>
> —*Anthony's obituary*

It is surprising what habits and traits family members and friends recall.

- She was the friend who would mail you a jar of precious Gustavus Nagoonberry jam. *(Wild Nagoonberries are native in Gustavus, Alaska.)*
- He wrote notes on baby blue notepads with a brown flair pen.
- She loved all things pretty, organized, and stored in Ziploc baggies!
- He liked to keep candy in his pocket to hand out, despite the protest of family that it was sketchy.
- She always made Jesus a birthday cake on Christmas.
- He particularly hated Daylight Saving Time, which he referred to as "The Devil's Time." It is not lost on his family that he died

the very day that he would have had to spring his clock forward. This can be viewed only as his final protest.

These people had some quirky abilities.

- He could identify the year, make, and model of almost any car ever made by its front grille.
- He was gifted as a mathematical savant. He could add, subtract, and multiply hundreds of thousands in his head.
- Gifted with a high I.Q. and an analytical mind, he could perform complex multiplication in his head and often amused his children by immediately alphabetizing the letters in any word they gave him.
- She would dazzle her children with her shorthand skills and her uncanny ability to write backwards.

> **"He was a sharp dresser, known for striking sports jackets with plaid pants combos, his penchant for ascots, and for wearing shorts all year long."**
>
> — *Hubert's obituary*

Uncommon clothing preferences are recalled with good humor: her dreadful taste in sweaters, his unique hats, his signature bib overalls, his dapper style with fedoras.

- She was best known for her colorful display of foxtails on her handbags.
- He wore a gigantic embarrassing cowboy hat to all important moments in his daughters' lives, but we see now that it was so we could identify him quickly in photos.
- He wore the same blue work shirts for more than 40 years.
- We will always remember his ever-present Panama hat floating down the street wherever he went.
- He was not a slave to fashion and focused on comfort before everything else. He believed white pants were acceptable regardless of the time of year, and that his infamous white and black shoes were appropriate for any occasion.

These men occupy the two opposite ends of the fashion spectrum.

- He took fashion cues from no one. His signature every day look was all his: a plain pocketed T-shirt designed by the fashion house Fruit of the Loom, his black-label elastic waist shorts worn above the navel, and a grass-stained baseball cap.
- A man of style, his sartorial panache included sporting cowboy boots with suits in the 70s, pairing Liberty of London ties with three-piece suits in the 80s, and developing his later personal signature of white jeans and striped dress shirts.

> **"He gave out silver dollars and troy ounces of silver for birthdays. He cawed a perfect crow caw. He was very allergic to onions."**
>
> — *Leland's obituary*

Obituaries may list unusual qualities or habits that will be missed, proving there are infinite ways to express a personality.

- He will be remembered for wearing pajamas under his tuxedos with red socks.
- He was known to have the best groomed roadside ditch on his road and a passion for old tractors. His backhoe was named Wilbur.
- He was an excellent marksman and once he shot a bat out of the rafters at first try from 50 feet—with a BB gun. He could do a perfect moose call, and a moose would actually come out of the forest.
- He was a lover of beauty and design, be it pruning a tree, crafting filigree, or choosing the correct bow tie for riding a tractor.
- He was known for doing knuckle push-ups on gravel and his extreme sit-up regimen. At the age of 78 he set a goal of 562,000 sit-ups for the year. He did 600,082.
- She was a unique individual that cared immensely about other people and she loved cats, and many people knew her as Meow. We believe she did this to put people at ease and break down communication barriers. It worked for her. MEOW!

> **"Those close to her will never forget her spontaneous playful sense of fun and adventure and the charming leisure with which she savored the beauties of life on earth."**
>
> *— Ann's obituary*

These obituaries capture the essence of a person.

- She was a small-statured woman as tough and stubborn as rusty nails. *(I love this analogy.)*
- He remained humble all his days, keenly aware of other routes his life might have taken. He was always grateful for the people around him and the fortuitous moments that propelled his life forward.
- Not only did he love his dogs and prefer their company, but like them, he was an insanely insightful judge of character. He had a keen sense of justice, was highly allergic to the cruel and the boastful, and didn't suffer fools. He was also a lifelong connoisseur of stand-up comedy, and this gave him a laser-sharp vocabulary and a wickedly irreverent sense of humor, with which he blessed his friends and tortured teachers, clergy, and jerks.
- He enjoyed creating small moments of joy for others, often anonymously. He would send cards and gifts under such names as the Birthday Fairy, Get Well Fairy, Appreciation Fairy, Car Repair Fairy, and Good and Naughty Elf.
- We will always cherish her marvelous mind, intelligent humor, contagious laughter, loving smile, comforting hugs, chaotic spontaneity, organized chaos, selfless compassion, and intense loyalty.
- Through his many years of ups and downs, good times and bad times, prosperity and hardship, he was a sponge. He learned and grew from every experience.
- He was the very embodiment of the strong, silent type with natural dignity, a self-assured masculinity, innate charm, a robust sense of humor, and a quick perception of the ridiculous.
- He was the second of nine children and his father had a 5th grade education and worked as a mechanic. The family lived in a two-bedroom home, with his six sisters sharing one bedroom, his parents and two baby brothers another. His father built a

bedroom for him from the screened porch. Eventually he led a Fortune 500 company and was part of the Conquistadors, an exclusive club of aviation and aerospace executives from around the world. Despite a lifetime of achievements that included career successes and multiple industry and management awards, including from *The Wall Street Journal*, he will be remembered for his extraordinary humility.

- Her joie de vivre was infectious. Her gift was her ability to fly like a hummingbird; up, down, backwards, and forward, hovering in mid-air so that all involved could experience a renewal in the magic of living. *(I'm not quite sure what this means, but it sounds as though she was wonderful.)*

> **"In the days, weeks, months, and years ahead, we will keep Ben in our hearts. We will see in our mind's eye his sun-freckled face, wide grin, muscular arms, and skilled hands as he stands in a mountain river gently cradling a glistening, glorious trout before slipping it under the water to make its way in the stream."**
>
> *— Ben's obituary*

Even when a loved one's bodily presence is gone, their physical attributes may be vividly and fondly recalled. To remember these details signifies an attentive love.

- We will always remember the way his shoulders shook as he giggled.
- He will be remembered for his gentle touch on the dance floor.
- We can't forget her "go-through-your-soul" piercing green eyes.
- He was 95 when he died, but we will miss his handsome boyish smile.
- He had expressive eyebrows.
- He shaved every morning and smelled clean and fresh.
- He had sun-kissed hair and a deep golden tan.
- She passionately illustrated stories with her long fingers fluttering, abundant rings glittering.

This man's demeanor was thoroughly studied. It seems to reflect his approach to life: "He was calm and steady as he moved through a room with never a jerky or rushed movement. When he sat in a chair, he folded his tall frame to fit, one leg over the other, back curved. His voice was soft. He listened. He remained calm."

> **"The memories strike hard, with vigor, and are soothing and cruel at the same time."**
>
> — *Wells's obituary*

A Portuguese word "Saudade" means having happy and sad feelings at the same time. Recalling feelings and experiences brings pleasure, but also pain. With nostalgic gratitude, families record what they will miss.

- We miss his whistles and songs around the house; his Southern charm and tidewater accent; his questionably-matched outfits; his mastery of movie, TV, and sports trivia; his love of auctions and antique junk stores; his ceaseless creativity; and of course, his hugs.
- She will be remembered most for her magnetic smile, inviting demeanor, engaging conversation, and her willingness to simply listen and be there for others.
- His boundless energy, unquestioning love of family, willingness to always help others, easy laugh, warm smile, and cheesy jokes will be missed.

A grief-stricken son wrote his mother's obituary: "Her half-eaten egg salad sandwich is in the fridge, waiting for her return that will never happen. Everything in her bedroom is just as she left it: her TV remote, a silent television, mismatched clip-on earrings, old newspaper clippings gathered in a worn rubber band, several watches with dead batteries. As dead as that house is now. As dead as the mom I loved and cherished. I sat on her bed and wept."

> **"This was no ordinary man. He had an easy, original, and irresistible charm. His rumbly, baritone voice could carry across a football field. He was extremely funny and didn't know how to tell a dull story. He swore constantly and effortlessly, outdoing any drunken sailor on the planet. It was hard not to love him."**
>
> — *Hans's obituary*

Sometimes people are remembered with a smile or chuckle. I admire people who, while grieving, are able to recall happy times and laugh lovingly.

- He was known for his seventh-grade sense of humor. He loved to perch on a bar stool, "Jim and tonic" in hand, and help solve anyone's problems.
- For a methodical engineer, he had a mean foxtrot.
- He had a lifelong appreciation for kind gestures, wildly inappropriate jokes, underdogs, spontaneous dance parties, curious minds, family games, old cars, pretty women, and long stories.
- He cheered for Alabama football, cooked eggs for his dog, loved coconut cake and pecan pie, ordered an old fashioned with a splash of Sprite, always preferred sweet over savory, loved eating haystacks and buckeyes during the holidays, introduced us to chocolate gravy and potato salad made with sweet pickles. He did a lot of right things right.
- What's most important to remember about him is that he had a horrendous habit of telling awful jokes to his grandchildren, making breakfast shakes using foods left over from the Cretaceous Period, and creatively describing fish he imagined he caught from time to time. He was also dangerous at a barbeque unless you liked your food well charred.
- She was a force of nature and known for her creative spirit and mischievous ways. She signed her children's school physician forms with P. D. Trician and concealed the real reason her mother's church circle loved her meatloaf containing special "oregano" that somehow found its way into the freezer.

- When she set her mind on something, she would accomplish it, which her daughters picked up and her sons couldn't seem to figure out. *(Let me guess who wrote this.)*
- Everyone who spent time with him knows of his well-tuned internal divining rod that would point him to ice cream on any continent. He was proof positive that one can live well into their 80s on an ice cream diet.
- For those who knew him best, he had the ability, and the matches, to light up a room. You've never really caught people's attention until you walked shirtless with him down the boardwalk.
- Throughout her life, she was fanatical about protecting her skin from the sun and loyal to *Dutch Tulips* as the shade of color for her toenails.

This man's family seems like fun: "He never met a dog he didn't like, the same could not be said for the wanna-be blue bloods, snoots, and summer barnacles that roamed about town. His words, not ours. Well maybe not exactly his words as those would be much more colorful. He was a frequent shopper at the dump, and he left his family with a house full of crap, 300 pounds of birdseed, and dead houseplants that they have no idea what to do with. If there was ever a treasure that he snatched out from under you among the mounds of junk, please wait the appropriate amount of time to contact the family to claim your loot. We're available tomorrow."

It's wonderful to see that meaningful memories and slices of life do endure—then pause to remember, and even smile.

Wisdom from Life Stories

What can we learn from those who have gone before us? What wisdom gained from their life experiences have they left for us? Some obituaries are rich with philosophical quotes from books, poems, and songs that inspired the person who left us.

- "How lucky I am to have something that makes saying goodbye so hard." (A.A. Milne, *Winnie the Pooh*)
- Above all she believed in the power of human connection. She liked to quote her understanding of the philosopher Martin Buber: "I would give anything for the touch of a human hand."
- She was tough, yet kind; steely, yet sentimental; earnest with a wicked wit; she embodied a line from Shakespeare's *A Midsummer Night's Dream*: "Though she be but little, she is fierce."
- "It is only with the heart that one can see rightly. What is essential is invisible to the eye." (Antoine de Saint-Exupéry, *The Little Prince*)
- "For of all sad words of tongue or pen, the saddest are these: it might have been." (John Greenleaf Whittier)
- He would want to leave you with the words of Bob Marley: "One love, one heart, let's get together and feel alright."
- When asked what life was all about, he would often repeat the words of Noel Coward: "Jolly good company, filthy stories and all that, but most of all, love."

> **"*Que Sera, Sera* was the theme song for her beautiful smile and loving heart."**
>
> — *Rosa's obituary*

Some well known and lesser known lines are a part of obituaries to reveal how the deceased lived.

- The arc of her life was a testament to the dictum from Saint Francis: "It is in giving that we receive."
- She personified the phrase "Derech Eretz," the proper way to conduct oneself with dignity, and honesty, and true concern for those around them. *(Derech Eretz is Hebrew for commendable acts of decency.)*
- She was game for every adventure and quick to jump up and dance. Once asked to describe her life, she offered this line from *Dream Girls*: "I want to be in the world . . . and of the world . . . but never to stand aside and watch."
- She lived a light-filled life as described by Edith Wharton: "There are two ways of spreading light: to be the candle or the mirror that reflects it."
- She lived up to Anna Sewell's words from *Black Beauty*: "There is no religion without love, and people may talk as much as they like about religion, but if it does not teach them to be good and kind to man and beast, it is all a sham."
- She lived by the maxim *Esse Quam Videri*: "To be, rather than to seem."

> **"She lived her 103 years closely following the lesson she passed on to her family: 'You can't change the wind, but you can adjust the sails.'"**
>
> — *Bel's obituary*

People's beliefs are influenced by their experiences. Quotes from those who have died that exemplify how they lived are at the heart of their obituary.

- As a former cattle rancher, my word is my bond. If I promise, I perform. No exceptions.
- Even in his last year, he was splitting and stacking his own wood. He appreciated a busy day. In the evening he would say, "Boy, we were busy today! What are we doing tomorrow?"
- If I can make you happy, then I am happy.
- "There are two ways to be rich in this world; one is to have more, the other is to want less." He belonged in the latter category, and in that sense he was rich beyond measure.
- "How can I help?" was his catch phrase; "Hello, friend!" was his greeting.
- Her VW bug bumper sticker said a lot about her: "Less Judgment, More Curiosity."
- "There's a little bit of good in the worst of us and a little bit of bad in the best of us." My father was a police officer.
- She was a brave and resilient woman whose motto was: "I may give out, but I will never give in."
- She helped many on their journeys through life and often said, "We are all whole, total, and complete."
- In the end she was taking care of us all, ordering us temporary tattoos that read: "It's going to be okay."
- She had a chalkboard in her kitchen where she wrote sayings that inspired her. Her last one read: "Other People Matter. Period." That was my sister.
- He told his children, "Whatever you do, do it with gusto." He certainly did.

"Aspire to inspire before you expire."

— Archie's obituary

Families use the occasion of a loved one's passing to capture and celebrate their humorous nature.

- Our mother's sayings kept us grounded and light: "If you have a cow in the front yard, you don't have to put a sign on it."
- He couldn't pass up a good Irish proverb: "Here's to a long life and a merry one; a quick death and an easy one, a pretty girl and an honest one, a cold pint and another one!"
- Wry and philosophical to the end, she wanted her tombstone to ask: "What was that all about?"
- He tried to teach his daughters the many important things in life, passing on advice: "Peaches in heavy syrup is just plain good," and "Never stand behind a coughing cow."
- Her favorite quote was from Mark Twain: "I'm glad I did it, partly because it was worth it, but mostly because I shall never have to do it again."
- When annoyed with her children she quoted Christopher Fry: "One day, I shall burst my bud of calm and blossom into hysteria."
- She loved lipstick and always told her granddaughter: "Never leave home without a little color on your lips."
- Her final words to her husband were: "Don't grieve for me too much and get out of the darn house."
- She would say to the ladies in her life: "Wear heels until you can't."
- Ever the educator her favorite phrase was: "Come here and let me show you something."
- As he remarked later in life: "The first 90 years were easier than the second."
- She would not want us to grieve, as she was always laughing. We know she is smiling and saying: "We had a good time, didn't we?" Yes, we did.

- "A bad day at the bridge table beats cleaning house." She valued people over the superficial.
- I assume this family recognized the irony: "He loved to remind us, 'Everyday above ground is a great day.' His final resting place will be in a columbarium."

> **"As she always wrote in her greeting cards, 'May your ship always sail in the sea of sunshine and happiness and anchor in the harbor of love.'"**
>
> — *Roselene's obituary*

Some memories of loved ones are upbeat and optimistic. As her life of 92 years was coming to an end, this woman's family asked her to share her thoughts on life: "I have been blessed in life from beginning to end, for I've been loved every day of my life. I'm very fortunate and very grateful."

- "How wonnnnnnn-der-ful," she often commented whether on a friend's accomplishments, a museum experience, or a scrumptious dessert.
- "Act as if what you do makes a difference. It does." And it did.
- Forever the optimist, as she lay dying she said, "Now I'm going to see all the places I've never seen!"
- "It'll be so much fun! Trust me. You'll like it." And we always did.
- Her personal quote in her senior yearbook reads: "They conquer who believe they can." This is how she lived her life until her death at 93.
- She faced each day with a prayer of thanks, a beautiful smile, and the belief learned from 102 years of life: "Everything is going to be all right."

> **"For her, the wonder and beauty in life emanated from the richness and splendor of relationships."**
>
> *— Annalisa's obituary*

These people lived with intentional kindness.

- Let those you love know you love them, share your knowledge, and always ask for one more hug.
- Speak with a smile in your voice and never belittle anyone. There but for the grace of God go I.
- You have to earn your day. Always do something kind for someone else.

Other people were known for their blunt or pragmatic views: "Life is not the way it is supposed to be. It is the way it is. The way you cope with it is what makes a difference."

- She was an avid gardener who said: "Beneath these beauties lay the carcasses of thousands!"
- Her attitude with bridge and life was: "If you don't come to win, don't come to play."
- His parting words to his daughters every time they went out were: "Use your good judgment."

> **"She died as she lived, concerned for the well-being of others. Her final words were, 'You'd better go to dinner. It's getting late.'"**
>
> *— Elizabeth's obituary*

Lessons are learned by observing how the deceased lived their life. It is not what they said, but what their loved ones witnessed that matters.

- Anybody who knew her knows she gave more than she could, and yet took less than she needed.
- She shared the beauty in her life and opened the eyes of her friends to the beauty in their lives.
- He also had one non-negotiable value; always tell the truth. His life reflected these values and he led by example.
- He was not one to hold a grudge; he felt that holding on to anger was just a waste of time.

- If he taught us anything, it was to live each day to its fullest, that kindness has no limits, and make sure your loved ones know how you treasure them.

> **"He was a lover of the Lord and all the mysteries of his creation. He was in awe of the world around him and bestowed that amazement upon his family. There were few things he appreciated more than a meadow full of wildflowers."**
>
> — *Darwin's obituary*

Some quotes focus on an appreciation of the simple pleasures of nature.

- Enjoy each day as it is; stay and admire the songs of the birds and the simplicity of a single blade of grass.
- She tended to her garden much like she did her family: watering with love, weeding with protection, and offering her hand in support where needed.
- He preached a philosophy of pay attention, watch trees grow, be a witness, listen to the earth, let people and animals be themselves, but you're allowed your own space and always be honest.

This tribute sounds as though she was a loving and successful wife, mother, and mother-in-law. That is no small feat: "She adored her husband, but more importantly, she understood him. Her sons were her sun, moon, and stars—she loved them unconditionally, challenged them regularly, and inspired them eternally. She was a model mother-in-law who never made a surprise visit or inserted her opinion on child rearing. She'd remind us to read more, vote, and mind our own business."

Maybe insights from those whose stay on earth has ended can help us clarify our own philosophy of life as we navigate the time we have been given: "It is all meaningless, but endlessly fascinating and achingly beautiful. All we can do is forgive quickly and be kind, to others and ourselves; know that we are all doing the best that we can. Cultivate gratitude; believe that enough is a feast. Be of service and generous; try to escape the prison of self. Know that your death is real and coming at blinding speed, so stop struggling to hold on to the intrinsically ephemeral and let go, relax, and remember to have fun."

Leaving a Legacy

"Success isn't just what you accomplish in your life; it's about what you inspire others to do. To leave a lasting legacy, inspire others to dream more, learn more, do more, and become more."

— *Mac's obituary*

The impact of a life is measured by what a person takes, gives, and leaves behind. That's their legacy. Even seemingly insignificant words or actions have long-lasting power. A friend may have complimented you on an article of clothing, and you remember that person each time you wear it. An especially thoughtful gift may bring someone to mind when you use it. We all have had the experience of recalling a person who seemed to be incidental in our life because something they did or said popped into our mind. They had more impact than they could have imagined. People would be shocked to find out how they were being remembered years later.

"He always had a kind word for the unnoticed in the world and brought smiles to perfect strangers whose days were made better because of him."

— *James's obituary*

I believe the wisdom of Maya Angelou: "I've learned that people will forget what you said, people will forget what you did, but people will never forget how you made them feel."

- Her smile brightened many weary souls and her encouraging words lifted numerous discouraged spirits. She could create the perfect impromptu gathering with a sleeve of saltines, a block of grocery store cheese, wine, and Popov vodka. The door was always open to her home with the promise of leaving feeling loved, included, and important in her life.

- In her presence, you stood in sunlight. She had empathy that was rare, insight that was uncanny, and was a consummate listener. You always felt better and nourished in her presence.
- He was known for his contagious laugh, warm smile, great hugs, and most of all his unconditional love. He always saw the best in people, forgave easily, and prayed nightly for every family member. Also, he always made a point to compliment women, talk to strangers, and make everyone feel important and noticed.
- He was a handsome man with a huge beautiful smile. Whenever he crossed your path it was as if he had been waiting all day just for you and was thrilled and delighted that you had finally arrived. He had a kind and generous heart, glad to make people from all walks of life feel better with generous compliments and a laugh or two.

> **"She had a broad, curious intellect, and a funny, quick wit; traits that she passed on to her children and grandchildren."**
>
> — *Ann's obituary*

Everyone leaves a legacy to their family and friends. It is not a trust fund or the family estate, but rather what one teaches through example.

- She taught us that genuine kindness is a powerful tool; it opens unlikely doors and softens the hardest hearts.
- She believed in persistence, frugality, and compound interest, values she imparted to her offspring with varying degrees of success.
- We aspire to the same patience and kindness that defined his life. They are the lights that lead us forward in our own lives.
- Her legacy lives on in each of us, as we choose to live as she did: caring for others, forgiving offenses, speaking words of encouragement, or taking someone to lunch.

- She mothered by example and allowed her children to explore their passions, believing they would come to their senses in the end. She taught her children how to actively belong to and engage in a community, and that civic duty is an obligation.
- She passed on her love of music, books, and animals, as well as her sometimes stubborn demeanor, to her sons. She sang her life's song lovingly, thoughtfully, fearlessly, and always with perfect pitch. Her sons are immensely grateful she shared her music with them.
- Mommy did the bulk of the training and nurturing. She taught us manners, good English, and all the proper ways things should be done. But she also taught humor, gaiety, music, art, independence, and tolerance.
- She was a child of the Great Depression and learned to be frugal for her family, charitable to the needy, sympathetic to others' struggles, and generous to a fault. She taught her children to help others and the value in working hard.
- He was an active listener and gave advice without judgment, inspired us without platitudes, and was strong without bluster. He built people up and never tore people down. His cheerful optimism, practical judgment, considered wisdom, zest for life, and Christian example are among the qualities that made him a role model for his family.

> **"Her legacy will live on through the hearts and minds of those who knew her, as well as those whom she touched but never met."**
>
> — *Kim's obituary*

People's actions also impact their communities and the wider world. These ripple effects spread long after one is gone and reach further than one might have imagined.

- His enormous generosity of spirit made the world a kinder place.
- At her core she was a faithful giver who contributed more than she took. Her impact on the world is immeasurable.

- He was a gentle and passionate advocate who was actively engaged in the battle against anti-Semitism, racism, and homophobia. He was known for his bright spirit, his willingness to help, and his insatiable desire to make the world a better place.
- He was a passionate volunteer about certain causes, especially those that dealt with helping abused and abandoned children. He did not shy away from particularly painful subjects.
- She devoted herself to supporting and giving voice to the unheard, the marginalized, and the powerless.
- He has been an activist or supporter of peace and anti-war movements, prison reform, and end-of-life rights, among other progressive causes.
- Advocating for kindness and compassion for all living things, especially animals wild and domestic, is probably the legacy most important to her.
- She completed an incredible arc that brought the world she traversed ever closer to justice, health, and peace.
- He was an extremely kind and gentle soul; a peaceful presence on this planet.

The tribute to this man sounds like a prayer: "We will honor his nature when taking special care of those we find ourselves privileged and able to serve. When we stand steadfast in the courage of our convictions, we will honor his spirit. He is as alive today as he ever was. His spirit and light are in all who knew and loved him. Together we are a powerful and righteous force for good."

> **"He made our lives happier, funnier, richer, stronger, and more loving than if we had never known him. He blessed us all and left each of us with our own unique memories and experiences, which are the best parts of his essence that can never be taken away."**
>
> *— Deon's obituary*

The moral principles by which the deceased lived are often noted: "He valued honesty, integrity, and hard work and passed down those traits to his kids." When these values are carried on by others, the legacy endures.

- He proved that a man with a penny can be happier and enjoy far more things in life than a man with a million.
- At a young age she became the lady of the house, thus beginning her strong family values and shaping her strong spirit and sassy attitude. She approached life with all the conviction of a lioness, and was a force to be reckoned with.
- She was practical yet classy, down-to-earth yet hopeful, and entirely no-nonsense while simultaneously enjoying the lighter side of life. She was motivated by the challenge of frugality and was a force of nature.
- Throughout his life, he strived to live by the principles of honesty, strong family communication, facing one's fears, and accepting his children and everyone he knew for who they were and on their own terms.
- She opposed the war in Vietnam. She embraced the civil rights movement and federal action to enforce racial and religious civil rights. A child of the 20s and 30s, and a woman who knew her own mind, she also embraced the feminist movement, supported passage of the ERA, and most recently, at the age of 94, proudly participated in the 2017 Women's March.

> "She would tell you that she lived a wonderful life. Her childhood was nurturing and rich in the Appalachian traditions of family and community. Her life passion was for the uplifting power of education. Her life story is the embodiment of that truth."
>
> — *Karen's obituary*

The value of education and the importance of learning are often part of a life story.

- She was a child of immigrants from Slovakia at the turn of the 19th century. She learned English in grade school and then taught her parents and siblings. Even as an adult, she remained a stickler for English grammar, usage, spelling, and pronunciation. No one ever heard her say "irregardless" or "ain't."
- His passion for education started during elementary school when he attended one-room school house. His experience there was the foundation for a lifelong enjoyment of reading and learning. He made certain both of his sons received a college education.
- She was instrumental in helping establish over 40 annual scholarships with contributions of over one million dollars. Her desire was to help others succeed through education.
- She supported the education not only of her five daughters, but the majority of her 14 grandchildren and 17 great-grandchildren.

These obituaries celebrate a long-delayed accomplishment.

- She left school at a young age to help support her family. When she was 50 years old, she earned her high school diploma with the honor of valedictorian of her class.
- After she raised her children, she received her high school diploma at the age of 29. She made all A's (except for one B) while taking care of her home and family.

> **"She cared little for material things. Her biggest joys came from people, nature, and the little surprises of everyday life."**
>
> — *Cathy's obituary*

These memories of the deceased hint at their character. How they lived told us who they were.

- He never locked his doors and always left his keys in the pickup in case a neighbor needed a ride. He would do anything for anyone and never complained a day in his life.
- Happy Jack was the kind of man that if he knew you were up to your knees in mud and whatever, repairing your sewer line in the cold, dark, rainy, snowy wind, he'd show up wearing boots with a shovel in his hand. And he never left until the job was done. He will be missed by Hells Angels from around the world.
- He played NPR for the seemingly perpetual brood of chickens he adored and cared for, even long after they stopped laying eggs.
- He turned on the church lights on Sundays for years, knowing he was playing a small part in allowing parishioners to see the face of God.
- She had many years of perfect church attendance and could be found in the same pew every Sunday morning.
- She gave her children freedom to roam the neighborhood, but used a referee whistle to call them home. She was a stickler about grades and chores, but also playful and affectionate. On Sunday mornings, children and pets piled into her bed to watch cartoons while she read the paper.
- He enjoyed the solitude of country living; being able to connect with nature was a blessing. He took life one step at a time and was never in a rush to see the day pass by. When patience was called for, he would relax with a cup of Navajo tea and a Louis L'Amour book.
- He was philosophical in the face of death. While he was ill, he was grateful for each day. When he entered the three-month reprieve he was given, he treasured the opportunity to sing and to work, which he said gave his life its savor. This was a radiant and blessed time for him. When the doctors gave him no hope, he gracefully acceded to his fate and passed away two days later.

- A spectacular beauty, she was even more beautiful on the inside. She had an incredible ability to "see" everyone around her, whether it was complimenting the nail color of the check out girl in the grocery store, noticing a new hairstyle on a waitress, or congratulating the dry cleaner on his son's college acceptance. She left a wake of kindness everywhere she went.

> **"He liked to say he chose to walk on the sunny side of the street. We feel fortunate to have walked some of the way with him."**
>
> — *Howard's obituary*

People are remembered for how their humor and laughter brightened lives.

- While approaching a red light with her kids in the car, she'd roll down the windows and sing opera in the loudest voice she could muster! Her kids would promptly disappear out of sight. Also, she had the ability to give the best impersonation of Mick Jagger—all for a good laugh. How she loved to laugh.
- Underneath his quiet demeanor, he had countless layers of raucous joy. He had a quick and wicked sense of humor, and no one laughed harder at his jokes than he did.
- Throughout his life, he demonstrated and passed on the importance of laughter (and sarcasm). Sarcasm and self-deprecation are the true signs of his offspring. It's even easily noted in his grandchildren.
- She had tremendous vitality and a very strong will, but she loved mostly to giggle, and if you could make her laugh, she especially loved you. Also if you were handsome!
- He was a wily prankster with a mischievous charm, endless charisma, and a laugh whose volume was exceeded only by the joy it spread.
- His humor served him well to the end. After his terminal diagnosis, when told by the nurses picking up his food tray that he should have eaten his vegetables, he would say to them, "What's the worst thing that could happen?"

This well written obituary captures the details of a strong personality: "He left us feeling that he'd had the most fortunate life. He had a wonderful crazy family, immediate and extended; amazing friendships; an eventful career; a life full of travel and great food; but mostly, he was always surrounded by people that he loved. His ability to see joy and wonder in everyone and everything, and his desire to share those things with everyone he met, will be greatly missed."

> **"She found great joy in her own life and brought love, laughter, and song to all she knew."**
>
> — *Elizabeth's obituary*

Some obits contain one perfectly worded sentence that concisely captures the essence of a soul.

- Her laughter was the soundtrack of our lives.
- He was the sparkle of every holiday and party.
- She led a life that blessed every person she met.
- She led a selfless life; your problems became her problems, and your joys became her joys.
- She was steadfast in her sense of self, her relationships with those she loved, and her desire to make the world a better, more beautiful place in her own way.
- She was a person of indefatigable good cheer who could talk and laugh with anyone.
- He had an infectious smile, a hearty handshake, an uplifting outlook, and a loving and caring heart.
- Of all the wonderful attributes that she possessed, there was always a common one that people would agree on; when she walked into a room, she lit it up like sunshine.
- May we learn from you to see those around us with greater clarity, less judgment, and deeper love.

> **"The world was a sunnier place with him in it."**
>
> — *Tim's obituary*

A few well selected words elucidate the spirit of a loved one.

- He was a totem of wit, warmth, and wisdom.
- He was a forgiver of offenses.
- He was a man of grit and grace.
- She was a wildflower.
- He was a beloved expression of life on this planet.
- She was a feisty bundle of energy and goodness.

Think about your own legacy because each day we have on this good earth, our words and deeds leave indelible imprints on the minds and hearts of those we leave behind: "She lived life with joy and exuberance. She made mistakes and learned. She helped others through their mistakes and pitfalls and never stopped loving. She was the goodness and kindness one wishes to have in the world, and she made us better people."

Portraits of Imperfect People

> "She was a source of unequaled kindness and venom; her presence was always fierce. Too often it pushed others away and made her life difficult. Our gift to her memory is to cherish the Technicolor life and even the battered confetti in the street, evidence a parade has passed us by."
>
> — *Laura's obituary*

Having read countless obituaries, I rarely found a person's less-than-flattering or even negative traits revealed. Most people subscribe to the adage that if you don't have anything nice to say, say nothing. No obituary that I found labeled the deceased as a brute, thief, murderer, child beater, or wife abuser. Rarely is prison time mentioned. Family members don't want the legacy of their loved one tarnished, so omission is a common method of dealing with faults. But no one is without fault. The challenge is to compose an obituary based on truth, even if creatively worded, so that the departed is honored, yet recognizable.

> **"Never one to sit on the sideline, she grabbed life and shook the change from its pockets, leaving a trail of stories, tears, and laughter."**
>
> — *Laura's obituary*

Some obits share aspects of a personality that weren't always pleasant. Honest descriptions included gruff, ornery, argumentative, difficult, a tremendous pain in the neck, and the like.

- Her vocabulary was vast and vulgar.
- He lived a long, full life bringing joy (and sometimes angst) to all those who knew him. He loved to complain about the silliest things.
- She was a stubborn, obstinate, argumentative pain in the backside who should probably have drank and smoked far less than she did.
- He was a jack of all trades and a master of none. He had his demons, but would always find time to help fix your furnace.
- He was a very strong-willed person; always right even if he was wrong.
- He was a tough competitor. He was irreverent, opinionated, fearless, disciplined, straightforward, curious, and fun-loving. He will not be soon forgotten by those who knew him.
- He was a brilliant curmudgeon and will be sorely missed by the eclectic communities of which he was a part.
- She will be remembered for her stubbornness and sass as she was not just sweetness and light, but came with a healthy dose of sarcasm and the deepest eye roll you've ever seen.
- Her favorite pastimes were complaining, yelling at her husband, and giving unsolicited advice regarding anything from how to break down a box to what shirt to wear.
- She was sweet, wild, and snarky from the beginning. She was fierce with an attitude all her own and would challenge any fool who stepped on her toes. She was restless, impelled to be on the move, and her nature could not be contained.
- He seemed to know about everything and if he didn't, he'd convince you that he did. He could drive his wife insane. Somehow he managed to be both a terrible curmudgeon and

a very jolly man. It was (almost always) a joy to be in his orbit. His powerful personality ruled the world around him.

- He could be a tough person to know and sometimes to like. He struggled with childhood demons and an addiction to alcohol which tested his bonds to family, friends, and co-workers.
- He could be a staunch friend or a bitter enemy.
- She was a deeply religious, complex individual with lots of angels, and yes, a few demons.
- He was a man who lived aloud, as himself, despite what society expected. He successfully embarrassed his son and daughter multiple times and on many occasions with his choice of outrageous attire.
- She was at times unpredictable, always controversial, and yet unmistakable. She was loved and feared, hated and respected.
- She was a force of nature. I suspect she will continue to be for those who knew her. She could be terrifying, and terrifyingly fun.
- You could call her bossy, micro-managing, opinionated, stubborn as a damn mule, outspoken, emotional, decisive, picky, and we wouldn't have had her any other way. In lieu of flowers, please send money to help contribute to lifelong therapy bills. No joke, they're going to need it. Oh, and screw cancer.

> **"In addition to English, he was fluent in sarcasm. He was also known for his wicked, dry sense of humor."**
>
> —*Jake's obituary*

A sense of humor is an appreciated trait often portrayed as sassy, infectious, quirky, offbeat, or wry. But it can get some people in trouble.

- She had a keen sense of humor and a sharp tongue. Her grandchildren kept a secret notebook of "Grandma's Best Lines," none of which can be repeated here.
- He led an unpretentious life lived to the fullest and a legacy of foul jokes.
- His wicked and often inappropriate sense of humor either offended you or made your day, either of which was fine by him.

For better or worse, he was an original who was always true to himself.
- Rarely appropriate but always hilarious, she was a classic Hollywood beauty and an exceptionally glamorous woman with a feisty sense of humor and a big affinity for life.
- He was known for his loud, often rude, sense of humor.
- She was known as being wickedly funny and was a feisty fire-starting provocateur on Facebook who had mastered the use of the "F word" in a way few had.

> **"He could be painfully blunt at times in his honesty. But an honest man he was."**
>
> — *Lee's obituary*

Some people are remembered for their lack of tact.

- She was quirky, opinionated, impatient, and well-meaning. Honest to a fault, she caused many a friend and family member to bristle at her remarks.
- He was a no-nonsense man who told it like it was. He would "break it down" for you so you always knew exactly where you stood.
- If you didn't desire to know an absolute and truthful response, you probably shouldn't have asked her the question! She was strong willed, honest, and demonstrated tough love.

This man must have been a real character, or maybe his entire family was hilarious since they wrote it. I can't imagine putting this in his obituary, but it is unique: "Perhaps most important to him was educating people on the dangers of holding in your farts. Sadly, he was unable to attain his lifelong goal of catching his beloved wife 'cutting the cheese' or 'playing the bum trumpet,' which he likened to a mythical rarity like spotting Bigfoot or a unicorn. He also mastered the art of swearing while being splattered by grease cooking his famous wings. In fact, he could weave a tapestry of obscenities."

> **"Tough as nails, yet ornery and cantankerous, best describes our mom!"**
>
> — *Doris's obituary*

Some people faced life head-on, not always with good results.

- He always marched to a different drummer. Percussion was his passion.
- He was an uncompromising man who taught his family the backcountry survival skills he learned as a child in German- and Soviet-occupied Lithuania during World War II.
- There will never be anyone like him. He was dedicated to his idiosyncrasies and we had to abide them.
- He had a demon in the middle part of his life when he had a love affair with Jack Daniels whiskey. He divorced Jack Daniels and never drank another drop of alcohol.
- He was known as "Bobnoxious" and will always be known for the endless toothpicks in his mouth.
- He was a complex and quiet individual. Throughout his life he struggled with demons that made it hard to be him.
- He worked hard during the day and partied hard at night. Struggling, with no clear path in his life, he fell into reliance on drugs and alcohol to quiet his demons.
- He did not go gentle into that good night. He loved a life of reckless adventure and provided it for his many friends.
- He made many friends "on the street" when he chose to leave our home. Incarceration was his lot for much of his life, and oddly, we think these were places of respite for him. He had more frequent contact with his parents when in jail or prison, always saying how sorry he was to be a disappointment.
- The Hard-as-Nails Bad Mama Jama had more lives than a cat, but still was taken from us too early. Never short on jokes, he didn't give a f*** what you thought, and if he wanted your opinion, he'd give it to you. He was the ultimate Alpha male.
- As he grew older he became more vocal with his short temper, often dropping the "F-bomb" when frustrated. It was always known in his household to never go near him when he was working on a project in the garage.

> **"She was not subtle in her preferences and her blunt interpretation of the world was a challenge for those in her life. From her earliest day to her very last, she was fierce, loving, wise-cracking, and critical."**
>
> — *Sally's obituary*

Family members address the unflattering truths of the deceased honestly: an eccentric personality, brutal honesty, headstrong attitude, offbeat humor, or an ornery side.

- His roar will never be forgotten.
- To call him a colorful character would be a vast understatement. Stubborn in his ways, he had strong opinions, which weren't always what he defined as the liberal way of thinking, and wasn't afraid to express them. "We don't always get invited back," he used to say. He looked like Santa, although he didn't like children.
- She was a feisty little package and made lasting impressions on people and friends wherever she lived. She had many adventures, memories, and stories to tell, most of which were quite colorful. She had a difficult life, battling addiction for most of it.
- She will always be known for speaking her mind with zero filter.
- He was named after both his grandfathers and definitely had their genius as well as eccentric personalities. Most people liked him, although most people didn't understand him and his strange mannerisms. He had a unique personality.

> **"Given what I know of my parents' backgrounds, it is frankly astonishing that they were able to stay together for all those years, and create a loving, gracious home full of such laughter and delight for my sister and me. It's a delicious miracle, really, and a testament to both my mum and dad's tenacity and deep capacity for love and relationship right through the middle of a lot of personal and family insanity. I'm grateful for this miracle."**
>
> *— Ben's obituary*

These writers acknowledge that family relationships can be challenging. Some obits make us wonder about the complete story.

- It was normal to have Dad gone for nine-month deployments. I remember one time Mom shared part of one of his letters from over there. The opening phrase was, "Water, water everywhere, but not a drop to drink." While too young to fully appreciate the sentiment at the time, I have slowly come to realize that he might have found a drop (or two or three) to drink after all.

- My dad moved to Alaska at the age of 23. I would always wonder why he left us three kids; I was age 5.

- He was bold, courageous, ostentatious, and charismatic and loved being in the limelight and would always be found being the "life of the party." God's grace allowed him to develop a bond with his family and his children.

- Due to his life choices, family and friends hold different views and memories of him, which helped create the loss of some relationships, finding new ones, and keeping some at a far distance. Few individuals know, care, or want to recognize that he also left behind another family.

- He was not an easy man to like. He was brusque, opinionated, and swore beyond most sailors. He was estranged from his younger daughter and her family. This was tough to accept because he could be fun, supportive, and so inquisitive about life. The end of his life was lonely. He missed his wife and unfortunately the love of grandchildren. He lived and died this life on his terms. The thought of what could have been will be missed. May we all be of better character but embrace his love for adventure.

- My mother was a hot mess of contradictions. Mom was physically one of the most beautiful women I have ever seen, and she never looked good in a photo. Mom was capable of conveying the most incredibly profound universal truths, and she knew the names and back stories of every member of the Kardashian clan. Mom could be the epitome of class, elegance, and grace, and she was an earthy, lusty woman who did things in her life which would have made a sailor blush. Mom was one of the kindest, most generous souls I've ever met, and she was also often insanely petty and self-absorbed. She was never one to shy away from what many would consider to be her shortcomings, and I will not do her the dishonor of hiding them now.

How surviving family members are listed and in what order can be interesting.

- He is survived by his son John and daughter Joan and another daughter and grandchildren.
- She was preceded in death by her dearly loved parents, her much-loved brother, her much-loved poodle, and her husband. *(The poodle before the husband?)*
- She is survived by two children born of a marriage.
- He is survived by his parents, brother, grandmothers, aunts, and two uncles he wouldn't want mentioned.

Nothing is hidden in the following obituaries. In one man's obituary, it stated he had been convicted of incest with his daughters. He had been married four times and had fathered 16 children with nine women. His daughters, the writers of the obituary, were identified publicly as the victims: "A prominent minister whose legacy was clouded by an incest conviction has died."

This excerpt left little to the imagination. It was deemed truthful and angry enough to be removed from an obituary website: "She had two children, and then became pregnant by her husband's brother. She moved away and abandoned her children. She passed away and will now face judgment. She will not be missed by her children, and they understand that this world is a better place without her."

Thankfully, you rarely read obituaries like this scathing account. It was written by two of this woman's children with the blessing of the other siblings. They said they wrote it to shame her, having all suffered terror from the time they were born: "She thrashed the maternal instinct out of her children and replaced it with the hate she had for us. Everyone she met, adult or child, was tortured by her cruelty and exposure to violence, criminal activity, vulgarity, and hatred of the gentle or kind human spirit. On behalf of her children, whom she so abrasively exposed to her evil and violent life, we celebrate her passing from this earth and hope she lives in the afterlife reliving each gesture of violence, cruelty, and shame she delivered on her children. Our greatest wish now is to stimulate a national movement that mandates a purposeful and dedicated war against child abuse."

Obituaries are written proof that people are fascinating, flawed, and leave behind complicated memories and legacies. As the adage goes, you can't make this stuff up: "Weary of reading obituaries noting someone's courageous battle with death, Mike wanted it known that he died as a result of being stubborn, refusing to follow doctors' orders, and raising hell for more than six decades. He enjoyed booze, guns, cars, and younger women until the day he died. Many of his childhood friends that weren't killed in Vietnam went on to become criminals, prostitutes, and/or Democrats. He asks that you stop by and re-tell the stories he can no longer tell. As the Celebration will contain 'Adult material' we respectfully ask that no children under 18 attend."

Glimpses of Life

> "If heaven is truly a state of eternal happiness, or even if it is only casual bliss, then it will surely include for him a plug of fresh tobacco, a spittoon, and an audience. And if we're real quiet now, and listen closely to the west wind, we can just about hear the loud guffaws and the ping of quid hitting the cup."
>
> — *Buddy's obituary*

Portions of obituaries captured my attention for a variety of reasons: They were sad, funny, unique, mysterious, unexpected, special, endearing, or just strange. They didn't fit into any other chapters, but are worth reading.

> "He was born in 1992 in a claw-foot, cast-iron bathtub at the family's home, a fact that made him very proud."
>
> — *Joe's obituary*

In some obituaries, an unusual birth upstages the death.

- She was born in 1915, two months early, so she was kept warm in a shoebox on the oven door!
- He was born on a small farm during a severe blizzard. The local veterinarian delivered him since the doctor was unable to reach the farm during the storm.
- She was born in 1923 to delighted parents who had given up all hope of having a child. With bright blue eyes and Shirley Temple curls, she was the darling of a network of banker and distiller German Jews.

- His father wrapped him in a caribou hide when he was born.
- Her mother was 18 when she was born. Her mother knew she was born at noon because she could hear the factory whistles blowing, signaling it was lunchtime for the workers.
- He was born in a tent on a drainage of the Black Hills, when muskrat and beaver lakes were icing over. He was one of 19 children.
- He owed his love of all things nautical to his mother. She had prompted his delivery by taking a speedboat ride.
- She was born in a car, the fourth girl in a row to a catastrophically dysfunctional family of five children.
- He and his twin brother were born on May 15 and 16, 1924, separated by minutes before and after midnight.
- She was born inconveniently on the opening weekend of deer hunting. Ruining the first week of the hunt, her parents were pretty damn happy even if no deer were bagged, a baby girl was.
- He was born in 1924, but afraid of losing their infant like previous babies, his birth parents put him in a basket with canvas and left him on someone's doorstep.

> **"So ... he has passed. That is the report we are going with, but deep down we all feel it is in the realm of possibility he will show up at a family event to critique his obituary and collect on the bet he will outlive us all."**
>
> *— Rick's obituary*

Obituaries can reveal quirky facts about the person's death.

- His last words were: "I'm dying for a Coke." His Coke memorabilia dominated the home decor.
- In a final bid to avoid eating white turkey meat, she permanently checked out of the skilled nursing facility early Thanksgiving morning.
- He died the golfer's dream; on his favorite course playing with the one he loved. He scored a 43 on the front nine. Though tied with his wife, he held hope of beating her on the back nine. On the 11th hole after he shanked his first shot, he duffed his second

into the sand, picked up the ball and called it a day, literally. With a glance to meet eyes with his wife, he passed quickly.

- She passed away peacefully in her sleep. Given her long list of vices, it must have irritated her to die of "nothing."
- He died due to a fall while attempting to hoist a 72-pound lawn mower up his front stairs with his commercial dolly while wearing socks.
- Like his brothers before him, he passed away in an unfortunate, dramatic way. All three died in tragic accidents. One of his sisters said she hoped they weren't setting a precedent for the rest of the family.
- He passed away the week following one of his heroes for justice and equality, Associate Supreme Justice Ruth Bader Ginsburg. We hope that she appreciates her new law clerk.
- She had a fruitful 31,576 days on this Earth and will be greatly missed by her family and numerous friends.
- He had a quiet lunch with his wife and friends, admired the beauty of the spring garden through the window beyond the table, went upstairs to take a nap, and never awoke. He died at 87 with the same elegance that distinguished his life.
- He could do the Eskimo roll in a kayak, but died from a fall off the roof.
- She was diagnosed with clear cell ovarian cancer six months ago, but she was clear with her family she wanted the cause of death listed in her obituary to be the Trump presidency.
- An 88-year-old researcher of magnetic superconducting, MIT professor, genealogical expert, active Democrat, tennis player, local actor, and author of multiple scientific publications died along with this wife from carbon monoxide poisoning in their new car, which had a keyless ignition.
- He died unexpectedly in Surprise, Arizona.

What a poetic description of death: "She left on a sunny, brilliant Pacific Northwest spring day. Quietly she moved from this world to the next as efficiently as a puff of breeze through the gossamer blossoms in her garden. She was beckoned by the spirit of her husband while a few birds chirped outside, acknowledging her ascent."

This obituary was written in a unique style for a beloved son: "The course of history has been irrevocably changed by his passing—a statement that, to a stranger, may seem grandiose, but to those who knew him, seems entirely inadequate. The Earth is 4.543 billion years old, and he arrived in 1992. For 9,710 beautiful days he loved learning, exploring, and testing the limits of his own abilities. Even as a child he was brilliant and determined, and damn, he was handsome. He was a paleontologist and died on a climb in Denali National Park. Whether the adventure was big or small, for him it was a sacrament to being alive and sharing meaningful moments with others. He found God's hand in the tiniest grains of sand. May the time of our separation from him feel no longer than the change of a season."

> **"He would like to let you know his work here is done. He received an offer he could not refuse. The new assignment comes with a huge sign-on bonus; and a reunion with family and friends not seen in a long time. Music, laughter, and love are guaranteed. Food is delicious and you never gain an ounce."**
>
> *— Guillermo's obituary*

Grief and humor are close companions. Humor helps us cope with life's challenges and imperfections.

- He briefly attended college, where he majored in socializing, at which he excelled.
- Her talent for cooking showed by her husband's pant size.
- He was preceded in death by his tonsils and adenoids in 1935; a spinal disc in 1974; a large piece of his thyroid gland in 1988; and his prostate in 2000.
- There will be a loss felt in sales of rubber bands, Ziploc bags, and plastic containers as his children have unearthed a collection that should hold them well into the next decade.
- He can likely be found forwarding tasteless internet jokes. (Check your spam folder, but don't open these at work.) Unlike previous times, this is not a ploy to avoid creditors or old girlfriends. He assures us that he is gone.
- She previously served on the Board of the Library Foundation.

Ironically, the only correspondence she has received from the library since her resignation has been notices for several overdue books (a true statement). Between ICU, dialysis, and physical therapy she selfishly refused to make the time to return them. Her last words were, "Tell them that the check is in the mail." Any gifts in her honor should be made to the Library Foundation to the overdue book fund.

- He was preceded in death by his own left leg; he liked to joke that he already had one foot in the grave.

- Our father made his last undignified and largely irreverent gesture, signing off on a life, in his words, "Generally well-lived and with few regrets." When the doctors confronted his daughters with the news last week that our father is a very sick man, in unison they replied, "You have no idea."

- He never missed a chance to use salt and pepper, but mostly he loved his family.

- His buddies described him as the type of guy you could trust with both your wife and your money!

- Fun? How about his never-ending collection of owls? HOO would ever have believed it without seeing it?

- Molson's stock price fell sharply on the news of his passing. Senior executives at Molson called an emergency meeting to brace for the impact of the anticipated drop in sales.

- Among his proudest achievements were couch-coaching both the Red Sox and the Patriots to their recent world championships, and purchasing a Fendi winter coat at Filene's basement for a fraction of its original list price.

- She was preceded in death by too many pets to include—all well-loved and overfed, as well as multiple non-pets, all also overfed.

- At 91, on a typical Sunday you could find him being wheeled around town by his grandson, in search of ice cream and a glass of Johnnie Walker.

This grieving wife mourned her husband in her own way with creative humor: "He died peacefully at home after years of crime fighting and a years-long battle with a nefarious criminal named Cancer, who has plagued our society for far too long. Civilians will recognize him best as Spider-Man, and thank him for his many years of service protecting our city. He is survived by his first wife Gwen Stefani and his current wife and their son, who will grow up to avenge his father's untimely death."

> **"When he was a young boy he had the privilege of opening a show with a traditional Native American dance for famed country singer Charlie Pride, after which Charlie requested his autograph."**
>
> *— Marion's obituary*

An obituary may broadcast the deceased's claim to fame.

- He served as Adjutant of the American Legion Post, including the Weasel Piss Lounge.
- She was the staple of the annual Fourth of July celebration where she served at different times as the Garlic Bread Queen, a member of the Barbeque Bean Team, and a major logistics supporter for the Methodist Pie Social.
- He had the historic oddity of having been a witness to the Japanese attack on the island of Oahu on December 7, 1941, and the terrorist attack on Manhattan on September 11, 2001.
- At one time he held the state high-jump record, but only briefly, as his record was beaten by the very next jumper.
- At age 12, she was the first ice skater to give an exhibition at Rockefeller Center on Christmas Day 1936.
- He was a two-time recipient of the President's Award from the National Potato Council for his dedication and service to the potato industry.
- As a young designer, he rocketed to fame with his design of First Lady Jacqueline Kennedy's iconic robin-egg blue dress. It is now part of the permanent collection in the JFK Presidential Library.
- He wrote 30-odd books exclusively on his beloved Olympia manual typewriters, Model SG-3. Many SG-3s gave up the ghost before he did.
- He was born on September 23, 1952, the same day Rocky Marciano won the heavyweight championship of the world. His

lifetime career was in boxing. He won many amateur fights and a tough man contest.

- He is most famous for inventing the childhood disciplinary tool of "Time Out."
- She was the last living person to have flown across the Atlantic aboard the German airship Hindenburg. When she was 88 years old, she climbed Mt. Washington, her most challenging ascent. Also, she may have been the only octogenarian to climb Mount Kilimanjaro three times.
- He was inducted into the International Towing Recovery Hall of Fame and Museum for the many contributions he made to the towing industry. He was a legend in his field.
- She loved *The New York Times* and read it with passion every day. She appeared in it a few times. Her first appearance was at the age of four in an article "Missing Child Found in Swamp." It is so good she was found.

> **"A beloved mentor to many, his name was appropriated for Dr. Spielvogel in *Portnoy's Complaint* by novelist Philip Roth, who often joked with Carl that he owed him lot of royalties."**
>
> — *Carl's obituary*

It's never too late to engage in name dropping.

- Her striking beauty inspired Batman's creator, Bob Kane, to create Catwoman. She died at 106.
- Her Uncle Hank was the legendary Hank Williams.
- He once played piano with Fats Domino, marched the last five miles of the Selma to Montgomery voting rights march behind Dr. King, and met Lech Walesa during a family trip to Poland in 1984.
- Born in England, family lore suggests he was a descendant of Robin Hood.
- She was a woman of the world and died just weeks shy of her 101st birthday. Her early professional highlights in textile design include a brief collaboration (and a chaste kiss) with Salvador Dali.

- She met John Wayne, her favorite movie star, on one of his fishing trips to Juneau.
- She was one of Hugh Hefner's Playboy Bunnies from the early 1960s to 1974.
- His mother was descended from Miles Standish, an English settler who came to America on the Mayflower.
- She taught George W. Bush in third-grade Sunday school in Midland, Texas.
- He cleaned President Eisenhower's teeth as a dental technician.
- She was a high school classmate of the author Larry McMurtry, who called her the prettiest girl in town, and loosely based the character Jacy Farrow on her in his novel *The Last Picture Show*.
- When WWII broke out she enlisted in the army and spent much of the war in Europe under the command of General Dwight Eisenhower. Her war experiences include typing the German terms of surrender and missing the plane that crashed with Glen Miller's band on board.
- She was her mother's youngest child and the inspiration for her mother's 1940 classic book *Pat the Bunny*.
- She felt that the farmer's wife role was not for her and proceeded to travel the world from age 16 as a nanny for some of the luminaries she met. She was in service to Gene Kelly, Greta Garbo, and Ernest Hemingway, who personally poured her a cup of tea in his Finca Vigia home in Cuba.
- She discovered rock and roll at a very early age and was a participant in many tours with Bruce Springsteen's E Street Band.
- At 26 she bought a Chevy Bel Air convertible. She took annual vacations with her girlfriends, and on one trip she met and dated John F. Kennedy.

> **"Despite all his gifts and talents, because of alcohol he lost his family and many of his dreams. But despite being a long-time alcoholic, Boe used his skills and talents to bless many others' lives. No one knew about his struggles or the demons in his soul. They only knew his smile and generous spirit."**
>
> *— Boe's obituary*

Obituaries reveal life stories both sad and tragic.

- He had an extremely compassionate heart and an occasionally troubled mind.
- An Austin icon is dead, and Austin just got a lot less weird. The city's flesh-flashing, cross-dressing, attention-loving, frequently homeless mascot died.
- He lived in foster care with his siblings until he was officially adopted at age 60.
- His much-loved cat Hobbes perished in the fire with him, and we can only pray that Hobbs is still flopped across his lap.
- He died at 62 years old as a result of domestic violence. He was stabbed with a filet knife in his home.
- Outwardly he had it all: humor, height, handsomeness, rap talent, fantastic wit, infectious smile, mechanical talents, and a mullet that left all others jealous. Inwardly he was had his own struggles that he hid from family and friends.
- He was largely self-taught, and despite being gay, bipolar, illegitimate, addicted, and victimized in a much more condemnatory time, his strength of character and determination overcame these obstacles and he shone in everything he set his mind to.
- He passed away after a lifelong battle with addiction. Among his inspirations and struggles were an ingrained aversion to conformity and a burning romance with street culture. For the gifts you have given us, we are truly grateful. And for everything else, you are wholly forgiven. You are finally and truly free.
- He was known by many as he chose not to drive and would walk everywhere, every day, throughout Fairbanks for the last 20-plus years. He was killed by a hit-and-run driver.

- He drew outside the line and never fit into a single box. He was a talented, tortured dreamer; traits that drew people to him yet made him inaccessible. He had his demons and that darkness was part of his allure and mystery. Until it wasn't.

- Melinda, given the name Matthew at birth, died at 48 years old. Just when the caterpillar thought the world was over, it became a butterfly.

- His values and morals were different than many. You didn't have to be blood to be family; he made his own family from the friends he treasured in the Jungle.

- The 2000s were his survival years. In 2003 he survived a fall and brain injury in the Escalante Wilderness, thanks to the heroism of his daughter. He also survived an attempted murder at the hands of an evil meth addict. Alas, he couldn't save himself.

- He passed away in Alaska. Anyone with knowledge of how to reach his next of kin is asked to call the funeral home.

- He was an integral part of the early Punk scene and a familiar face in that world. He was outrageous to a fault and danced to his own special drum.

- U.S. Navy musician killed Dec. 7, 1941, during the attack on Pearl Harbor, was accounted for Sept. 5, 2018. He was among 394 previously unidentifiable sailors and Marines whose remains were interred in mass graves at Pearl Harbor, Hawaii. He was 20 years old when he died.

This was a unique approach to announcing a death: "Sedalian takes fork, ends journey on Bird Day. *(The deceased was born in Sedalia, Missouri.)* Despite overcoming alcohol and cigarette addictions, he waged lifelong battles against other ailments as well: Toxic Shame, Generalized Anxiety Disorder, Depression, and finally, his two most relentless opponents, Dementia and Cancer. He opted not to endure further illness; he refused medical treatments, choosing, instead, to end his earthly journey and mortal suffering on a Sunday, his 'Bird Day!' just a few hours before the dawn. As I always say, 'When you come to a fork in the road, take it!'"

> **"He mostly wore yellow shirts and ate off yellow plates because yellow is the color of the bright side of life."**
>
> — *Don's obituary*

These parts of a life story were deemed important enough to be included in an obituary. Aren't people endlessly fascinating?

- His conviction that extraterrestrials have arrived on Earth led him to leave his career as a nuclear physicist to lecture widely about alien visitations.
- In his spare time, he enjoyed hanging out with his buddies, drinking a cold beer, and riding side-by-sides. He was the Man. The Myth. The Legend. Men wanted to be like him. Women wanted him.
- Born in Alaska, she preferred to store her baby blanket in the freezer between uses.
- She gave up trying to teach writers the difference between "foregone" and "forgone."
- He was a master of arcane facts and distant memories. He could recite his locker combination from seventh grade.
- She leaves a five-foot-tall hole in the world that will never be filled. She may have been short but she cast a long shadow. She was a Liberal who didn't suffer fools or Republicans and spent the last four years alternately raging at the state of the world or hiding under the bed.
- He never went to school but trapped in the Black Hills of Alaska to support his large family. In 1946, he got the first car in the village. He loved to drive and drove until he was no longer able to. He continued to enjoy life in the passenger seat.
- She was known as much for her glitz and glamour as for her love of Hershey's chocolate that she carried everywhere with her and ate before every meal.
- His will, to the miffed admiration of his family, specified no bequest to them and approximately 36% to the federal government, 18% each to New York City and New York State, unrestricted, to reduce debt. He disapproved of debt, and in the end, put his money where his mouth was—to the tune of between one and two million dollars.

- Only a few weeks before his death he bagged a 12-point deer. He then field dressed it and pulled it out of the woods by himself. He did not go gently.

- She died in the early morning hours, but her age is None of Your Business. She was a force of nature and left those who loved her simultaneously amused, frustrated, grateful, and more whole. She stood by her choices, even the regrettable ones, and demanded that others do the same. She will remain a mythology of contradictions. She was fine with this and proud of it. She honored tradition, law, and order, but if the situation called for it, she unapologetically violated them.

- He dazzled many maitre d's in many a Manhattan restaurant as he swept in wearing a colorful vest, a silk ascot, a large silver medallion hanging from his neck, sometimes a velvet-lined cape, always ordering two portions of pasta all'Amatriciana, and leaving lavish tips. He was a complicated man of all seasons.

- A confirmed bachelor until the age of 55, he favored petite blondes, reminiscent of his mother.

- He adored the ladies, and they adored him. There isn't enough space here to list all of the women from his past. There isn't enough space in the phone book. A few of the more colorful ones were Momma Margie, Crazy Pam, Big Tittie Wanda, Spacy Stacy and Sweet Melissa. (He explained that nickname had nothing to do with her attitude.) He attracted more women than a shoe sale at Macy's.

> **"He was a dentist who kept a two-gallon jar filled with molars he's removed, which was a source of fascination to his children."**
>
> — *George's obituary*

Singular traits and personality quirks provide interesting detail in an obituary.

- He was legendary for being able to hammer a nail home with a single blow.
- She was a talented sleeper.
- He was an ardent whistler.

- He loved his dogs. He taught them sign language and his commands were in Spanish.
- He had a brown eye and a green eye. Even when he lost the use of his brown eye, he saw the visible and invisible world with the clarity few people have. He also saw what people did not see; the consequences of poor political and human decisions.
- He was the humble creator of a formula which was rumored to have almost bankrupted Saratoga Race Track.
- When a feral cat showed up at his house, he worried about him so much he started feeding him daily so he wouldn't starve. After a while he built him a house on stilts so he would not be harmed by any predators out there in the country or by nature's wrath. He even equipped the house with a heating pad so that the cat would not be too cold at night.
- He was a larger-than-life dynamo. He would make a friend before the elevator doors closed.
- Steeped from birth in Irish wit, humor, and fatalism, and gifted at observation and brevity, she had the consummate ability to drive home a verbal nail.

> **"He is survived by his nagging wife and his smartass children. It did not take much to get under his skin, and most of us enjoyed pushing his buttons daily."**
>
> — *Hugh's obituary*

Family relationships are nearly always included in obituaries, even when they are atypical.

- She had four sisters: Patty the elder, Kitty the cook, Lisa the lawyer, and Piji…the…piji. The sisters dearly loved her, spoke often, and as one family photo proved, all preferred Clairol Blonde in box #47.
- I met and married a Canuck in 1962 and was freed at last in 1986. *(Canuck is a nickname for a Canadian, sometimes with a negative implication.)*
- She is survived by her screen and television roles, as well as her children.

- He is survived by his daughter who shares his characteristic exuberance and problematic sense of humor.
- She married in August and in January had a very healthy eight-pound "premature" daughter.
- Doodles loved to spend time with her sister Beatles, going to the casino and just enjoying life together. You could say they were two peas in a pod.
- His demise will now allow his siblings to emerge from his shadow. A variety of nieces and nephews with a mediocre upbringing would complete the list of those left to embellish his memory.
- He is survived by his mother, father, sister, and brother. He is also survived by his estranged, but not forgotten brother.
- He is survived by his children and grandchildren, and an ever-burgeoning population of squirrels and chipmunks. His retirement included plotting the demise of the local squirrel and chipmunk populations.
- She is survived by two sons, the strikingly handsome Greg and the slightly less handsome Ryan. She is also survived by her really old mother and two sisters who are not exactly spring chickens themselves.
- We were the brothers that neither of us had. May he find eternal peace liberated from the hardships that invaded his final years.
- She was a mother to some crazy and oddball kids.

> **"Her marriage decayed and the couple divorced; it was a three ring circus—engagement ring, wedding ring, and suffering."**
>
> — *Ida's obituary*

Marriage—or marriages—are significant parts of many lives.

- After four practice wives, he married his true love.
- Even his ex-wives praised him for his easy smile, natural generosity, great heart, and of course, his exuberant dance moves.
- His wife once claimed that it would be a cold day before she married him, and she got her wish; the night before

their wedding there was a heavy frost, which cemented their unwavering love.

- He was married five times, and in a testament to his great heart, most of his exes continued to regard him fondly, most of the time.
- She married Lee and they stuck by each other for almost 50 years. *(How romantic.)*
- She was always partial to the men in her life and often said she was happily married for over 50 years, just not to the same husband. She seldom met a good looking man she wouldn't flirt with. All the men, past and present, will miss her charm, wonderful personality, beauty, and style. She was predeceased by her four husbands.
- She was never married, but had two children with her first love and high-school sweetheart.
- He married his wife on October 13, 1957. Fifteen minutes later, they were pregnant with their first son.
- He graduated from high school in 1953, where he met and married his first of three wives. He was heard to say on occasion, that he had enough adventures for three lifetimes, and he just happened to have had three wives to share those with.
- He was a loving and caring husband, but he and his wife realized that they were better off friends. They walked into divorce court holding hands and laughed when the judge said, "I think you have the wrong courtroom, this is divorce court." They both replied, "We know!!!" They had their ups and downs, as best friends often do, but their 40-year friendship was always very special to them and admired by their close friends.

> **"He possessed incredible parking karma in the middle of Manhattan."**
>
> — *Gerald's obituary*

Some facts of life included in obituaries cannot be classified. These are just random.

- He attended Miami University where he majored in being expelled.
- In life, as in her papier-mâché artistry, she made the best from what she found. A discarded microphone stand? That's an ostrich neck. An old bar stool? Looks like the legs of a giraffe.
- For the last 20 years of his life he was on a crusade to educate others on the correct use of the term "weightless."
- She was an accomplished artist who loved circus peanuts.
- He attended Catholic primary schools and prided himself on staying left handed against the nuns' strong persuasion.
- He leaves behind an extensive hoodie collection, several pairs of ripped jeans, 23 Bic lighters, many broken hearts, and a car that is proof he never once littered.
- He was a young farmer who fell out of the hay mound and lay on the ground for two days where he was attended by the piggies.
- A master of social graces, she was a former Miss Putt-Putt who never showed up empty handed or without an opinion.
- He had strong opinions, mostly food related. He refused to eat chicken breasts or cumin.
- In his memory, watch online to learn about the destructive and life-giving aspects of volcanoes.
- She was a long-term resident of zip code 92014.
- I welcome his soul's wonderful, positive, and happy energy to our cemetery. (From the cemetery caretaker, as written in the funeral home's online guestbook.)

These excerpts are longer, but they're worth reading to appreciate how a person is memorialized in detail with love and humor.

- His family is devastated and deeply saddened by his sudden death while out on his regular morning run. But we are grateful that he remained vital and in full control of his faculties until his unexpected heart attack. Anything else would have been unacceptable to him, and we are relieved that he went out on his own terms. Although he never regained consciousness, and likely would have preferred to be better dressed, we hope that he somehow knew that his first responders thought he was only in his 50s. He made the world a better place. And he always looked damned good doing it.

- He was locally sourcing his food years before chefs in California starting using cilantro and arugula (both of which he hated). He excelled at growing camellias, rebuilding houses after hurricanes, rocking, eradicating mole crickets from his front yard, composting pine needles, living within his means, outsmarting squirrels, never losing a game of competitive sickness, and reading any history book he could get his hands on. He loved to use his oversized "old man" remote control. He took extreme pride in his two grandchildren for whom he would crow like a rooster on their phone calls. He despised phonies, know-it-all Yankees, Southerners who used the words "veranda" and "porte cochere" to put on airs, eating grape leaves, *Law and Order* (all franchises), cats, and Martha Stewart—in reverse order.

- To relieve stress, he preferred smoking and drinking over yoga, although he did cut a fine figure in yoga pants according to his partner and an undisclosed number of female (and male) admirers. He also loved playing pool, fishing, stalking Jennifer Lawrence, and looking at boobs. He will be remembered for his contagious smile, sparkling blue eyes, gentle heart, and inappropriate sense of humor.

- He escaped this mortal realm leaving behind 32 jars of Miracle Whip, 17 boxes of Hamburger Helper, and multitudes of other random items that would prove helpful in the event of a zombie apocalypse. He is preceded in death by his parents, a 1972

Rambler, and a hip. He despised "uppity foods" like hummus, which his family lovingly called "bean dip" for his benefit, which he loved consequently. He couldn't give a damn about most material things, and automobiles were never to be purchased new. He never owned a personal cell phone and he had zero working knowledge of the Kardashians. He died knowing that hot sauce can be added to absolutely any food.

There are no duplicates among us. A well crafted obituary celebrates a person's fascinating complexity. It transforms the deceased into a one-of-a-kind human being who filled this world with richness.

Substance Use Disorder: Drugs

"As we all do, he struggled with demons.
His addictions ended his life too early. We are sad."

— John's obituary

In researching this chapter, I used "addiction" as a search term in on-line obituaries. Up popped many innocent addictions: animals, football, chocolate, small purses, reality TV, bridge, Starbucks, watching CNN, shoes, shopping, golf, needlework, dogs, college football, crossword puzzles. One obituary writer admitted: "In his later years he became an Amazon addict. Jeff Bezos is a little less rich because of his passing." Another was described as happily "addicted to the marrow of life."

But the addiction explored in this chapter is more serious. Addiction occurs, as this obituary declares, when substance use crosses the line between pleasure and compulsion: "For those who think drug addiction is strictly a choice—yes, it is at first. But for some, drug addiction changes their brain chemistry and develops into something which gives them very little choice in the matter." Another obituary described addiction: "It is the only prison where the key is inside."

> **"Early in her life, Jessica experimented with OxyContin and later became addicted to heroin. She was a strong woman and devoted mother, but her addiction permanently altered the way she was able to think and perceive the world. She battled her opioid addiction for over 10 years. She continued to battle each day but, in the end, her addiction claimed her life too soon. Some people may think an overdose is a peaceful death, but I assure you it is not."**
>
> — *Jessica's obituary*

Addiction takes on a life of its own with a sway so strong that a person can lose their way, then their entire sense of self: "His battle with addiction clouded his light." It changes how a person thinks and feels, how they act, what they say and do. In diagnostic terms, addiction is now referred to as a substance use disorder. "Jonathan passed away after a fierce battle with opioid use disorder at age 30. Though he succumbed in the end, he fought his battle with ferocity."

> **"The word addiction is such a cursed word meaning shame, loneliness, hopelessness, loss of family and friends. Please educate yourself and others about addiction, nobody asks or wants to be an addict. Help stop the shame and stigma of addiction. Our son, like all others suffering from this disease, was so much more than his addiction."**
>
> — *Matthew's obituary*

Addictive substances change lives in fundamental ways. The craving for drugs, alcohol, or other substances causes one to be cruel to people they love, lose jobs they really want, spend money they don't have, and damage their physical bodies and mental health.

A person may be addicted to several substances: "Over the years, she quit alcohol, she quit smoking, but how does one quit food?" Addiction is less about which substance a person craves than why they crave it. Sometimes it is the desire to numb physical or emotional pain.

- The death certificate will say she died of a heart attack. In reality her addictions were the cause of death. She always said she used the drugs and alcohol to make her feel normal. After she was diagnosed with bipolar disorder, the drugs and alcohol stopped when the medicine started. The addiction was replaced with nicotine, caffeine, and sugar. Year after year her consumption of these was greater and greater, so in the end, her body shut down. She had little peace on earth, so I hope she finds it in heaven.

- In her later years, she was happy to finally have arrested her food addiction problem through a 12-step program. (She died at 92 years of age.)

Very few obituaries mention another addictive drug: "Her life was shortened by lifelong tobacco addiction, and she passed before her family was ready to say goodbye."

> **"She had a tenacious ability to survive and a fearless instinct to take risks. She died unexpectedly."**
>
> — *Kim's obituary*

When a loved one passes away, the family wants to portray them at their best, writing an obituary that will present them in a positive light. The writer carefully selects words to reflect the deceased's life contributions and all the love and care that was showered on them. But what if your loved one died of a heroin overdose or lost a long struggle with addiction? What do you say then? Should you omit these difficult facts and pretend they passed away peacefully? Not being comfortable sharing what they perceive as a secret and shameful struggle with addiction, families may exclude the cause of death or use phrasing that leaves the cause ambiguous. Perhaps they feel more comfortable sharing how their loved one lived, rather than how they died.

> **"In the spirit of love and sharing, which was very much a part of who he was, it is important to note that he has had a long struggle with addiction that stole this beautiful person from our world."**
>
> *—John's obituary*

There are too many young faces in the obituary pages, and many deaths are due to substance abuse. In one day's obituary section of the local paper, there were two 22-year-old men who "passed away suddenly." Other words sometimes chosen are "died unexpectedly" or "died at home." While those phrases may be true, they may not be the whole truth. With drug overdoses such a common killer, this terminology may signify a drug-related death or suicide.

Some families venture toward the truth. While the cause of death is not divulged, from additional obituary information, a reader is able to draw a reasonable conclusion.

- He died in the emergency room. Donations may be made to Addiction Recovery.
- Our 27-year-old son died unexpectedly at his home. Memorial contributions may be made to an addiction retreat program.
- She was excited about attending college this fall, but died in July. Contributions are suggested to Stop Heroin Now.

> **"If our son's story can help one addict push even harder for another day of sobriety, encourage an active user to choose recovery, or shine a light on this horrible epidemic, then it is worth coming out of the shadows."**
>
> *—Adam's obituary*

When composing an obituary, families are sometimes concerned about how readers will react to their honesty. Family and friends will not be shocked—they most likely knew—and reaction from the general public is often sympathetic. Here is an eloquent and poignant testament to a family's enduring love and heartbreak: "Although he had a zest for life and loved his family dearly, he battled mental health issues and addiction. If you are lucky enough not to understand addiction, then you are, in fact, very lucky. I hope you never have to. I hope you never see someone you love disappear before your eyes while standing right in front of you, and yet your love for the addict endures. I hope you never have to be awake all night praying the phone doesn't ring, yet hoping it does at the same time, and yet your love for the addict endures. I hope you never know the feeling of doing everything you thought was right and still watch everything go wrong, and yet your love for the addict endures. I hope you never have to live as an addict. I hope you never know what it means to be afraid of yourself, to never trust yourself, to fight a raging war inside your own mind every moment, to both feel unwanted and unworthy, to need something you know is destroying you and do anything for it, to trade your life, your soul, and still end up broken and alone, to give away everything and everyone you had, to have no answers, to always question, to have no choice yet have to choose to fight your battle. Our son lost his battle with addiction. May the four winds blow him safely home."

Online responses to this truthful portrayal of a troubled but much loved son and husband were unanimously positive.

- I was struck by the eloquence of this loving tribute to a son who, while obviously loving, also caused you pain and sorrow. I know your difficult and brave honesty will be of solace and hope to others.
- I do not know your family, but this is one of the most amazing obituaries I have ever read. So honest. Most families hide the fact that their family member is an addict. Whoever wrote this should be congratulated for putting this information out there for other addicts to read.

I was curious about this obituary: "He was a father, son, grandson, brother, nephew, cousin, friend, and he was loved. He died suddenly at home and will be sorely missed." Further online research revealed his death from was a drug overdose. The complete story was his little brother and sister found this young man dead on the floor of their home from an accidental fentanyl overdose. According to a social media post by his sister, while the coroner was removing his body from their home, she actually took the rest of his drugs, snuck out of the home as the coroner was putting her brother into a hearse, and used her brother's drugs in the bathroom stall of a neighborhood fast-food restaurant. That's the horrible reality of addiction.

> **"His addiction became bigger than his own life. He is now free from pain and the weight of the demons he has carried for so many years. Recovery is hard, regret is harder."**
>
> *— Vaughn's obituary*

Drug addiction is at epidemic proportions in our country. Obituaries name and blame heroin, opioids, synthetic opioids, or addiction as the cause of death. Substance abuse is no longer a deep, dark secret. Tens of thousands of Americans die each year from an opioid overdose—or about 200 people a day. During 2020, 93,000 deaths were attributed to drug overdoses. An increase of nearly 30 percent over 2019, that is the highest number recorded during 12 months.

- Addiction took so much from her. It took her desire to do the things she loved. It took her smile. It took her sparkle. It took her sense of humor. It took and took and took until it took her life. One of the things it couldn't take is the joy and love she spread to all she knew.
- His life included periods of incarceration, periods of addiction, and a long disabling illness that resulted from both of these. Despite this, he continued to look at the world with hope and happiness. His last words, on the arrival of his eighth child to his bedside were, "I'm happy."
- Our loved one left this life at 33 years old. She always did things her way, that's for sure. Along the way, events in her life led her down a hard, dark road; one that would lead her astray and away from all those she loved and loved her. Regrettably, most of her adult life was defined by addiction. Her death was sudden and unexpected. Addiction stole her life.
- Substance abuse is everywhere and is often used as a means of coping with grief. The line between use and misuse can be blurry and hard to recognize. Opiate misuse disorder is a ferocious and punishing illness. It is fierce and greedy and it did not leave her time to keep fighting. She kicked ass until the very end. We are all blessed to have known her and to love her always.

> **"She shared her story with the world, hoping to dismantle the shame and secrecy about the disease of addiction."**
>
> — *Emily's obituary*

Loved ones try to change the negative judgment directed toward addicts. Addiction is the only medical illness that is criminalized. People suffering from addiction receive punishment more often than treatment.

- Our beautiful daughter was quietly taken from this world after an accidental overdose. Her pain and embarrassment from her addiction have ended. Heroin is a nasty drug.
- The day he died, a part of us died along with him. The pain of his death is heartbreaking and intolerable, which is why stories like his should not be ignored. The only way we will conquer the opioid epidemic is to share our stories, raise awareness, and fight for our children's future. Please help End the Stigma.
- One thing we would like to see change more than anything is the stigma attached to addiction. Society is so geared towards viewing those suffering with addiction with such shame; it only further perpetuates a world steeped in hate. Let's take more accountability in making this world a better place, and understand them, because they too are people, and they are suffering.
- Our society shames and hides away those who need us the most, until they are displaced by regret. Tell those who struggle you love them, and make sure they are not alone.
- As a recovering addict, he maintained his sobriety for 18,765 days and taught that drug addiction is a disease, not a human failing or character flaw. He led a movement to change societal attitudes toward addiction, to correct misinformation, and to eliminate the shame and stigma often unfairly attached to addiction.

> **"If a parent's love could fix addiction,
> it would have been eradicated years ago."**
>
> — *Chase's obituary*

The heartbreak suffered by families is palpable. But their love persists.

- At only 23, he died quietly in the bedroom of his father's home of an accidental opiate overdose of a mixture of heroin and fentanyl that he purchased easily and cheaply earlier that day.
- She had no doubt how much her family cherished her; and we have no doubt she loved us passionately. She was in between sober houses, waiting in an upscale coffee shop, and wanted just one more hit. She had one last hit of fentanyl. Family is asking for privacy at this time but requests that you share her story.
- Our beloved son passed away after a long, cruel battle with addiction. Though we feared his death for more than a decade, we had hopelessly believed it would never come. He spent too long in an unspeakable darkness he never once asked for, his joy being constantly threatened, constantly eradicated, never safe from the torment of addiction.
- In a fitting end to the saddest story in the world, our son died as a result of an apparent overdose. The last 15 years marked a painstaking, heartbreaking, harrowing journey though the legal and medical systems as he and his family battled the disease. He has died despite dozens of stays in rehab facilities, hundreds of thousands of dollars invested in the hope of his recovery, and countless hours of heartache felt by him and by those who loved him so deeply, yet couldn't save him. This is the disease. That was his reality.
- He came to us and asked for help—he was addicted to heroin. He wanted to get clean and get his life back. His last evening was spent talking with his parents on their front porch, looking forward to a new future, returning to work, talking about his love for his family. The perfect night. And then the unthinkable happened. We will never know or understand why. Rest peacefully, our sweet child. You take a piece of our hearts with you forever.

This is a brutally honest obituary. Despite their pain and anger, the family was able to find peace: "To say his death was unexpected would not be truthful. Multiple overdoses within the last six months became so commonplace that they started to lose their shock value. Being revived each time with Narcan made him feel invincible. He overdosed on what was presumed to be fentanyl-laced heroin. Suffering irreparable brain damage and then being placed on life support for 14 days was not something we ever prepared for, and we know it was not something he envisioned. It was the final gut punch that, while truly agonizing, was at the same time a blessing as it gave us the peace we need and the grace he needed from us. We were finally able to forgive him for the past and all the anger and resentment melted away, leaving only space for unconditional love."

> **"A pen and paper were found by his body. He died mid-sentence. A letter written before he died by an addict: 'It rips my heart apart knowing it's my actions and decisions that have caused a separation from my family. I am a dope fiend, a heroin junkie, a drug addict, or just cursed by a disease of the mind. It's taking a toll on me...there seems to be no escape. I'm stuck, trapped, owned, miserable. Almost like I'm possessed. Mom and Dad, it hurts me to hurt you.'"**
>
> *— Adam's obituary*

As Paul said to the Romans: "I do not understand what I do. For what I want to do I do not do, but what I hate, I do." These obituaries share what the deceased thought of themselves.

- I just want to be a regular guy with a decent job, a woman I love, and a nice place to live.
- Don't hate the addict, hate the disease; don't hate the person, hate the behavior. If it's hard to watch it, imagine how hard it is to live it.
- I wish for all people to hear that I am a good person with a bad disease. I kept getting back up each time I fell, but I hurt so many people in my life, primarily my daughters, all whom I will love dearly in spirit.

- He told his mother he could not get the devil off his shoulders; the devil that was telling him to do it just one more time, it will feel so good. "Momma, I am scared that he won't leave." The grief is over, but so is he.

> **"Addiction is a horrible disease, not a crack in character. It does not discriminate among our children. It often strikes those who are most familiar and among the most fortunate. No parents could have been prouder of their blue-eyed wonder."**
>
> — *Murphy's obituary*

All of us are vulnerable. There are no "other types of people" who become dependent on drugs. After reading at least a thousand obituaries of people who died of substance abuse, it is apparent to me that addiction is a pervasive battle. It does not discriminate. It takes the old, young, weak, strong, poor, wealthy, highly educated, uneducated, and people of any race, nearly any age, and from the city or country.

- Our beloved 24-year-old daughter died as a result of a heroin overdose. She didn't look like an addict. You can't tell an addict by looking at them.
- Our son died from complications due to a long, hard battle with drug addiction; he was 35 years young. He was a dedicated journalist, a brilliant freelance writer, and a culture sponge.
- She spent the first 16 years of her life as a happy, witty, straight-A student. Then heroin and other drugs took over that beautiful mind.
- She graduated from college with highest honors and went to work in the White House for President Reagan, ending her career as a political consultant. She died of addiction at age 54.
- An attorney and the father of four sons passed away prematurely in his apartment. After years of recovery, he sadly succumbed to his disease. Instead of mourning the loss, his family and loved ones want to use his memory to help others by raising awareness that the opioid crisis can strike anywhere, including the professional community.

- Our wonderful son died suddenly at the age of 38. He could have been your child. We went to all his games and sat down to home-cooked meals at night. He loved to learn and read, and was considered gifted. But unfortunately, once he started taking meth, he could never let go of it for more than a few years, and his gifts slid by the wayside.

- He was a warm, loving, kind, and loyal person. He was college educated and a computer genius. He loved life and lived it to the fullest. Unfortunately, his drug addiction destroyed his life and took everything away from him. Eventually, drugs also took his life.

- Our daughter spoke in a public recovery forum using the title, "Addiction can even happen to a golden Girl Scout," addressing the delusion that drug addiction doesn't happen to people like us or in a town like ours.

- She loved sports. She played soccer and volleyball. She loved the outdoors. She loved music. She played the piano, flute, guitar, and sang beautifully. She liked to read and to watch movies. She loved her pets. She had a great sense of humor and loved to laugh. At 22 years old, she succumbed to the disease of addiction.

- He had everything a 19-year-old could want. But once drugs took control in his life they changed him, destroying so much of the hope and promise in his future. Ultimately he lost his five-year battle, and is now another heartbreaking reminder of the heroin epidemic in this country.

"Unfortunately he had an addiction he could not overcome and died from an accidental drug overdose. We are choosing to be open about this so others will understand that even with treatment, he was unable to break the hold those substances had over him. We do not wish that his memory be defined by his mistakes as he was dearly loved by family and we have many good memories of him."

— *Alex's obituary*

Those with substance abuse issues don't want to be reduced to being seen as only an addict. The bereaved insist that the whole person is remembered, the person who was different when not in the grip of addiction. These parents included words to their son from his counselor in his obituary: "I cannot tell you how much I admire and respect you. You are not your addiction. Sure, your addiction is a part of you, but it is just that—a part of you."

- He was a tall, handsome, charming, remarkably bright, charismatic person suffering from the demon of addiction from the age of 11. He died of a heroin overdose with his family and friends loving him and encouraging him to seek recovery.
- My son died this week. He was sweet, he was kind, and he had a good sense of humor. He was very articulate and passionate about politics and the causes he supported. He was a very talented musician and gifted artist. He was also mentally ill and a drug addict.
- A happy baby, a spunky little girl, a beautiful woman, a gentle person, but she struggled with addiction. She coped the best she could with the demons inside, always with a hopeful heart, but the addiction was stronger. She never wanted to leave this world or those she loved.
- She is defined by more than her addiction or manner of death. Like all humans, she was a mosaic of almost 32 years of life experiences. She felt all her emotions extremely strongly. She loved her way of escaping from her complicated little self and life. And had she not lost her last battle with addiction, she would have chosen to remain with her loving husband and their newborn son.
- His time with us on earth is not defined by the addiction, and his character is not defined by time spent incarcerated. He will be remembered as charismatic, smart, courageous, funny, handsome, and loyal. He felt the emotions of life deeply, often too deeply. The chemical comfort offered by opiates has beguiled us for millennia and will continue to dim some of our brightest lights. Addiction is not to be ashamed of or criminalized. He tried for years to shake the beast for himself, for his family, and for his friends; as time pressed on he felt less and less compassion and energy for himself.

- Many knew him only through the lens of the addictions he battled for years. That wasn't the real him though, and those fortunate enough to truly know him knew he was funny, smart, creative, and compassionate. You are a beautiful soul who fought a hard battle.
- He was a son, brother, father, friend, painter, cook, reader, student, practical joker, musician, and also a compassionate, nonjudgmental human being who sought to help others until the last day of his life. He was also an addict. Perhaps that is what people saw first, and the chaos that carried into his brief life, but it is certainly not the whole person.

> "She passed away 22 years and a day after she first lit up the world with her green eyes, blonde curls, and bright smile. Despite her soaring dreams and zest for life, her bright star was dimmed by struggles with addiction. She was proud to be seven months clean and sober; she had a job she loved, sober friends to rely on, and a family who loved her. Sadly, it was not enough; she died from a drug overdose. Our girl was magic. She is barely survived by her mother."
>
> — *Claire's obituary*

An unattributed definition of addiction describes the high cost of pain that others must pay: "It is the disease that makes you too selfish to see the havoc that you created or care about the people whose lives you shattered."

- He could have been anyone's son. He was mine, and I loved him and my heart is broken.
- In college she began to experiment with drugs, as a result, she was on and off drugs her entire life, resulting in a fatal overdose at the Hard Rock Casino at the age of 52. She gave birth to three boys. Realizing her challenges would prevent them from having the quality of life they deserved, she allowed them to be adopted into loving families.
- He died of a heroin overdose. His wife is now widowed, his children fatherless, and his family heartbroken. I am sorry if this obituary offends, hurts, or shames some people. I hope that it

might help save some people from the incredible heartache we are experiencing and help open everyone's eyes to the extreme control and impact drugs have on not only you, but your family too.

- He attended one year of college until his parents pulled him out due to failing grades. Shortly thereafter, his heroin addiction took over. Over the course of his life, he made many bad decisions including experimenting with drugs. Unfortunately, his five-year addiction and battle with heroin took over. His family and friends truly loved him and tried everything from being supportive to tough love as he struggled with his own inner demons and heroin.

- He was a vibrant and energetic child who grew into a curious and easily influenced young man. As his addiction tightened its grip, he estranged himself from any family and friends who sought to help him. He leaves behind his greatest joy and accomplishment, two beautiful daughters who will never remember their father's embrace.

- As with any unexpected death, there may always be stories unfinished, relationships left incomplete, jokes left unsaid, and embraces never felt, but he had reason to be proud of himself and we will pray that he always knows how much we loved him and how special he was to us, both in good times and bad, both in periods of addiction and sobriety. We may never know what tortures he felt internally that drove him to abuse drugs, but we do know that despite the bad feelings he may have kept buried deep, we always tried our best to show him love even when it was difficult.

> **"Ty's death marked the end of an ongoing heroin addiction that left a long path of destruction. He leaves behind two beautiful children in the wreckage of his death."**
>
> — *Ty's obituary*

Some pain is too just much to bear.

- She was on her way to re-hab; she never made it. She died in a bathroom stall at the airport with a needle in her arm and her boarding pass in her hand. She was 23.

- He came into the world, a golden boy, born on Mother's Day. After a wonderful weekend with him, I thought we had made it to the other side; but it was just his last gift to us, and I thank him for that. He relapsed in the following days. Our beautiful son died of a heroin overdose. He was 23 years old.
- He passed away after a long battle with drug addiction at 30. His father tragically passed away from drug addiction last month.
- Both of our sons lost their battle with heroin addiction on the same day.

The raw eloquence breaks your heart. It is impossible not to feel the loved ones' despair and pain. While addiction ends some lives, it forever scars the lives of survivors: "The path you were on was dangerous, dark, and scary, therefore so was my path. My heart dragged in the dust as you walked this path of a million tears and now it is broken in two."

> **"He struggled for many years with drug addiction. Mercy on all families that struggle and suffer with them."**
>
> — *Shaun's obituary*

Some families suffer to the point of anger, bitterness, and hopelessness.

- My brother died from an overdose. It was easier to just not say I had a brother versus try to explain his mental suffering, his homelessness, his times in lockdown, how he tried to self-medicate. He died alone like he lived; feared and rejected by people, when really it was him who feared what was around him. Sometimes it seems easier to say you had no brother when the reality is you have grieved for him each day before his death.
- With his untimely and early death, worlds have been shattered and prayer left unfulfilled for the hope of having the long-lasting recovery.
- Our son grew up in a lovely family devoted to his success. He earned a graduate degree from Harvard as well as a law degree. However, during the past 25 years he had been unable to escape his drug abuse. He ill used all those who loved him.

We all suffered the weight of despair, shame, deception, and estrangement such addiction inflicts. We will try to remember the good, but having lived with the ugly, it will be difficult. Drugs stole his spirit and he died isolated from those who loved him.

- Over the past several years, he struggled with addiction, but recently his mindset took him to depths of darkness that magnified his dependence on alcohol and drugs. In addition to taking his life and our hopes for his recovery, his disease of addiction leaves behind the broken hearts of his family that loved him dearly.
- Her addiction struggles took her from us years ago, but took her life on May 25.
- If you are lucky enough not to know or understand what addiction is, then good for you. I hope you never have someone you care deeply about disappear right in front of you.
- Our son died of an overdose. He is survived by a few treasured friends that stuck with him through thick and thin, and many friends that turned their backs on him in his darkest hours.

This obituary was shocking in its detail and heartbreaking in the pain it revealed: "At about 9 a.m. he injected methamphetamine into his veins, walked into his parents' backyard and shot himself to death. He was a kind and generous soul, but it was also a soul tormented by drugs. We will never know what depths of despair drove this sweet and considerate man to believe himself unworthy of living. Parents, beware for your children. Meth is not a recreational drug; Meth addicts and Meth kills. His grieving parents are crying for what should have been."

> **"Our young son died as a result of an accidental heroin overdose. No one sets out to be a heroin addict. He did his best and will be forever loved, missed, and remembered."**
>
> *— Ryan's obituary*

Obituaries tell of lives that spiral out of control until they hit bottom.

- He lost his marriage, relationships with his children, connection to family, his friends, his business, his health, his smile, his reputation, and every scrap of enjoyment in life. Missing out on important family events, intervention, rehabilitation, even jail time and all the love in the world could not stop his addiction. Days turned into years, until it all ended by taking his life. He has forever changed the lives of his loved ones.

- Our father was used to calling the shots and doing everything pretty much his way. Eventually the medications he needed for his health took control of his life, his business, his judgment, and his relationships. His addiction ran unchecked and he ended up living on the streets.

- Ironically, one of the longest periods of time where we truly had him back in our lives was during a five-year incarceration. At the time, we thought it was horrible that we were separated, but the separation was only physical. He was sober, mentally present, clear-headed, grateful, loving, and focused with his eye on the prize, which was a second chance at life. Sadly, once he regained his physical freedom, he soon became imprisoned by his addiction.

- When his problems with drugs resulted in several years of homelessness, he showed great understanding and compassion for the community he found on the streets and in the shelters.

- At 20, his drug use led to behavior that landed him in the criminal justice system. He was in and out of prison for 12 years. He voluntarily attended rehab at least 25 times to combat addiction, but he was still unable to stay clean. He died at 33 of an unintentional overdose.

> **"She never hid her addiction and would want her story to be told to help even just one addict to push even harder for another day of sobriety. She would want to shine light on this horrible epidemic of addiction."**
>
> — *Patricia's obituary*

Families of those who have died of a drug overdose express their hope that others struggling with addiction will learn from their honesty.

- Our son battled addiction and would want everyone to know his story in the hope that he could save someone else from pain. He said many times that if he could not be healed of his addiction, that he wanted God to take him home. He was found by a pot of freshly brewed coffee and a slice of pecan pie. His family believes God heard his prayers.
- Our family considers it our duty to speak freely and honestly about the merciless addiction to Benzodiazepines, now at epidemic scale, and to participate with action.
- If you're struggling with addiction, know that you are loved more than you can imagine, and that you are truly worth fighting for. Please accept help.
- We think that our daughter, given her brave and compassionate heart, would want her death from an overdose to be known to provide a warning so that others can safeguard themselves against situations like the one that stole her from us. Please take care of yourselves and each other—that's what she would want.

> **"Ben's mother, father, sister, and brother send a message of love and support to others who navigate the path of addiction."**
>
> — *Ben's obituary*

Obituaries like this one warn others: "Our 25-year-old son did not want to die."

- For those that try drugs, please know, it only takes using heroin one time to get hooked. Heroin is a demon that affects the way your brain processes pleasure, taking over not just your brain, but your life, and destroys families.

- Please take our beloved son's death and beat the trap of addiction. There is NO shame in admitting you are human and made bad choices. There is ALWAYS a way out.
- For all of you struggling with addiction please know that there was nothing my son wanted more than to defeat the devil. He wanted to live. Please live.

This family is blunt: "For many years he suffered with addictions, but for the last 23 years of his life, he was clean and sober. His family asks that if you do not have enough respect for him to show up at his services straight and sober, please do not bother to attend. Also, if you did nothing but cause him misery during his life, do not show up and pretend to mourn him."

These families seize the opportunity to make a difference in other parents' lives, pouring out details of their loved one's struggle. Maybe they are trying to understand their own needless loss, pass along hard-won insights, give families hope, or maybe save just one life.

- Pay attention to your children and the world that revolves around them. Even when the surface is calm, the water may be turbulent just beneath.
- If you are a family member, support your loved one without enabling them. Do not stop giving the words of encouragement they need. Realize, however, that you have no control over what is happening inside them. Seek support for yourself. Say "I love you" because you never know when a conversation may be the last.
- Our charismatic and beautiful son and brother died from a drug overdose. While we always felt we had some grip on his issues, his ability to hide and disguise his addiction proved superior to our parental sixth sense.
- Someone you know is battling addiction; if your "gut instinct" says something is wrong, it most likely is. Get involved. Do everything within your power to provide help. Don't believe the logical-sounding reasons of where their money is going or why they act so different. Don't believe them when they say they're clean.
- It is with a heavy heart that we announce our mother passed away from an accidental drug overdose. She was 63. If you have a loved one who is battling this monster disease, please get help for yourself and your loved one.

> **"We're sure you didn't know the danger or the years of pain you would endure when you took that first pill. You were just a teenager looking for a reprieve from life. We didn't want to talk about those pills. You lost close friends and family, and those losses sunk you even further into the sadness that kept you hooked."**
>
> —*Jennifer's obituary*

Families left with unanswered, and perhaps unanswerable, questions seek reasons why their loved ones started down this path. It may have been a prescription for a legitimate medical reason that became the entry point to abuse: "Those early prescriptions when she was a teenager altered her life permanently."

- Free of opioids for 11 months, he thought he had it beat this time. He was reintroduced to them by a prescription pain medication after a recent injury. Within two weeks he was dead.
- He earned a PhD in Policy Analysis, managed a $40 billion portfolio, and at the young age of 42 he attained the rank of Colonel in the Air Force. His remarkable life and stellar career were tragically cut short by opioid addiction stemming from a surgical procedure.
- She was in a life-altering car accident and her medical treatment included prescribed opioids. Her whole life was turned upside down. The darkness and loneliness of her addiction lasted approximately 24 years.
- Our son attributed his addiction to drugs as having stemmed from the use of pain killers prescribed for him following the removal of his wisdom teeth while a teenager.
- His life was like a storybook. His life's dream was being lived every day making a living by doing the things he loved. His knee had to be rebuilt because of an old injury and he was prescribed opioids. He became addicted and his life went downhill. He eventually lost everything.

> **"All of the wonderful blessings that he had: talent, friendships, positive outlook on life, and most importantly, family, were sidelined by a wrong decision to do drugs."**
>
> — *Justin's obituary*

Families admit the hard truth. Their loved one made bad choices and bad decisions.

- Sadly, our son's introduction to drugs and alcohol in middle school led him down a path that, despite his family's love and his own attempts at recovery, he never succeeded at conquering all of his demons.
- He struggled with addictions, which created a cloud of bad luck that followed him wherever he went. Unfortunately this bad luck was of his own creation.
- He was born unexpectedly three months early and he died unexpectedly at his home from a heroin overdose. He was almost one year clean, his future looked so bright, yet one poor decision ended it all. We were all stunned by his death; he always came back. Yet an addict's death should never be unexpected.

One family, upon the death of their daughter, made a statement: "Some will say that an obituary shouldn't be the place for a commentary on the opiate crisis. You wouldn't have died but for opiates, and we wouldn't be writing this if it wasn't for the drug companies that made billions off addicting people just like you. This isn't to say you weren't responsible for your actions; you were. But the drug companies are complicit in your death."

The people with whom a person chooses to associate make a difference in the direction a life can take: "Our son died of an overdose. He was preceded in death by his many friends who also lost their battles with addiction: Elizabeth, Dan, Trevor, Jake, Travis, Ryan along with many others. May they all have found their peace." Choosing a partner carefully is also essential. This couple left behind a six-year-old daughter: "She was joined in death just two days later by her husband, also of an overdose."

> **"She was diagnosed with the very challenging diagnosis of Borderline Personality Disorder. and so begins a pathway to hardcore drugs, living on the streets, and self-destruction. She overdosed on heroin/ Fentanyl. She leaves behind a family that has been mourning the loss of sweet, sweet Alexx for over half her life. This hardcore drug addict was once a blonde four-year-old with a bowl haircut."**
>
> *— Alexx's obituary*

Addiction and mental illness are often entwined. Self-medication is another reason people misuse or abuse drugs.

- He struggled with paralyzing shyness and was bullied by many as a result. Early in his teens, drugs promised an escape and so began his life with addiction.
- He started using drugs to make him feel normal, to feel accepted, to feel worthy because this is what the drug told him, at first. What it didn't tell him was how it would devastate his family, take his education, take his jobs, take his future, take and take until it would take his life. Addiction will take hold and destroy anyone in its path including families and loved ones of those afflicted.

> **"With great sadness his family announces his passing after a long battle with drug addiction. Upon his return from Iraq, he was subsequently diagnosed with PTSD and a traumatic brain injury. He was a kind and sensitive soul."**
>
> *— Mark's obituary*

Related to self-medication, life-altering experiences from serving in the military can also prompt abusing drugs to cope with PTSD.

- He served proudly with the United States Army and has struggled with PTSD and substance abuse for years. Heroin came into his and our lives and stole him from us.
- He was a warrior who faced every challenge with a fierceness and determination to do his best for his country as a Marine

and for his family. After returning from Iraq, he took on perhaps his biggest challenge, overcoming PTSD and addiction. Like battles he fought overseas, there were victories and defeats, none of which kept him from getting up and fighting again. Unfortunately, his battle ended on Tuesday.

> **"He fought hard to overcome addictions, entering rehab on many occasions—each time leaving a deep imprint on staff and clients, each time leaving hopeful that this time, life might be different. In a perfect world maybe it could have been...one day."**
>
> *— Ron's obituary*

Many people who struggle with addiction have gone through rehabilitation, fighting the battle for years. This long and discouraging struggle is referred to in many obituaries.

- He drank and did drugs but he still functioned. He had nice friends and lived his life. Then he found his way to heroin. Life was never the same. He was in and out of rehab and our lives were a living hell.
- His moments of sobriety were washed away like the changing tides of the ocean with the cycles of relapse and recovery. In recovery he was a hard worker, confident, caring, and loving, but while in relapse, he was distant, ashamed, and embarrassed. He did not want to be an addict. No one ever does.
- Our son was one of those people who spent so much time giving his happiness away he didn't seem to keep enough for himself. As an adult he started to pursue happiness in his own way as he struggled with drug addiction. After nine years of struggle we thought he might have won. He relapsed for the final time last week. His search for happiness is over.

> **"Addiction can be a hard road in life, and kindness is a beautiful gift."**
>
> — *Sticky's obituary*

Families seek increased awareness and empathy: "We loved our son with all of our hearts and would like to express our gratitude to everyone who stuck by him through the battles of his drug addiction and did not judge him."

- Our son's legacy invites us to come together to hold each other up with love, and have meaningful conversations with one another, even when it's hard.
- The best way to honor him is by educating yourself and others on the disease of addiction; by treating strangers with empathy, generosity, kindness, and compassion; and by respecting this disease and the basic human dignities of those afflicted by it.
- If you are reading this and lack the empathy to relate or think that drug addiction is a choice, please read more about addiction and understand that this disease can start innocently and legally and can affect anyone, anywhere.
- Those drug addicts you're judging are not just some junkies and losers who deserve to die. They are actually some good people with good hearts who made some bad decisions as we all do. So if you can't help them, don't hurt them. Pray for them.

> **"What a truly tragic thing it is for a parent to write an obituary for a child who has just died. As parents of a son battling addiction, we knew full well that the time might come when we would have to sit down and perform this gut-wrenching task. That awful time has arrived. So, we sadly dedicated ourselves to writing our son's final farewell with intermixed feelings of shock, grief, anger, appreciation, and hope."**
>
> — *Eric's obituary*

- It is a monumental feat to write your child's obituary. Yet to write your child's obituary that succumbed to the beast of addiction after 10 years, practically impossible. But to write a second obituary for yet another child, that fought addiction for 14 years, an indescribable catastrophe.

- Hi Johnny—Mom here. A lot of people have been asking why there hasn't been an obituary announcement, but you know why, don't you? You know that this is the most painful task imaginable—we talked about this more than once. We have both danced with your devil. You tried; I know. It's okay.

This moving obituary is educational: "Sadly, this obituary is one of thousands that are the end result of addiction. Each weaves a different story with identical thread, but in each story there is a beacon of determined hope that the ending will change. So, if you are reading this with judgment, educate yourself about this disease. It is not a choice or a weakness. No one chooses this disease. Chances are very good that someone you know is struggling with addiction, and that person needs and deserves your empathy and support. If you are reading this and are struggling with addiction, know that every day brings a fresh start. There are hundreds of thousands of families that have lost someone they love to this disease, and we are all cheering for you. Know that we believe that you can and will make it, because it is never too late."

> **"Healed and whole at last. Everything in its right place."**
>
> *— Jordan's obituary*

Despite their pain, families find consolation in knowing death has delivered some peace.

- Now he has peace, love, and happiness, three things that eluded him here on earth.
- How well I know your sorrow and how helpless I was to ease your pain. Rest in sweet, gentle peace, my son. I will try to find peace in your peace.
- Loved by so many, with his booming voice, beaming smile, contagious laugh, and sincere hugs, his passing leaves a crater-sized hole in our hearts and our lives. We are comforted by knowing also he is now at peace and in the arms of God.
- My beautiful daughter died after relapsing during her brave fight against the disease of heroin addiction. She leaves behind a beautiful nine-month-old daughter, a heartbroken younger

sister, and a devastated mother. At last she is at peace; she struggles no more.

Families appreciate the good in the life of their loved one.

- He was a leader in the recovery community, helping many successfully overcome the disease from which he, himself, suffered. He died of an overdose.
- Our beautiful girl was taken from us by heroin. After six days on life support, she was unable to be saved. But because she was an organ donor, she will be able to give at least seven people a chance to live.
- He drifted for many years and struggled with homelessness and addictions. However, he provided his friends and family the unique opportunity to understand addiction and homelessness in a powerful way. He taught us to reach for each other with whatever goodness we have to offer: a warm cup of coffee, a smile, a warm coat, a meal in time of need. The family invites you to reach for someone in need in whatever way feels best.

Unconditional love shines brightly in these final love letters.

- We are not ashamed or embarrassed by his struggles. We know the courage he had in rising daily to fight the good fight to overcome and endure. He was never afraid to share his experience when he felt it would benefit another. He possessed a beautiful soul full of light, and he left his mark indelibly etched in the hearts and minds of all who knew him.
- He lived a full life that included long meaningful relationships, struggles with addiction, serious legal trouble, disconnection and reconnection with his sons and, at the end of his life, good times with his granddaughter. He could be arrogant and hard-nosed at times, but he could also be generous, loving, and fiercely loyal.
- In full transparency, he struggled with addiction. It inhibited and ultimately ended his career and, at times, strained his personal life with family. But he was always loved, and he loved us back. His parents and family loved him fiercely and unconditionally over the decades until his passing. It has been written that the opposite of addiction is not sobriety but connection. That resonates.

- Loved by all, those close to him remember his good heart and gentle soul. For the last 15 years, he fought a brave battle with addiction. Addiction affects the whole family, and his family fought with him and for him every day. We saw glimmers of hope, but the disease dominated. He finally found peace; his war ended. We will miss and love him forever.

One family's message is almost more than one can bear: "Our third son has struggled with the disease of addiction for the past six years along with his two brothers, who also struggled with addiction. He has now reunited with his brothers who await his arrival to heaven. Things got extremely tough for him after losing his brothers, as it would for any one of us. His light would shine through time and again, but it was apparent his soul was dimmed forever. He is with them now, and we pray that his soul is at peace."

> **"It is impossible to capture a person in an obituary, and especially someone whose adult life was largely defined by drug addiction. To some, he was just a junkie, or a criminal, or a thief—when they saw his addiction, they didn't see him. What a loss for them because he was kind, and warm, and funny, and thoughtful, and loyal, and hopeful, and determined, and resilient. He believed that everyone had potential for change and that everyone deserved forgiveness. He was adored, and being loved by him was a gift."**
>
> *— Adam's obituary*

This chapter was extremely difficult for me to research and write. Throughout this project, the obituaries I have read are usually for people who have lived happy, long lives. But those hundreds and hundreds of obituaries of overdose deaths stacked up and eventually blocked the sun for me. It was heartbreaking to learn of people so full of promise who needlessly died, and the suffering of those who loved them. The magnitude of the drug epidemic cannot be whitewashed or ignored.

Substance Use Disorder: Alcohol

"We expected to be proud of his success in traditional ways. Instead he challenged us to stretch our hearts and minds, learn about mental illness and alcohol addiction, and develop compassion instead of passing judgment. This may be one of his greatest gifts to us."

— *Michael's obituary*

Public health experts have focused extensively on overdose deaths from opioids, heroin, and prescription painkillers. Deaths from these drugs have risen rapidly since the early 2000s. But each year, alcohol kills more people than drug overdoses—through cancer, liver cirrhosis, pancreatitis, accidents, suicide, and other ways. Researchers estimate that deaths from alcohol-related problems have more than doubled the past 20 years. One blunt example from an obituary: "He left us as a result of injuries sustained from being a dumb ass. He drank, drove, and didn't wear a seatbelt. Please don't be a dumb ass!"

Culturally, we separate alcohol from other drugs, usually referring to "alcohol and drugs." It seems that being addicted to a legal substance is more acceptable than being addicted to an illegal one. This may be why more Americans are addicted to alcohol than any other drug.

When I started researching obituaries for this book, I didn't see many references to alcoholism, or alcohol use disorder. But as references to drug overdoses became more common, the mention of alcoholism seemed to appear with regularity. Maybe this is a good thing. Death by drugs and death by alcohol are equally tragic.

> **"On the full moon of December 30, with 48 years of sobriety and 84 years sailing 'full and by,' he raised sail one last time and said goodbye."**
>
> — *Bob's obituary*

Alcoholism is sometimes mentioned in an obituary even when it is not the cause of death. Evidently families of the deceased are proud and thankful for sobriety: "Among his proudest achievements was 37 years of membership and service in Alcoholics Anonymous (AA)."

- She endured many health issues, but she was a fighter, especially with her addiction with alcohol. In 2019, she celebrated 43 years of sobriety. She loved her ladies' meetings and the many special friends from that group.
- He was a champion drinker and smoker until he gave them both up and became a dedicated and passionate member of AA. He went to meetings every day, sharing his experience, strength, and hope with many friends who have benefited from his raw wisdom.
- He was best described as a free spirit and was well liked by everyone. He was proud of his Irish heritage and frequently enjoyed a beverage at the local (or non-local) tavern. He was famous for having a story for every occasion; fact checking was prohibited. In his later years, he retired his drinking uniform and became a devoted member of AA.
- Those who really knew him knew he fought a very heavy alcohol addiction for many years. But please know that he was sober from alcohol for six years and that should be acknowledged and celebrated. His body has been donated to a science program to help educate about alcohol abuse.
- He was a dedicated member of AA, but passed away unexpectedly at home. In lieu of flowers, please consider making a donation to the memorial fund, which has been created to honor his memory and to support his beloved wife's recovery treatment.
- From the age of 30, when she was given only a few months to live as a result of alcoholism and damage to her liver, she stopped drinking and was a grateful, lifelong member of AA. Countless people will tell you her outrageous tough talk and

brash language helped them be happier and more human.

> **"The family would like to help any families that may be fighting the demons of addiction. Many families are embarrassed to speak of issues within their families but if we could help save even one life, then this is all worth it. Cheryl's son battled and lost his fight with opioid addiction and abuse. Her personal demon was found in the form of far too many Budweiser cans; her passing was due to alcohol abuse."**
>
> — *Cheryl's obituary*

Even when not celebrating the years of sobriety their loved one enjoyed, families acknowledge the addiction.

- He believed in second chances, maybe because he craved another chance for himself, along with other addicts he met and supported whenever in recovery. As many a gentle and sensitive spirit experiencing love and loss, he battled alcoholism. He longed to be rid of the demons and to be worthy of the love he received from family and friends.
- He waged a long and sometimes terrible battle against alcoholism and is finally at rest. He would want everyone to know that addiction is a terrible disease which he suffered from along with many other family members, friends, and loved ones.

> **"Even though he was only 22 years old, over the last several years he had battled depression and dependency on alcohol. He remained strong in his desire to leave the world a better place. His life and accidental and untimely death are not defined by his addiction, but by his steadfast love and sense of humor."**
>
> — *Bo's obituary*

As with drug addiction, the family wants the deceased to be appreciated and remembered as a whole person. Alcoholism was only one part of their life.

- He died from natural causes related to chronic alcoholism. While his addiction to alcohol informed many of his decisions, it did not define him. He continued to be the same kind, generous, and intelligent individual we all knew.
- Our son, age 27, passed away after a long battle with alcohol addiction. He wouldn't want to be defined by his addiction and mistakes; he was so much more than that. He was a kind, intelligent child, who could be feisty and outspoken, but would do anything for anyone and could light up a room with his smile and eclectic sense of humor all while struggling with his addiction. He loved his family. This was the real person and he should be remembered for this, and not the mistakes that were made. He definitely wanted to live, while at the hospital he had talked about changing his life for the better but didn't get the opportunity.

People may think there is "type" of person who becomes an alcoholic, but that is not the case. As with other addictions, everyone is vulnerable.

- She died at 69 years old after a long struggle with alcohol addiction. She earned an MBA from the Wharton School and taught in France and worked as a management consultant. She was also an accomplished potter and water colorist, and won a sculling gold medal at the National Women's Rowing Associations championships, and dove on the Great Barrier Reef.
- My husband confronted his alcohol addiction in a very open way. Before the State Bar of Texas formally recognized the unique challenges practicing professionals faced when suffering from addictions, he formed an informal lawyers' AA group. Immediately, other prominent attorneys came forward, admitting their own struggles. He believed AA saved his life and saved the lives of others who were suffering in secret. Some attorneys swear he saved them from death or complete professional destruction.
- He was a veteran and recipient of a doctorate in organic chemistry. He struggled with alcohol addiction for much of his life, but through the support of AA he was sober for more than

20 years and was very active in the organization up until the end of his life. We would like to extend our sincerest gratitude to all of the men and women of the organization who helped put him on the path back to our family.

- While in law school she struggled with alcohol abuse, and delayed her graduation to join AA and enter recovery. She had to explain how she could be in AA and still be a good lawyer to pass the bar. When she passed, she joined Lawyers Concerned for Lawyers to advocate for greater acceptance and support in the legal community for other lawyers recovering from addiction. She stayed sober the rest of her life, until at 35 she was struck by a bus while riding her bike.

> **"Our 40-year-old daughter died unexpectedly. She suffered from alcohol addiction, an isolating disease she kept extremely private for many years. She ultimately lost that battle, devastating and blindsiding all those to whom she was close."**
>
> *—Ariel's obituary*

While those who succumb to alcohol abuse include adults of all ages, I was unpleasantly surprised at the number of young adults.

- Our 33-year-old daughter died after a long battle with alcohol addiction and an eating disorder.
- Our 29-year-old son was an alcoholic who was desperately trying to break free of the tenacious hold which alcohol had taken of his life. He simply went to sleep expecting to wake up the next day, but his last relapse mixed with medications made that his last sleep.
- He suffered many troubling years in his struggles with alcohol addiction. Although he didn't take his own life, his addiction significantly shortened it. He was 34.
- She died in the arms of her husband at 33, following a decade long battle with alcohol addiction.
- Our 38-year-old daughter died unexpectedly. She thrived through high school and college, until approaching graduation, when a dark cloud was forming on the horizon. The recreational

drinking of campus life became something more. With great hope she was married, but her struggles with alcohol worsened, and the challenges became insurmountable. She was beautiful inside and out. She loved her family fiercely, as we did her. But in the end, her light and promise were overcome by a disease more powerful than her. May your spirit soar free, precious child. It was a privilege to be your family and we pray that like you, we will be lavish with love wherever we go.

> **"Our son tragically and unexpectedly passed away at 32 years old. The severity and duration of his addiction to alcohol was almost entirely hidden from his friends and family. He passed just hours before family intended to bring him to a medical detoxification facility."**
>
> — *Eric's obituary*

Alcoholism is a disease of isolation marked by attempts to keep it hidden from others.

- The alcoholic can hide it, and our daughter hid it well. But eventually it becomes too big and oftentimes too late.
- He had struggled with alcohol abuse and tried to continually hide it and bear the brunt of it on his own. During his struggles, we tried to help him as best we could. He was proud and did not want those outside of his immediate family knowing about his demons. We continually told him that we loved him, but it was not enough to cure him of his deep depression. Every family hopes that they will beat this disease, and we honestly believed this until the moment we received the phone call that he was gone.

Some families just can't hide their pain.

- He was intuitive, gentle, and powerful. However, he suffered from an addiction to alcohol for much of his life. The care and love of all those around him couldn't save him from those dragons, and he was unable to save himself.
- With profound sadness we announce the unexpected passing of our only child. He faced many challenges in his short life, and

was successful in conquering all of them but one, his alcohol addiction. He tried over and over, but the disease was more powerful than he. We remember his smile, kindness, and how he always stood up for the underdog.

- Our son passed away at 45 due to heart failure after a lengthy battle with alcohol addiction. Please remember to treat others with kindness and patience; you never know what others are dealing with under their tough exteriors.

- He was a wonderful father, husband, brother, and friend, but at some point, alcohol addiction slowly took over his life and he lost many of the things he loved, and we lost him. It was such a struggle for him and those who loved him. Hoping he is now at peace.

> "Her life took a wrong turn and her struggles with drug and alcohol abuse began. It would be easy enough to sweep this chapter of her life under the proverbial rug, but I think she would like people to understand how adversely these struggles came to affect her life and relationships, both with family and friends. As much as I mourn the death of my sister, I mourn the loss of a life that could have been, even more. I will always regret she never had an opportunity to do more with her life, but as we all know, that is a clear consequence of alcohol and drug addiction."
>
> *— Julie's obituary*

Sharing their discouragement, some families mention relapses.

- He fought hard against alcohol addiction most of his adult life. But in the end, after 18 months clean, he relapsed and lost his battle. The light of a loving, intelligent, kind-hearted spirit was taken from our lives.

- She was the perfect child when her ongoing battle with alcohol addiction began. The thing about alcohol is that it is legal and socially accepted. For most people it is never a problem. Alcoholism is a thief; it stole her family and friends. It stole her job and eventually stole her life. She had too many admissions to hospitals, detox, and rehab; too many to count. Each time she came out motivated and ready to change, and each time she was not able to sustain the change. She did not always allow us in her life, but we never stopped trying. Our faith and hope were big; her hope and faith were big; the addiction was bigger. She died at 38, leaving behind a daughter and a husband who loved her unconditionally.

Individuals who abuse alcohol are also likely to abuse other substances, including legal prescription drugs and illegal drugs. Drinking and drugs exacerbate the effects of each substance and can leave a person at risk for physical, behavioral, financial, and emotional health complications.

- His minimalistic lifestyle often left him without a home. After living with alcoholism and anxiety, at the age of 49, he began to suffer liver failure and untimely death.
- Alas, he was vulnerable to alcohol addiction and his long, sad decline led to him spending his last years disabled in a nursing home.
- She developed emotional disorders which sadly led her to self-medicating, which led to alcoholism and drug addiction issues, which cut her promising life short. She began an unconventional lifestyle living on the streets. She suffered serious domestic abuse injuries, life-threatening homeless fights, and became disabled from injecting heroin into the main nerve in her arm. She passed away peacefully in a dry tent curled up in a warm sleeping bag.

"Our father was 66 when he died. In 1980, while incarcerated, he graduated from college with a degree in aviation science and became a licensed pilot. His license was eventually revoked for flying under bridges. A gregarious person, he got to meet a lot of famous and infamous people, both in and out of prison, which provided him with many entertaining anecdotes. A lifetime of alcohol and drug addiction destroyed all his relationships, his health, and whatever human potential he possessed. He spent half his life incarcerated, and the rest of the time hustling and conning to support his habits."

— *Gary's obituary*

The pain and anger of survivors is apparent. Perhaps there is comfort in sharing.

- His death was unexpected and has ripped a hole in the center of our tight knit family.
- He died following a lifelong battle with alcohol addiction. Addiction to alcohol is a disease that destroys the addict and their relationships with family, friends, and neighbors. As per his wishes and those of his family, there will be no services.
- He had four children throughout the course of a couple marriages. In the midst of all that, he was acquiring a severe case of alcoholism that would stick with him until he was 57 years old. That addiction left him with a life full of bad decisions, legal issues, regret, guilt, and basically no family.
- She made poor choices, often surrounding herself with the wrong people—people who did not have her best interests and those of her innocent children at heart. Her struggles led her to inflict pain on her family for so many years. Her addiction culminated in this very sad ending.

Survivors try to sustain other families with warnings and words of encouragement, despite their own suffering.

- To the families of the addicted: They need and deserve your empathy and support. Please love them through this, even if they don't want it. There will be anger, but be angry together, rather than apart.
- In 2014 he lost his wife to a long battle with alcoholism, and he struggled with alcoholism himself for much of his later years, which took its toll on many aspects of his life—most importantly his health. The disease of addiction shows no mercy. The battle he has fought and lost is a reminder to us all how important it is to seek help and help others we know who may be struggling, and to support them to the best of our abilities. Love you, Dad.

Families address those who struggle with alcohol.

- We lost a son, brother, and uncle to alcoholism. He expressed regret for decisions he made in his life. He was still a young man. We ask that if you're having a problem with alcohol/addiction, please reach out for help through a treatment center or 12-step program of AA/NA. You are not alone. Don't become another statistic. The life you save will be your own.
- If you are struggling with any type of addiction, know that your family and friends love you and want better for you. Don't hide or feel ashamed, talk through it until you are blue in the face. Embrace the people you love and believe with all your heart that you can and will make it through to the other side.

Obituaries that disclose alcohol-related deaths reinforce the fact that addiction does not discriminate. Unbeknownst to you, people around you are struggling. Be kind, always.

I loved the honesty of this tribute to a flawed but loving and much-loved parent: "The body of our father was discovered by dear friends. He had died of natural causes related to a lifelong love of beer and bacon. He had recently proclaimed it was exactly the way he wanted to go: quietly, peacefully, and quickly. He was 66 years old. He was a kind soul with a wry wit and an often crude sense of humor. Despite the sharp edges of his personality, he was all softness inside. For most of his life, he struggled with alcoholism and social anxiety. This could make him difficult to love and even more difficult to include in activities. His family would like you to know that this is a symptom of the disease of addiction, not an indication of his character. He did his best, he loved us fully, and even when it was uncomfortable for him, he showed up. We learned posthumously of his large circle of friends, many of whom had similar struggles. To all of his friends, new and old, thank you for loving him, too."

A Life of Struggle: Mental Illness

"Please remember to pray for those who struggle with mental illness and addiction. It is a hard life."

— *James's obituary*

Just as survivors are honest about deaths resulting from drug or alcohol abuse, there is no shame in acknowledging that mental illness ravaged the life of a loved one. According to the National Alliance on Mental Illness, one in five American adults experiences mental illness in a given year. Mental illness is far more widespread than we might think.

Families may feel that mental illness reflects poorly on the deceased or even the family and omit or refer to it in vague terms in an obituary. But some families seek to remove any stigma associated with these issues by including them in the obituary.

- To honor my son, it will be my mission to shed light on the impact of mental illness, especially in children and young adults, and the importance to break the stigma of shame that surrounds it. Please don't assume, don't judge, and don't brush off another's feelings because they aren't the same as yours. Instead, listen, be open, care, believe, accept, and help.
- She was our star. But as she grew older she struggled with depression. Her struggles led her to a dark place and ultimately drug addiction and overdose. Although the past several years were very hard, we never gave up hope she would push through the darkness and come out stronger. As sad and tragic as this is, please know that she is finally at peace with her struggles with addiction and mental illness.

- The mentally ill person and loved ones tragically have to deal with stigma. Individuals are "crazy" as well as their family having "crazy" genes. Mental illness is as real as diabetes or heart disease. It is a disease of the brain that can be treated with public awareness, understanding, and proven medical practice.

> **"She battled mental illness and drug addiction for 24 years. She was brilliant and beautiful, but could not shake her demons. She died suddenly at 37."**
>
> — *Elizabeth's obituary*

This obituary eloquently illustrates how our choice of words can negatively impact a person living with mental illness: "So often people who have a mental illness are known as their illness. People say that 'she is bipolar' or 'he is schizophrenic.' Over the coming days as you talk to people about this, please do not use that phrase. People who have cancer are not cancer; those with diabetes are not diabetes. She was not bipolar—she had an illness called bipolar disorder—she was a beautiful child of God. The way we talk about people and their illnesses affects the people themselves and how we treat the illness. In the case of mental illness there is so much fear, ignorance, and hurtful attitudes that the people who suffer from mental illness needlessly suffer further. Our society does not provide the resources that are needed to adequately understand and treat mental illness. Please know that our daughter was a sweet, wonderful person that loved life and the people around her."

> **"Flamboyant, classy, and more than a little naughty. Don't forget the red lipstick, the cleavage, and never call her Norma. So many people were kind to her, wowed by her, intimidated by her, and a few (shall we say) 'wooed' by her. Thank you to all who spent a little time with her, cared about her, and those who forgave her. Please remember that mental illness should not define or devalue a person. Love and forgive, forgive and forget, but never forget the very unforgettable Norma."**
>
> — *Norma's obituary*

As with other challenges in life, survivors do not want their loved ones labeled or summed up in a just a few words. Families want the person they loved honored and remembered in all their fullness.

- My husband lost a long and courageous battle with depression and addiction. He was an extraordinary educator and touched the hearts and minds of hundreds of young students during his 21 years teaching. He was also an avid reader of books, doer of crosswords, renowned cook capable of turning a leftover into a gourmet meal, and traveler of the world. He left a smile on the face of everyone he touched.

- Although he struggled with anger, alcohol addiction, and undiagnosed mental illness, friends and family remember him as intelligent, sensitive, thoughtful, and articulate.

- Our 27-year old daughter was one of a kind: a powerfully intelligent, passionate, talented, independent, resilient woman. For many years, through terrible suffering caused by mental and physical illness, she did absolutely everything in her power to heal and to be healthy. She found the strength to resist drug misuse for the better part of six years. When she was feeling well, her impact, her achievements, and her lust for life were formidable. When her depression worsened, she mustered all her strength to try to dig herself out of it, and she never stopped seeking help.

> **"He battled depression his entire life and struggled with alcohol addiction in his adult years, ultimately succumbing to his demons."**
>
> — *Philip's obituary*

Mental illness compounds life struggles. These obituaries reveal the pain some people faced for years.

- She fought anxiety and the cruel reality of living in the relentless grip of depression for many years. She soaked up pain like a sponge and it often got the best of her.

- Her 37 years were filled with joy, but mostly great sorrow and suffering. She bravely fought for over two horrendous decades with addiction and declining mental health. Unfortunately she was found too late this time. She died of a heroin overdose.

- He passed away by himself, which is partly how he felt every day of his life. He battled vices, but the biggest one was within. Depression and anxiety took away our son. He chose a path that ultimately ended his life. No matter how much we as parents tried and tried over and over to help him, he still went back. He always said, "Devil on one shoulder and angel on the other." Devil won. Fly away with the angels.

- Despite his achievements, his optimistic nature, and his kindness and compassion towards others, mental illness slowly began to make appearances in his life. It gave him no breaks for all the goodness and hope he brought into the world.

- Our beloved son joined the angels before him in heaven after struggling for many years to battle the darkness within. Mental health and substance abuse are battles that are both silent and dangerously loud.

- Starting in his mid-teens through to the end of his life, our son was plagued by the demons of mental illness and drug addiction. One of his poems about homelessness read, "Unaddressed, it came with my life in a bag weighted with an emptiness that made my shoulders sag." For our son and all others like him, mental illness was, and is, the worst and cruelest fate.

> **"Trevor lost his battle with mental illness and decided to end his life. He spread joy in the world with his open energy and bursting smile. He loved the wind in his ever-changing-colored hair."**
>
> — *Trevor's obituary*

Suicide is a leading cause of death in people with addictions. Many substances lead to mental health problems, including anxiety and depression, making it hard to know which one caused the other. Suicide is considered a mortality of depression. Some just want relief.

- A much loved son, brother, and friend made peace with his demons by taking his life.
- Our beloved son passed away of a broken heart and soul. He is finally free from his earthly demons and depression.
- Our amazing, handsome, brilliant tough fighter chose to leave the darkness of his five-year battle with mental illness in search of light and peace. He fought valiantly against the demons that came at him relentlessly. He hid his pain behind that perfect smile and those beautiful eyes.
- He went to be with our Lord after a courageous battle with depression. He died in a place that he deeply loved, the mountains of Montana. He was ushered into the loving arms of our Lord where he no longer has to endure any more pain, where he can fly fish, hunt, and flash that incredible smile to the full healthy extent it was before his battle began.
- No matter how many times he was told he was special and he mattered, he couldn't see through the darkness of depression to believe it for himself. He struggled with the embarrassment and shame he felt about his depression.
- We take comfort in knowing he has escaped the strangling grip of schizophrenia.
- He died inside of our love, even as we feel frustrated that our love could not do more to help him. He lives now, still, inside our love and affection, and God willing, inside a peace and security that so much eluded him in this life.

> **"The memory of his bright smile, quick wit, argumentative need to be right, and most of all his kindness will never be forgotten. Our broken hearts will forever feel the loss and emptiness of his absence."**
>
> — *Christopher's obituary*

Struggles with mental health affect not only the sufferer. They leave loved ones in its painful wake. Families bear the brunt.

- Mental illness would dangle pieces of his laughter and his heart in front of us, only to snatch them away for good. The pain that he endured in living is now our pain to bear in living without him.

- Our daughter died instantly when she was struck by a car. Tragically, she was mentally ill and homeless. She was diagnosed as bipolar with schizophrenic tendencies and had received extensive treatment, with little success. Typically of the mentally ill, she self-medicated with alcohol and drugs. Her illness became graphically evident when she burned our family home to the ground at age 22.

- He struggled for many years with mental illness and addiction. These demons that he faced took hold of his life, changing him and destroying so much of the hope and promises of his future. He leaves behind his three children and another one on the way.

- My son passed from this life alone from an overdose. The end was inevitable, as it is for all of us, but for those left behind, we are never prepared for the end. My son suffered from schizo-affective disorder which means the reality you and I understand was not the same for him. One of the ways he coped was to self-medicate with street drugs. He chose drugs because they soothed the demons in his head, made him feel better, and gave him meaning. The high was high and the low so low. He was caught in the trap of need and want. He thought he was invincible. If he expected the inevitable we will never know.

> **"We need to come to terms with the fact that as a society we've done little or nothing to address the mental health needs of our citizens, which in turn leads to crime, homelessness, addiction, suicide and much more. We need to break this chain of heartbreak. "**
>
> *—Jaclyn's obituary*

Some families use the obituary to educate readers about the scarcity of treatment in our country. One family wrote that their dearly loved 30-year-old son died: "The family suggests donations to local charities and organizations providing treatment for mental health, addiction, and substance abuse."

- Her doctors said my daughter's future life would be most difficult because of the closure of mental hospitals, inadequate replacement facilities, and prohibitively expensive private hospitals. As her mother I write this obituary to make mental illness a reality in all of our lives, and advocate for an expansive treatment program, now sadly inadequate.

- He had schizoaffective bipolar disorder, and as we discovered, our mental health system is truly a mess. Our county has no residential long-term mental health housing (except for jail!) unless you can afford $30,000 a month. Mental health and drug addiction are intertwined and it's our hope that one day our government institutions will take seriously the treatment of individuals who are suffering from these sometimes deadly ailments.
- He died after an extended battle with mental illness and addiction. To honor his memory, the family asks you to support improved treatment options for mental health and substance abuse at the ballot box.

> **"Our son suffered from addiction and depression for many years. Although he found comfort and peace at times, he was never able to fully overcome a disease that medicine could not cure, counselors could not quiet, and our love and affection could not adequately soothe. He is free now from the struggle that haunted him. He lives now, still inside our love and affection."**
>
> — *Chase's Obituary*

Obituaries of those with mental illness often point out co-occurring substance abuse. Among the 20 million adults in the United States who experience a substance use disorder, about half also suffer from a mental illness.

- Behind her amazing smile was severe anxiety, panic, depression, and bipolar disorder. She fought her entire life to overcome these demons that dragged her down. Like many, she turned to drugs and alcohol. In 2017, she hit rock bottom, overdosed, and went for addiction rehab. Her strength was that of a warrior. She relapsed, but was able to get her life and work back, and become a survivor. The last months of her life were very happy. She was living her dream of living by the beach and water. The mental health issues and addiction proved to be too much, even for the warrior she was. She drowned 50 feet from her apartment while in drug toxicity. While we are all broken, what keeps us going is knowing her suffering and struggle are over.

- He was an old soul from birth, who never failed to share his beautiful smile and unconditional love with all those he came in contact with. He fought a long, hard battle for many years with the demons in his own head and the demon of addiction outside.

- Those who cared about her witnessed her wounded heart and mind become ravaged by unspoken, undiagnosed psychological issues which lead to alcoholism and drug addiction beginning as a preteen. In her silent screams for help, the only relief she could find was escaping her inner demons, but those demons couldn't be suppressed. So while her loving heart remained, it was buried and she was lost in a world of destruction, obsessive-compulsive behavior, bouts of violence, and chaos. People were forced away from her as it became clear she couldn't be helped. Her complicated life ended before she could find the healing and clarity she sought, but she lives on in the hearts and minds of the people she touched, and now she is free to rest in peace and love.

- After several attempts at rehab, he found his way to sobriety ten years ago. He was a hero having overcome life-threatening challenges and having built a path of strength and purpose in sobriety. He was a role model for recovery and inspiration for accomplishing life's goals. After struggling with lifelong depression, he was human, all too human.

"Everyone knew Joe. Unfortunately, Joe, as some of us do, had demons that he just couldn't shake. As lighthearted as he was, those who knew him were troubled by his struggles until they finally took him from us. We don't like to lose our loved ones, but we can rest in that our dear brother and friend is finally at peace."

—*Joe's obituary*

After witnessing the toll that mental health challenges had on their loved one, these families are thankful at last for peace.

- Our son struggled with mental illness and drug addiction. Our hope is that the noise in his mind is hushed and the anguish in his heart is at peace.
- Known by his street name "Teardrop," he left behind the pain and evil in this world and entered into paradise. He had fought a lifelong battle with addiction and mental illness and spent many years in and out of treatment and on the streets where he had built a large street family who loved and cared deeply for him. He was found unresponsive along the harbor shore, taking his last breaths in the very place he sought out peace for so long. Teardrop will be greatly missed and can now be at peace.
- Our mother died at 49 after a long battle with addiction and mental health. Now she is finally able to run wild and free with the horses.
- Our 38-year-old son died in his home. We simply ask that you remember that individuals in torment are someone's family and a child of God. Offer a gentle smile, a warm hello, or a loving act of kindness to our walking wounded. The demons of addiction and mental health are powerful and last night those forces defeated a once kind and gentle soul.
- Our 18-year-old son struggled throughout his life with depression, anxiety, PTSD, and survivor's guilt related to his tumultuous childhood in Russia. He had worked for years to overcome mental illness. It is right to acknowledge and honor the progress he had made while recognizing the toll that struggle took on his life.

> "His life changed ours for the better. He brought fierce love, laughter, brilliance, and passion to the world. His death saddened us beyond measure, but has also reminded us that life is short, and we need to love each other every day—like we don't have any more tomorrows."
>
> — *Nathan's obituary*

Surviving family members seek solace in their loss and in their loved one's life of pain. They also seek to comfort others.

- Yet even through all the struggles, he maintained his unending love for his fellow man and worked at helping others to battle their addictions.
- Our son was diagnosed with Undifferentiated Schizophrenia. God had a plan for him and my son carried it out with vigor.
- Despite battling unimaginable demons, he never complained or failed to bring a smile to those around him.
- Our son's legacy is one of hope and courage. For most of his adult life he suffered from the devastating effects of mental illness, and in that suffering became the inspiration for a sanctuary for those like him who need a place they can call home. Countless members of the community have had much of their lives stolen from them by a disease that knows no boundaries.
- On our daughter's behalf, we encourage you to talk about anxiety, depression, and addiction with an open mind and a loving heart. While this might be difficult to understand, her struggles aren't for us to understand or judge. She knew grace and now she knows peace. We will hold on to that with our whole hearts as the sun brings light to each new day.

I applaud the honesty of these families. Sharing private pain can bridge the distance between us. In the end, following the struggle and anguish, there remains hope and enduring love: "Beyond darkness and pain there is light and joy. If you are struggling there is help for you. There is always an ear to listen, a shoulder to lean on, and a hand to hold. Celebrate small victories. To our daughter, it wasn't easy and you weren't perfect, but, damn, did you give it hell."

Died by Suicide

"He had a perfect heart, a perfect soul, a riotously outrageous
and relentless sense of humor, and a dazzling, radiant mind. He
began to be tortured by a blindingly painful and merciless disease
called depression. On the last hellish brutal day of that god-awful
miserable year of 2020, we lost our dear, dear, beloved son. He left
us a farewell note: 'Please forgive me. My illness won today.'"

— *Tommy's obituary*

Suicide is the tenth leading cause of death, with 132 Americans succumbing each day. How do grieving, shocked families deal with such heartbreak? Sometimes they use euphemisms to hide the hard truth. When terms are used—including died suddenly, died at home, passed away unexpectedly, struggled with depression, or could not find peace—without further explanation, one suspects something tragic may have occurred.

- She ended her battle with pain, suffering, loss, and addiction.
- Our son passed away suddenly at only 22 years old. Addiction and mental illness are real and there is no shame in asking for help.
- He passed away suddenly after a long and very courageous battle with PTSD, anxiety, and addiction. His family remains committed to breaking down the stigma related to behavioral health and suicide.
- He wrapped up the cancer story on his own terms at home.
- He struggled with mental illness and addiction until he could no longer struggle.
- After struggling with bouts of illness for many years, he eventually said goodbye to this world. His loving family will honor his strength in confronting adversity.

> **"He left us way too young, leaving us with far too many questions and no apparent answers. He was loved and will be greatly missed. Contributions may be made to support Suicide Awareness."**
>
> — *Colin's obituary*

Obituaries may not mention the specific cause of death, but the family implies the circumstances by their choice of memorials.

- Our beloved son died unexpectedly. He leaves a complex legacy. His friends and family knew him to be an incredibly unique and gifted individual, making his passing all the more difficult, and the depth of sorrow all the more profound. Memorials for those interested may be made to American Foundation for Suicide Prevention.
- Our son died at home. If you have lost a loved one to suicide, you are not alone. There is support through Heartbeat.
- A loving father and professor passed away unexpectedly at 32 years old. Donations can be made to the National Suicide Prevention Lifeline in his memory.

A man and his beloved wife passed away together at their home. His obituary suggested memorial gifts to support addiction, which led one to assume that was his issue. I researched his wife's death, and it hints at suicide: "She held this world, her children, and her life with hands that have cared for the skin and hearts and bodies of so many people. When holding it became too heavy, she quietly let go."

While obituaries do not always mention the taboo word, lately some are addressing suicide with openness: "Helen died by suicide." (*The preferred language of mental health organizations is "died by suicide," rather than committed suicide.*)

Words of condolence were left on one young man's online obituary. Although the writer was a stranger to this family, she connected with their pain: "My only child also made a decision. He was in unbearable emotional pain. He died by suicide. I wish I had the courage then to be as brutally frank about his death in his obituary. You have shown strength that I just didn't have."

"**Our daughter fought bipolar disorder since 2005, but she finally lost the battle to suicide. She sat in her car in a remote spot in her apartment parking lot and shot herself. She left a brief note: 'This life is not for me.'**"

— *Katie's obituary*

Most suicides are connected to some form of mental illness, often accompanied by drug or alcohol addiction.

- You're probably looking at this picture and thinking, "Too young!" He was only 28 when he left us following years of struggling with anxiety, addiction, depression, and sleep issues, all a slippery slope.
- Time after time, this courageous warrior pulled himself up from the ravages of the war within to battle his destructive demons of alcohol and drug addiction and depression. Unfortunately, this time the pain was too great, too difficult to face again, and on Friday night in New Orleans he ended his life.
- Our son succumbed to his addiction and depression and left his life here with us. Although he battled rough storms during his adult life, he brought great joy to his family.
- Our daughter lost her life after a long struggle with bipolar illness. We were proud of her many talents and accomplishments. She did not allow her illness to define her or prevent her pursuing the next opportunity, until her struggle became too painful.
- My beautiful son took his own life in his fraternity room. He was 21 years old. He worked hard on understanding what he was doing wrong, how he could be a better person, and a better friend, and I think he was really beginning to get it. Drinking sabotaged all that: seductive, deadly alcohol. The drug that brings down the walls and helps us feel close—as long as we're drunk. The drug that circles back and rakes out your heart. He said he would never do such a thing. But he did, because of alcohol. That drunken impulse in a moment of despair can never be taken back.
- His body, a canvas of tattoos, gives insight into how conflicted he must have felt in different times of his life. His life was a series of hard knocks, disappointments, and fears. His decision killed this dear and troubled man.

> **"How did his life end so tragically? By all appearances he was a man who had it all."**
>
> — *Matt's obituary*

Suicide can stalk anyone.

- She ended her life following a long struggle with alcohol/prescription drug addiction and related depression. She had been a National Merit Scholar.
- My hilarious, kind, generous, helpful, silly, and loving sister died of depression and suicide.
- Our beautiful daughter was a student, an accomplished competitive horseback rider, and enjoyed hiking and yoga. She had an uncanny ability to reach out to people to help in a positive way. She passed away unexpectedly.

The tragic death of a veteran police officer reminded his mourning community: "We are all human beings with various needs, frailties, and response strategies. We must follow his work ethic and life's calling to step in and help others in times of need. We are deeply concerned about the wellbeing of our officers, and want our loss to help save others."

> **"After a long and courageous battle with depression and addiction, the pain became unbearable and he took his own life."**
>
> — *Keith's obituary*

Family members stress that the suicide was a choice.

- He died at 19 of a self-inflicted injury.
- He died after deliberately shooting himself during a trip to the desert with friends. If someone you know exhibits warning signs of suicide, he or she should not be left alone.
- Looking ahead to continued physical decline, he chose to gently pass over to the Rainbow Bridge and we honor his choice and we honor his life.

- Our son chose to end his journey on earth. Over the past ten years he struggled with mental illness, depression, and addiction.
- On December 6 I lost my person. He chose this day, and everything he did was purposeful. Violence broke his soul and he was desperate to rejoin with the part he lost.

Despite their heartbreak, survivors offer forgiveness: "As your wife, I want you to know I forgive you for what you have done. Rest in peace, my sweet."

> **"Taken in the prime of his life by his own hand is a statement he did things his own way without permission. He left a deep chasm of his own pain to those he loved and left behind."**
>
> — *Blake's obituary*

Some writers of obituaries share their brokenness and anger.

- Our son ended his life because he couldn't withstand the pain of addiction any longer. He lost everything in order to support his addiction. Heroin made him give up life as a father, son, and brother and made him believe that it could make him feel normal. Heroin was more powerful than words a mother could say to her dying son; more powerful than a five-year-old boy could say to his dying dad.
- Outwardly our beautiful son had piercing blue eye, an infectious smile, and a heart of gold, but internally he suffered many years with deep battles of depression which eventually took his life. He is now free from his pain and suffering; however, he has passed on his hurt to his loved ones. Life will never be the same again.

"Some things are just too powerful to overcome. Sometimes we just don't have the effective communication skills to explain the struggles of mental health and suicidal ideation to the ones we love the most before it is too late."

— *Richie's obituary*

Families share tragic stories to reveal the lack of resources available to the vulnerable.

- He was a wild, free spirit who marched to the beat of a very different drum. The family would like to recognize the seriousness of addiction, mental health, and suicide and encourage open discussion around these issues. Those struggling like him are too often faced with far too many challenges and far too few resources to overcome them.
- Severe psychological stress led to our son's suicide. He turned to self medication as have so many of our children who are disabled, have brain disorders, develop addictions, or endure psychological suffering. Society's respect for life does not often extend to our loved ones who experience these conditions.

Understandably with tragic deaths, loved ones seek a glimmer of light and look for the good that came from a senseless loss. Their hope is that the deceased has found peace.

- Before ending his life, he recorded a message for loved ones. He told us he loved us. He was proud of us, and he was so, so sorry but he was in too much pain. In his last words, he lamented the current divisiveness and negativity and said the news actually hurt him physically. He really wanted us to be kind, to be positive, and to be good to one another.
- She was 55 years old. The cause of death was suicide, following a lifelong struggle with mental illness. During her last years, as she struggled increasingly with her own lifelong mental illness, she became a vocal advocate for those suffering from mental illness and suicidality.
- He loved fiercely. He also struggled immensely. What he did not like was dealing with his mental health, addiction, and medical issues. He hated fake people and social injustices. He was a

fighter and he was tired of all his ups and downs. He was worn out mentally, emotionally, and physically. His struggle has ended and he is now at peace.

- He was an organ, eye, and tissue donor. His family would like to acknowledge that he gave the most precious gift anyone could give; the gift to save the lives of others.

An obituary can offer comfort to other grieving families and support to anyone contemplating this act.

- After a long battle with depression and addiction, my sister took her own life at 22 years old. If you know someone who is struggling with depression please reach out, let them know they are loved, and you're here for them even if it's just to listen.
- As we mourn the loss of all the potential our son had, we want others that may be dealing with similar circumstances to know they are not alone.
- Our 24-year-old son died by taking his own life after a long battle with depression and addiction. His final wishes were for other young people to avoid drug use and to understand the devastating and detrimental effects it has on so many lives. The family asks that friends spread kindness to one another and educate loved ones on the dangers of drug use.

This obituary absolves all who knew their son of any guilt: "Never look back with regret, wondering what you missed or could have done because of the choice he made. No one could have seen this. We all miss him terribly."

I read with admiration a lengthy obituary for a larger-than-life man who knew much success during his 75 years. Only at the end did you learn: "He lost his battle with well-concealed depression by taking his own life. The family shares this in hopes it stirs others to share their mental health challenges and seek help. It is a crisis in our times, and one that needs to be brought out of the shadows. He gave love and received love in abundance; this will be his greatest legacy."

> **"Sam left us in the springtime of his life. We who laughed with him and loved him dearly will forever wonder how glorious his summer, fall, and winter would have been. But for now, let's appreciate the daffodils bursting forth in unexpected spots, as they will every spring, tall and lean and bright-eyed."**
>
> — *Sam's obituary*

This family wrote such a beautiful and hopeful tribute to a son. Remember that things are rarely what they seem. Afford people the gifts of grace and kindness. Many souls are struggling.

Death During a Pandemic

"What doctors described as a mild case of COVID turned deadly in a 24-hour period as the coronavirus attacked her lungs. She was 75."

— *Betsy's obituary*

I don't recall the particular day I realized that the world was quickly and drastically changing. In early 2020, there were hints that something was going on in China. By March, life in the United States was different. Before long, people began to understand that their lives would not be "normal" again. The novel coronavirus, referred to as COVID-19, cast gloom over all of us. It caused distress, anxiety, and fear as it altered daily life. COVID reminded us that death is all around us.

"Please follow COVID guidelines. Wear a mask and social distance with no handshakes or hugs."

—*Erin's obituary*

COVID changed protocols regarding sickness and death. Because of its contagiousness, those infected usually died alone, deepening the suffering and guilt of survivors. Adding more sorrow, people were not allowed to grieve communally. Bereft families and friends were not able to be comforted with hugs. Safer but more distant and impersonal ways to mourn the dead became the norm.

Obituaries reflected this reality.

- The family gathered by conference call with the priest to say prayers by his bedside.
- The family wishes to reinforce to everyone that the pandemic is real and asks everyone to please wear a mask.
- The family has asked that in lieu of memorials, everyone spend time enjoying and protecting their families.

Families conducted services via live stream options, if at all. In-person memorials specified social distancing guidelines.

- The family will host a one-day Zoom Shiva/Memorial.
- Due to current restrictions concerning COVID, a private graveside burial will be held. Only 10 family members will be allowed at the gravesite. All others are welcome to attend by staying in their vehicles near the gravesite or standing a minimum of 30 feet away from the gravesite.
- The family will hold an outdoor visitation and masks and social distancing are required. Please bring a pen if you want to sign the guestbook. We completely understand those who do not feel comfortable attending considering the COVID pandemic we are facing.
- The family will receive friends prior to the service by the following method: 11-11:30 a.m. last names A-G; 11:30-12 p.m. last names H-N; 12-12:30 p.m. last names O-Z. *(Oh my goodness!)*

This obituary was quite specific: "Consistent with the actions taken by many churches, congregations, and places of worship across the state, attendees must wear cloth face coverings (over the nose and mouth). When seating please skip a row, members in the same family may sit together, and then every separate family should sit six feet apart."

"In her honor, and when it's safe, hug your loved ones."

— Carolyn's obituary

Some families decided to postpone services.

- Family and friends will celebrate his life at a later date this summer, which is how he would have wanted it—with sunshine, music, dancing and laughter.
- While we would like to gather for a fitting celebration of his life, he would not like the idea of masks hiding smiles or hugs stifled by social distancing. When we can celebrate the way he would have wanted, there will be a grand celebration in his honor.
- When it is possible to congregate freely, his wife hopes to plan a get-together to honor him at the new iteration of the restaurant where they had their first date. COVID has robbed us of the opportunity to celebrate his life in the fashion we desire.
- A celebration of her life and the legacy assumed by her sons and grandchildren will occur after light and decency enter the White House and COVID is vanquished—just as she would have wanted.
- A memorial celebration will be held at a later date for family, friends, and the community with storytelling, a bit of poker, lots of loving agitation, and big fun.

"Age 97 and 101, they had recently celebrated their 77th wedding anniversary and died from COVID within five days of each other."

— David and Hilda's obituary

Obituaries increasingly cited the cause of death as COVID.

- She died at 81 of coronavirus on the last day of her 58th year of marriage to her adoring and heartbroken husband.
- He died fighting for his life in a New York City emergency room when COVID-19 overpowered him. He was in perfect health a week before.
- Our beautiful and precious son died at 33 of complications of COVID. A newlywed, he leaves his heartbroken wife.

A professor of neuroscience and physiology died as a victim of COVID at 90 years old. Ironically, he advanced the knowledge of the olfactory system (sense of smell). He would have been fascinated to know, had he not been too sick to hear about it, that loss of the sense of smell was identified as an early symptom of COVID.

A particularly sad obituary caught my attention. A 90-year-old woman died from COVID. Her obituary said prior to testing positive, she had been cared for by her daughter. The obituary next to hers in the newspaper was for her daughter, age 63. She also died from COVID: "She spent six weeks in the hospital, including three weeks in the ICU on a ventilator and ECMO machine, then on dialysis before a stroke stopped her tremendous, strong will to fight and live."

Obituaries can make social statements. This daughter's obituary for her father drew national attention. It listed two causes of death—COVID and the ineptitude of government officials: "My father, like so many others, should not have died. His death is due to the carelessness of the politicians who continue to jeopardize the health of brown bodies through a clear lack of leadership, refusal to acknowledge the severity of this crisis, and inability and unwillingness to give clear and decisive direction on how to minimize risk."

This woman's grief was mixed with anger at how the country failed her family: "He leaves behind his inconsolable wife and five children. His family members believe his death was needless, they blame his death, and the deaths of all the other innocent people, on Trump and all the other politicians who did not take this pandemic seriously and were more concerned with their popularity and votes than lives. Also to blame are the many ignorant, self-centered, and selfish individuals who refused to follow the advice of the medical professionals believing their 'right' not to wear a mask was more important than killing innocent people. Shame on all of you, and may Karma find you all!"

For whatever reason, some families want to make clear that COVID was not the cause of death.

- He died at 89, unexpectedly yet peacefully, at his home of heart failure unrelated to COVID.

- The medical examiner's report has not been released, but he did not die from COVID.

Even if a person's death was not directly attributed to COVID, the virus was at least partially blamed.

- Even at 94 he did not retire. Only COVID kept him from working every day.
- Her 11 months spent in isolation due to COVID was difficult.
- He never got COVID, but the circumstances of it surely hastened his end.

Obituaries tempered with humor were found even during these dire times.

- His positive attitude was a gift to the world, especially during COVID-19. He missed his friends, family, and a good hamburger and a scoop of ice cream from the Burger Bar.
- He enjoyed explaining Newton's Third Law or Einstein's Theory of Relativity to his grandchildren being homeschooled via Zoom because of the COVID shutdown.
- During the pandemic, she was able to stay in touch with her family through frequent Face Time and "Grand-Pad" calls.

> **"The passions of his life dwindled during the pandemic; unable to socialize, travel, or visit family made life very difficult in his already dire condition. He died from his alcohol addiction at only 32 years old."**
>
> — *Eric's obituary*

COVID caused spikes in alcohol abuse and drug overdoses. Increases in overdose deaths were reported in 42 states during the pandemic. Addiction is a disease of isolation. Social distancing cut off much-needed human connections. Stress and anxiety were compounded by unemployment and financial devastation.

- Our son was blessed with high intelligence and talent but was troubled with darkness. Sadly we share with you his struggle with depression and an alcohol addiction. Despite treatment and the support of his family, he just could not take this world any longer. The forced isolation and loneliness during the pandemic was more than he could bear.

- Last year our son finally acknowledged his drug addiction and was in a recovery program. He was excelling in the program until the COVID pandemic, and he had to come home. Once at home, he finally succumbed to the pressures of his addiction.
- He died while at home on winter break from college. He was 22 years old. The cause of death was suicide and the family believes that he struggled with the isolation of the COVID pandemic.
- Our son passed away after losing a long and painful battle with addiction. For those fighting COVID isolation or depression, you are not alone.

The goodness of people shines through.

- In the last weeks of his life during the COVID pandemic, he organized donations of personal protective equipment for frontline hospital workers.
- She made more than 1,000 face coverings to help out during the COVID pandemic. These masks were sent to a variety of groups. She made masks with clear coverings for deaf people and their families as well as masks that were sent to the Navajo Nation.

The alarming death toll from COVID reached 100,000 within the first three months. To mark this loss, the front page of *The New York Times* on Sunday, May 24, 2020, had no articles, graphics, or photographs. It became the first *NYT* front page in modern times with no images. Reporters had scoured COVID obituaries from around the country and found phrases that captured the uniqueness of each person. The front page listed names, ages, and places of death, and something special about each person who died.

- She died on the same day as her husband.
- He shared his produce with food pantries and his neighbors.
- He had a million-dollar smile.
- He enjoyed long drives, late nights, and huge meals.

On Sunday, February 21, 2021, half of the front page of *The New York Times* was a large graphic containing 500,000 dots. Each pixel represented a life lost to COVID in the country in less than one year.

This sad obituary, published in December 2020, offered powerful testimony about the devastation caused by COVID: "He passed away in isolation at a nursing home. Infected with COVID, he died in a room not his own, being cared for by people dressed in confusing and frightening ways. He died with COVID, and his final days were harder and scarier and lonelier than necessary. He was not surrounded by friends and family. He died in a world where many of his fellow Americans refuse to wear a piece of cloth on their face to protect one another. He was a farmer and a veterinarian and filled his life with an understanding of the science of life. The science that guided his professional life has been disparaged and abandoned by so many of the same people who depended on his knowledge to care for their animals and to raise food. He was a family man and a man of the community."

The deaths and dark days of 2020 will not be forgotten.

Writing an Obituary

Death is not an uncommon occurrence. Worldwide, 55 million of us die each year. At some point, each of us will be faced with having to memorialize a loved one. We want this final love letter to be as special as the person we are remembering.

For various reasons, often financial, families choose a death notice. These announcements are printed in a newspaper based on public records or information provided by funeral homes. They contain just the facts—name of the deceased, date of death, where the deceased lived, and the name of the funeral home. Newspapers have different procedures for death notices so it is best to check with your local publication. Death notices are less expensive than a full obituary.

> **"He read the Sunday *Times* obituaries every week, 'to see if his was in there yet.' He called me often to discuss its hypothetical contents. 'Make sure it's funny and original, the rest of these are depressing.' So here it is, Dad. I hope it lives up to your expectations."**
>
> *— Kevin's obituary*

What is an obituary? It is a written narrative that summarizes the time between two mortal life events—birth and death. Death is the reason you have an obituary, but it should only tangentially be about death. It is the life that matters. One purpose of the obituary is to celebrate that life.

Most obituaries are prepared and written by the family or the funeral home and may be accompanied by a photograph. They cover the same basic information as a death notice, but also include highlights and moments of the deceased's life story. Obituaries must be paid for, and this service can be expensive. Therefore, some families opt for two versions of an obituary: An abbreviated obit in the newspaper and a more detailed version on the funeral home's website or other memorial sites. Fewer obituaries are now published. I've come to believe that the obituary is a "dying art."

Obituaries, usually of public figures, can be deemed newsworthy and are reported in an objective manner using information provided by the family and other sources. These obituaries don't include funeral information or much about survivors or other elements of a standard obituary. The best known professional obituary writers work for *The New York Times* and *The Washington Post*. The writers compose these life stories, usually in advance, and they make for interesting reading about influential people.

> **"Though this details what he did through some of his life, it does not capture who he was."**
>
> — *Dave's obituary*

The primary purpose of an obituary is to announce the loss of a loved one. But it can be so much more than that. Obituaries should not be limited to just information—degrees, jobs, and affiliations. While biographical facts have their rightful place in describing a person's life, those details are not what made a life. They fall short of capturing the spirit, character, and legacy of the deceased. Significant events and attributes of the deceased and their impact on family, friends, and the wider world should be noted. An obituary is a well thought out tribute that is truthful, informative, and heartfelt. It acknowledges death, expresses loss, and celebrates a person and their life story.

After reading thousands of obituaries, I have developed some personal preferences. Following are some ideas of what to do and what not to do. But this is a deeply personal decision, so do whatever moves you if it is what best honors your loved one.

> **"She lived a life genuine and real. She sat on no boards, for she was a bored sitter. Ever armed with a list, she worked her way through what needed doing, collecting as a reward the satisfaction of an accomplishment and maybe a Blue Bunny ice cream sandwich or two."**
>
> *— Margaret's obituary*

Do mention significant contributions and recognitions. But if there are many, choose carefully and encompass as many as you can in as few words as possible. This strategy works well for someone who was involved in numerous service and social organizations or who had many places of employment or residence.

Do be judicious with superlatives. One obituary I read had legendary, brilliant career, impeccable ethics, stunning good looks, Commodore of the yacht club, consummate husband, comprehensive knowledge, mentor to everyone, and brilliance shone on all, among other accolades. You can adequately express love, admiration, and the extent of a person's accomplishments in a concise and modest manner.

> **"If you asked a hundred people who he was, they may all tell you a different story. Beloved husband, decorated Vietnam vet, devoted father, practical joker, adored grandfather, squirrel whisperer, Christmas light addict, lover of popsicles and popcorn, guardian of the galaxy, and needed by all who loved him unendingly."**
>
> *— Wayne's obituary*

Do provide meaningful examples that reflect the singularity of the deceased. Enliven the obituary by sharing a quirky habit, a favorite hobby, and other details of their life. The more specific the examples are the better. This unusual obituary was written by an observant and eloquent person: "He was born in their yellow frame home in 1929. Aunts attended, downstairs the men smoked. There were three brothers, drillers, business partners, descendants of colonials with rumored Seneca blood. Among his earliest memories is men's wash day in Buffalo Creek; naked, being passed down the slippery bank with squirming boy cousins for a raw home-cut lye soap scrub from his powerful grandfather. His home town was a small place, in old days hosting large family reunions; Civil War veterans, racing children, tables of farm food and canned relishes. It was there, on a draft horse yanking the family car along a red clay road, that Charley heard the news of Pearl Harbor. If he was a bit vain; well, Lord, you made him handsome. And if he was proud, it was an often expressed pride in us. The boy baptized in Buffalo Creek became our Patriarch, became his community's inspired and generous soul. We are proud and we delight in the legacy of your spirit."

> **"Her sensitivity and individuality were not always understood and accepted. For her, we must continue to educate ourselves to reduce the stigma around mental illness."**
>
> — *Ali's obituary*

Do address difficult personality traits or life issues with honesty. People are not perfect. Difficult truths can be respectfully included: "He lived in the moment most of his life and had a charismatic way of getting what he wanted. He was an angel and a terror all in one. His biggest demon was himself. Rest easy, you can now fly with the angels."

Do list survivors and those who predeceased the person, most commonly in order of importance, to the degree you wish. Some people go all the way down the family tree, to the very roots. Others limit these names. Most funeral homes and online sources provide detailed suggestions for these and other issues.

Do provide details about any memorial services. Know that there is no one right way to plan a service, Mass, or celebration of life, or even if you should have one. This is a personal family decision. Include suggestions from the family whether flowers or memorial contributions are appropriate. For contributions, make it easy for the donors by providing the complete name of the organization and address or website contact information.

"His father was a friend of Ernest Hemingway, his mother was the granddaughter of the founder of Woolworth stores, his paternal grandfather was a first cousin to Winston Churchill, his grandmother underwrote Amelia Earhart's transAtlantic flight, and his great-grandfather was a partner of industrialist Andrew Carnegie."

— Frederick's obituary

Do focus on the deceased. This seem obvious, but in the middle section of a 29-year-old woman's obituary, between where she attended school and her survivors, there were 20 lines listing her ancestors going back to 1637. It even stated that one ancestor founded the largest steam engine company in the world. The deceased was her parents' only child. The overarching theme of any obituary should be the personality of the deceased. The focus should have been on her story.

Do give yourself permission to use humor. It can be an appropriate part of a loving tribute: "If you're about to throw away an old pair of pantyhose, stop. We were blessed to learn many valuable lessons from our mother during her 85 years, among them: Never throw away old pantyhose. Use the old ones to tie gutters, child-proof cabinets, tie toilet flappers, or hang Christmas ornaments. Go to church with a chicken sandwich in your purse. Give the chicken sandwich to your homeless friend after Mass. Go to a nursing home and kiss everyone. Keep the car keys under the front seat so they don't get lost. Make the car dance by lightly tapping the brakes to the beat of songs on the radio. Believe the hitchhiker you pick up who says he is a landscaper and his name is 'Peat Moss.' She is survived by her children and grandchildren whose photos she would share with prospective friends in the checkout line." This is a stunning tribute to a clearly wonderful person written by family members who knew her deeply and remembered her with fond humor.

Do avoid the bland and formulaic approach to an obituary. Instead, replace facts with feelings and generalizations with detailed examples. Which excerpt reveals more of the deceased person? "He held advanced degrees from Princeton University and served on numerous committees in the title insurance industry." Or, "He adored his wife. Every morning they walked to work, hand in hand, for over 40 years. Every evening they had cocktails together until she died on his birthday."

> **"He used to tell people, 'My wife collects houses. I collect cars.'"**
>
> — *Michael's obituary*

Don't mention the number of homes, the long list of country club memberships, the 24 cruises they took, or their 38-foot-long sloop. Some words you might want to avoid include: lavish, pinnacle, first class experiences, storied career, titanic, unsurpassed, and iconic. Death is the ultimate equalizer. Obituaries are not the place to brag.

- She lived in the house that was built for her grandfather, heir to a family fortune. They summered at another family residence, where she enjoyed sailing lessons. She made her debut in Boston, and then worked in New York City until she met her future husband, who also has two residences. After their marriage ceremony, they took a wedding trip to Morocco, and then lived in a lovely apartment overlooking the East River. In their leisure time they traveled and sailed and retired to the homeport of their cruising sailboat, which they owned for 28 years.
- He was a regular presence at his country club where he enjoyed a celebrity of his own making among the club's glitterati. His sartorial splendor made him special in any setting. *(Significantly edited for brevity)*

Don't use the verb "expired" instead of died. It sounds as though a person has passed their "best by" date from the supermarket. How you describe death is up to you. "Died" can't be beat.

Don't delve into the minutia of their profession. No one cares as much as the deceased did. One man's career listed every position he held, with nearly job-description detail. The obituary was 16 column inches in *The New York Times*. I shudder to think what it must have cost and wonder how many people read those tedious details. At the end of the full-column obit was a mention of his wife and children. (*Ouch.*)

Don't list grade point averages (3.9 GPA with honors) after the names of the colleges attended. Heaven doesn't have a Dean's List.

Don't say "Never met a stranger." It is overused and doesn't say much. Look deeper and use a specific example of what you are trying to convey.

Don't make this spelling mistake: "Interment" is placing remains in a place of rest, while "Internment" is confining a person to a place against their will, such as jail.

Most likely you will have to write an obituary at some point. This can seem like a daunting task. I hope this book serves as a resource for how hundreds of people have paid tribute to their loved ones. Learn how others shared memories, expressed love, and vividly described the personality and life story of the deceased. Some obituaries were a sheer pleasure to read. The poetry and eloquence of this tribute was a loving goodbye to a mother: "There's a precise moment in the early mornings when the temperature reaches its coldest point and a ribbon of pastel pink clouds kiss the tops of the evergreens. It is at that specific time when the cold Elysburg mornings coaxed our blue-eyed Polish Mom to rise and head to work. She was the first one up every morning having her coffee, toast and jelly and the last one home. At the age of 92, she passed away of old age; her tires were well-worn and she was ready to see her maker. She lived a long, simple, quiet and comfortable life in her little white house, breathing her final breath in her sleep. May this obituary ignite fond memories of her; she is smiling down upon us, hoping that we respect each other, take a moment to say hello, and mind our manners."

> **"She was not famous or important in the usual sense of the word, but will be greatly missed by her family and those who knew her."**
>
> —*Carol's obituary*

The obituary is one of the oldest forms of a biography. It offers loved ones a heartwarming and meaningful way to participate in the celebration of a life. The most effective obituaries capture the singular magic of the loved one who has died and declare that this person's life story has been told and will be remembered.

Writing Your Own Obituary

Not many people attempt to write their own obituary. One man who wrote his commented to a friend: "I think everyone should write their own. It makes you think about what's important." There is benefit in thinking about the life you are leading and the legacy you will leave behind.

"'I was born, I lived, I died.' That is how Grandma wanted her obituary to be written, no more, no less. Her rationale was simple: 'I've paid for a newspaper my whole life, why spend more money on it when I'm gone?'" Despite Grandma's wishes, the family added their memories and observations to the suggested obit.

This woman made the difficult decision to discontinue cancer treatment and to head back to her beloved farm. She wrote this shortly before her death: "We came back to the farm to celebrate our final time together. The stories and laughter and ice cream socials we had along with movie night, the flowers, butterflies, birds, bees, cats, friends, and gigantic delicious meals made it just delicious for me. Who cares about manners! For me the sense of wholeness that comes from friends and family just resting in each other's company without any sense of either strife or disagreement is simply divine." In the end, she moved on to her next journey with amazing grace, teaching one final life lesson: "Despite life's inevitable struggles with pain and confusion, it can also give way to peace, companionship, healing, and love."

Here are examples of self-written obituaries. All have been edited for brevity, unless otherwise specified.

- Dear friend and beloved family, my heartfelt prayer is that your grief is short-lived and your memories of our good times together are everlasting. Thank you for making my life wonderful. I chose to write my own notice of passing; my loved ones would overstate the good and ignore the not-so-good. I, on the other hand, have always been a stickler for truth and facts. It is true I attended local schools; however I completely wasted my high school years and was lucky to even receive a diploma. Not only were my grades deplorably low, but so was my character during those four years. I have few regrets, but my high school period has always been an embarrassment to me. Career accomplishments aside, the most meaningful and most rewarding position of my life was being Poppie to my three wonderful grandchildren. Few people realize it, but I was an alcoholic for most of my adult life. I defeated that addiction in 2006 and lived the rest of my life alcohol free. I am very blessed to be able to enjoy and experience all that "stuff." But deep down inside my core I am a very simple being and don't need stuff to be happy and feel fulfilled. My favorite meal of all is a juicy hamburger and fries. I am perfectly content to wear the same old shirts and shorts year after year. Not surprisingly, the folks I enjoy golfing with the most don't even notice, or if they do, they certainly don't care. I was blessed and privileged to be born into this life, and look back upon my time on earth with much joy and few regrets. I have had a wonderful life. Note to kids, when you think of me, do not do so with grief. As long as there are memories, I am alive!

- I finally made it to the obituaries, my favorite part of the day. Every morning, before putting my teeth in, I'd flip open the paper and go straight to the obits—undoubtedly my most exciting read of the day. I never cared for the run-of-the-mill obits. If I were boring, this is what mine would say: "He came into the world in 1956 and passed away peacefully in 2020. He was a beloved son, husband, father, and professor."

- Surviving me isn't easy. If you had the pleasure of knowing me, you'd know that I was the biggest pain in the ass in the world. I think I've read every book on the planet and watched every episode of *The Walking Dead* religiously. I took great joy in collecting thousands of CDs to rotate the same ten over and over again on full volume so the neighbors could enjoy it, too. For now, you can find me in mismatched pajamas, shuffling down the aisles of a Borders bookstore in the sky.

- It pains me to admit it, but apparently I have passed away. My family and friends have made the fabulous story of my life. Love, Bill

- I'd like to tell you a little about my life here on Earth. I excelled not the least in things athletic or musical, but more than held my own in academics and frivolity. Unlike many teenagers I loved my parents as well as my sister very much. No one was more surprised than me that I made it all the way to college without jail time or drug addiction. I continued my education earning an MBA and a commission in the Army. Upon discharge I married and had three terrific children. Following divorce, I met my forever sweetheart. For over 15 fabulous years we worked together and this was the happiest chapter of my life. Working side by side with my beautiful wife offered many opportunities for vacations, job-related experiences, and ultimately, 30 wonderful years of domestic joy. In addition, I welcomed two beautiful daughters to my family and loved each of them thoroughly. The current tally of grandchildren stands at 23 but one never knows; the final count may go higher. I found something different and special in each grandchild and one of my great joys in life was watching them grow and blossom at each stage of development. I had a blessed life, but it was all my close friends and family accumulated along the way that really put the condiments on the sandwich. I truly loved and enjoyed all my great buddies. My heart-felt thanks to each of my friends and family members for making my life awesome!

- My story has no remarkable achievements or one-of-a-kind successes, no daring adventures or great expeditions, but it has

258 - Life Stories: The Book of Obituaries

found deep roots from my upbringing, in adult life from my marriage and the birth and continuing delight of our daughter. I never sailed the Pacific Ocean, climbed Mt. McKinley, or hiked the full Pacific Crest Trail, but my life, like so many, has been filled with poignant moments, earned achievements, unhappy surprises, bear hugs with loved ones, and all the other circumstances and events that characterize what I think of as an "ordinary" but purposeful life. It was neither the result of a grand plan nor an early certainty, but instead has grown incrementally over the course of many years.

- So, the world doesn't have me to kick around anymore. I'm gone! The devil finally called my name. The grim reaper came for me. I bought the farm. I bit the dust. So I guess I'm off to the Promised Land, eh? The Promised Land! Imagine! So anyway, I think I was a pretty nice guy, despite being a former punk and despite what some people would say about me. What did they know about me anyway? I loved my family and cared for them through good times and bad; I did my best. I had some serious health problems the last few years, but survived them (up till now anyway) with the help of my wife. I don't want a funeral. A funeral is a waste of harrrrrrd earned and harrrrrrd saved money that my family can use now. I was a very private person in life, so I don't want to end that life with people gawking at me while I lay in a coffin. I'm being cremated and my ashes are being scattered (somewhere). So instead of going to see the great creator, I will be going to see the great cremator.

- Some time ago the late comedian Carl Reiner did an HBO special called "If you're not in the obit, eat breakfast." Well, I'm not having breakfast today.

- My regrets are few but include eating a rotisserie hot dog from a convenience store in the summer of 2002, not training my faithful dog to detect cancer, and that no video evidence exists of my prowess on the soccer field or in the bedroom. Although I had a less than average life span, I did not live an average life. I traveled where I wanted to travel, laughed inappropriately at every chance, learned what I wanted to learn, fixed what I wanted to fix, and loved whom I wanted to love. Cremation will take place at the family's convenience, and my ashes will be kept around as long as they match the décor.

- I died of throat cancer. I was a true scientist, auto mechanic, wood worker, artist, inventor, business man, ribald comedian, husband, brother, son, cat lover, and cynic. I had a lot of fun. It was an honor for me to be friends with some truly great people. I thank you. I've had great joy living and playing with my dog, my cats, and my parrot. But the one special thing that made my spirit whole is my long love and friendship with my remarkable wife. I loved her more than I have words to express. Every moment spent with my beloved was time spent wisely. Over time, I became one with her, inseparable, happy, fulfilled. I enjoyed one good life.

Now that I have gone to my reward, I have confessions and things I should now say. As it turns out, I AM the guy who stole the safe back in 1971. I could have left that unsaid, but I wanted to get it off my chest. Also, I really am NOT a Ph.D. What happened was that the day I went to pay off my college student loan, the girl working there put my receipt into the wrong stack, and two weeks later, a Ph.D. diploma came in the mail. I didn't even graduate, I only had about three years of college credit. For all of the electronic engineers I have worked with, I'm sorry, but you have to admit my designs always worked very well, and were well engineered, and I always made you laugh at work. To Disneyland, you can now throw away that "Banned for Life" file you have on me, I'm not a problem anymore—and SeaWorld San Diego, too, if you read this. My regret is that I felt invincible when young and smoked cigarettes when I knew they were bad for me. Now, to make it worse, I have robbed my beloved wife of a decade or more of the two of us growing old together and laughing at all the thousands of simple things that we have come to enjoy and fill our lives with such happy words and moments. My pain is enormous, but it pales in comparison to watching my wife feel my pain as she lovingly cares for and comforts me. I feel such the "thief" now; for stealing so much from her. There is no pill I can take to erase that pain.

If you knew me or not, dear reader, I am happy you got this far into my letter. I speak as a person who had a great life to look back on. My family is following my wishes that I not have a funeral or burial. If you knew me, remember me in your own way. If you want to live forever, then don't stop breathing, like I did.

- One of the few advantages of dying from Grade 3, Stage IIIC endometrial cancer, recurrent and metastasized to the liver and abdomen, is that you have time to write your own obituary. (The other advantages are no longer bothering with sunscreen and no longer worrying about your cholesterol.) To wit: I believe we are each of us connected to every person and everything on this Earth, that we are in fact one divine organism having an infinite spiritual existence. Of course, we may not always comprehend that. And really, that's a discussion for another time. So let's cut to the chase: I was given the gift of life, and now I have to give it back. This is hard. But I was a lucky woman, who led a lucky existence, and for this I am grateful. I first got sick in January 2010. When the cancer recurred last year and was terminal, I decided to be joyful about having had a full life, rather than sad about having to die. Amazingly, this outlook worked for me. (Well, you know, most of the time.) Meditation and the study of Buddhist philosophy also helped me accept what I could not change. At any rate, I am at peace. And on that upbeat note, I take my mortal leave of this rollicking, revolving world—this sun, that moon, that walk around Green Lake, that stroll through the Pike Place Market, the memory of a child's hand in mine. My beloved friends and family, how precious you all have been to me. Knowing and loving each one of you was the success story of my life. Metaphorically speaking, we will meet again, joyfully, on the other side. Beautiful day, happy to have been here.

- My family is publishing this obituary against my better judgment. I did not want a memorial service or an obituary (although I read them faithfully each day to be sure I was not listed). They were convinced that being an interior designer for 61 years would leave behind folks who cared I was gone. They said it was not just about me. That became perfectly clear during the last several days when so many of you stopped by to give me a hug, reminisce, and tell a joke. Thank you for the visits. When my housekeeper recently asked how I was, I told her, "Slightly better than dead but not by much." Kill them with laughter—always. Typically you read about all the deceased accomplished in their lifetime. I'm not doing that either, but I will tell you that from birth to design school in Los Angeles, to a life in Interior Design with all of my wonderful (and some not so wonderful) clients (you know who you are), I have loved life and had a good time. I brought up a great family with my dear former wife that includes two daughters and five incredible grandchildren. The travel was fun (everyone should go to Paris at least once) and the career was rewarding (always got a kick out of telling clients, "You will learn to love it," even when they doubted me). The challenges were tough and to those who struggle with addiction you can reach within yourself to take back control with the help of those who love you. I am thankful for my new healthcare friends and caregivers that have been so helpful the last few months. Their patience, gentleness and compassion changed my life. I am thankful for the employees, colleagues, tradesmen, and clients that made my job so enjoyable. God has our backs, folks, and now He has me. Live and be well and love even "weller." There has been some speculation that the room God has prepared for me will not meet my design criteria; perhaps He will tell me: "You will learn to love it."

- Doug died. *(Not edited for brevity)*

- As you read this short synopsis of my life, I want you all to know that I lived a wonderful life. I wasn't rich monetarily, but I was rich in life. I just celebrated my 20th birthday and of course I surrounded myself with my family. When we're together it's always laughter, mainly me being the cause of it. I longed to create my own family and to do right by them. I was blessed with a fighter! My son was born months before his due date and it was scary. However, with prayers and family support he pulled through and that's who I lived for. He will be nothing less than great because that was his mother's and my plan. I trust that she will fulfill my dreams.

- I died on January 22, 2019. My mother died giving birth to my still-born brother when I was three. I was raised by my great aunt and uncle. They loved me as if I had been their own child, encouraged, and rejoiced in my every endeavor. I married Mary whom I had met and loved from that very first meeting. Her support and guidance were crucial in every task I undertook and every challenge I met. She was my compass, my guide, my conscience, my partner, and my lifelong best friend. Our six children, nine grandchildren, and four great-grandchildren were the source of great joy, pride, shared love and happiness throughout our married lives. I was fortunate to be invited to join the law firm where I found a second family and work that I loved for more than 55 years. I loved life and believed that you should live fully in the moment. I believed that laughter is the leaven of life. I truly cared for people; all people. And I wrote this obituary without a list of major professional accomplishments in order to emphasize that material matters pale into insignificance when compared to the love of family and friends. Please do not send flowers or make contributions in my memory. If you want to do something that would please me, take someone(s) you love out to dinner, tell them you love them, and say the things we unfortunately wish we had said before they died. Use the word "love" frequently, laugh a lot, and enjoy the moment. I did.

- I have laughed, loved, and lived a lengthy spell and now the lamp is out!

- I suppose that most people do not write their own obituary, but while my beautiful and successful daughters were a bit reluctant, I decided that after all that they've done for me, this is something I wanted to do for them. I was born to loving parents, and was welcomed into the world by a midwife. Being the third-born daughter, I was always facing the challenge of living up to my sisters. During my college summers, I worked at Mt. Rushmore to put myself through college. I was able to climb the mountain and stood on President Lincoln's head. It has been a wonderful life, if not quite long enough, but I am most grateful for all that has been. I die happily with my dear family around me. What more could I ask? Grandchildren are the icing on the cake of life and I am privileged to be partaking of this era of my life now.

- It has been a great journey in spite of many physical ailments including tuberculosis, a collapsed lung, a brain tumor, and a heart condition. Thank goodness I was blessed with a great sense of humor. I love chocolate, shopping, staying in motels, little children, Halloween, visiting rest homes, and helping the elderly. My epitaph will read: "I told you I was sick."

- My husband and I raised four daughters and gained three sons-in-law, ten wonderful grandchildren, and two great-grandchildren. I know on occasion the sons-in-law affectionately called me the monster-in-law, but someone had to keep them in line. We spent much of our time enjoying our grandchildren's many sporting events and musical performances. All in all, it's been a great life on this earth. I took a ride in a hot air balloon and went white-water rafting down the Rio Grande with my family. But, in the end, my favorite place to be was at our lake house enjoying our family time and boat rides. I have raised a family, been a psychotherapist, and have lived a rewarding life. However, there is no place like home, so please don't be sad because that is where I am now. God bless and keep you all safe until I see you again.

- Carol has died. Car for sale. *(Not edited for brevity)*

I was struck by the beauty of these obituaries. People facing their imminent death displayed a perspective from which we can learn. Most expressed gratitude for all they had enjoyed. They recognized that in the end, what they valued most was the love of family and friends. Having lived a life that was not perfect did not prevent them from appreciating it in its fullness. Amazingly, many still had a wonderful sense of humor. This may be my favorite obit: "I was born in 1938 (boy, have I said that a lot over the last three months) and died in September 2019, just shy of my 81st birthday, after a short and futile battle with pancreatic cancer. Now wait, there's a story behind this. What a wonderful life I had. Wonderful family, wonderful friends, wonderful adventures. I could go on and on. I met my husband of 58 years on a blind date. It wasn't exactly love at first sight. It took him three dates before he realized what was going on. I wonder if he ever did. I married the man of my dreams and from that day on I was proud to be his wife, Queen of the Castle and Grand Diva of all things domestic. I loved reading and kept a running list of every book I ever read. Shopping, carting the kids around, making Halloween costumes, going out to lunch, and movie nights all were fabulous. Just when I thought I was too old to fall in love again, I became a grandmother. I knitted a flock of hats, socks, and sweaters with love in every stitch. My greatest treasures all call me Grammy. There are simply not enough superlatives in the English language to describe my grandchildren. I am incredibly proud of each and every one—the people they are and the people they are becoming. All my life I have loved to laugh. My mother told me my laugh was not very lady-like but it was my only laugh so I stuck with it. My life has been full of stories and laughter, and for that I am grateful. So I was born; I blinked; and it was over. If you want to, you can look for me in the evening sunset, amongst the darting hummingbirds, or see me in the smiles of my children and grandchildren. You know I'll be there in time for cocktails. I'll leave you with this. Please don't be sad because I'm gone; instead be happy that I was here. I really did have a wonderful life. I was raised by family who loved me and was loved by the family I raised."

That obituary says it all, doesn't it?

How to Say "Died"

"Your last journey is over, Ken."

— *Ken's obituary*

Life and death are not opposites but part of the same continuum. Death is the price we pay for life. While the length of a life journey varies, everyone is headed for the same destination. This truth troubles many people, to the point that the actual word died is avoided in most obituaries despite being the most straightforward way to announce a death.

"She passed away after over 90 years making people smile."

— *Mary's obituary*

Members of the deceased's family writing obituaries often use passed away and other euphemisms, which are usually elaborated upon—courageously, in faith, suddenly, gracefully, quietly, recently, tragically, with dignity, unexpectedly, and begrudgingly. A combination of phrases is often used to personalize the death.

- She passed away relaxed and empowered at home with both her children present.
- She passed away from a broken heart.
- He passed away peacefully after a long and unexpected journey.
- She passed away suddenly but peacefully in the evening at her parents' home.

Rather than died or passed away, some writers use more creative phrasing.

- Crossed the bar.
- Cast off the lines and slipped away for one last sail.
- Finished building his legacy.
- Traded time for eternity.
- Ended his wonderful journey.
- Left the range.
- Left us to decipher unusual car noises all on our own.
- Left us in the early morning, his banjo in hand, for an eternal folk festival.
- Walked into the forest with his family by his side.
- Passed through the veil.
- Signed off for the last time.
- Was gathered to her people.

Deaths often occur in hospitals, senior care homes, or hospice facilities, but the final wish for many is to die at home: "Our mother died in her home in Mexico where she loved the beauty and simplicity of life."

Usually the age at the time of death is specified.

- He passed away at the age of 75 years, 11 months, and 18 days.
- She passed into eternal life at the wonderful age of 103.
- She died peacefully several months after her 100th birthday.

Women's obituaries sometimes do not include the date of birth, allowing them to take their secret into the great beyond.

Specific times of death might be included: "She passed at 4:44, a sign that she was in the company of angels and in harmony with the universe."

Most obituaries mention the general time of day.

- He passed gently in the early evening.
- She passed away at sunset on a beautiful autumn afternoon surrounded by family.
- He died early on a cold morning.

Some obituaries are more poetic in noting the time of death. One obituary used two words: "Suddenly, Sunday."

- He passed just in time to greet his deceased wife and mother for Mother's Day.
- She died peacefully in her sleep once she learned that Biden had won the election.
- He died on an innocent Saturday afternoon from a senseless act of violence.
- He passed away at home in his easy chair watching his morning TV shows.
- He died before sunrise of old age aggravated by the New Hampshire winter.
- He died peacefully on Halloween night under a blue moon.

> **"He died on his skis doing what he loved best; the avalanche that caught him gave him no chance."**
>
> — *Pete's obituary*

Some obituaries keep the reason for the death private. Most do reveal the cause, reflecting the heartbreaking vagaries of life.

- He was killed instantly as he was crossing the street in his wheelchair. He was hit by a driver who was texting.
- The professor and his wife passed away while they were sleeping due to accidental carbon monoxide poisoning.
- He died after battling a long fight with mediocrity.
- He died following an accident while playing pond hockey.
- She died in the blink of an eye after a long battle with substance abuse disorder, which led to addiction.
- He died after a two-year walk on the pancreatic cancer road.
- He passed away at 25 years old, the victim of a homicide.
- He passed away after a tragic snow machine accident.
- He was killed in an accident at a rural railway crossing.

Most obituaries mention how their loved one had been comforted at the end of life.

- He passed away peacefully with his daughter by his side reciting the silly songs he sang to amuse his children when they were young.
- He died peacefully in the loving embrace of his wife and surrounded by the love of family and friends.
- She died surrounded by the love and compassion of her children.
- She died with her family by her side, along with an unexpected snowfall.
- He passed at his home with his nieces holding his hand for his journey on to a pain-free life.

This obituary is particularly poetic: "She died sitting next to her husband in the serene setting of their sun porch at their beloved lake home. And so in the surrounds she adored, near the man she shared a lifetime with, her loving heart, at last, gave its last."

Because pets can offer unmatched solace, they are often included: "Passed away unexpectedly and peacefully with his dog Peanut by his side."

This strikes me as a lonely man's death: "He passed away surrounded by his beloved Art Deco collection." *(His obituary made no mention of people in his life. I wonder who wrote it?)*

"She was held tightly by those that loved her most, cradling her head, hands, and arms; holding her tight as she slipped earth's surly bonds. Painless, peaceful, resolute."

— *Ginger's obituary*

Some obituaries, though sharing news of a death, leave the reader with a sense of peace.

- He died in the shadow of the mountain range he loved so much.
- She passed away while enjoying the spectacular views of ocean, mountains, and birds.
- She died peacefully 11 days shy of her 94th birthday, holding hands with her loving husband of 70 years.
- He passed away doing what he loved; playing the piano.
- He passed away with dignity and a peaceful heart in the early hours of the winter solstice.
- She passed on to her final resting place after experiencing the joy of holding her newborn grandson.
- She departed this life at home surrounded by her two daughters, her books, and the things she loved.

This description is poignant: "He passed peacefully in the comfort of his daughter's home surrounded by family, in a room filled with love, with his hands held tight."

Other obituaries share circumstances which are hard to read.

- Our son passed away suddenly at home with four resolute EMTs working intensively to revive him.
- He passed on early in the morning due to an unexpected and shocking accident.

Attempting to soften the finality of death, obituaries may speak of reunions to come.

- He left his earthly confines to join his wife and family in heaven.
- Our father departed this earthly life to be with his eternal sweetheart.
- She was reunited and greeted into the heavens by her former poodles.

Religious words or phrasings reflect the departed's spiritual beliefs. Angels evidently play a significant role.

- Guardian angels came to lead her into heaven to meet her Lord.
- She stepped into heaven and joined the choir of angels, praising her Lord and Maker.
- He surrendered peacefully into the arms of angels.

Other times, the deceased *becomes* an angel.

- She has left the earth, and heaven has a wonderful new angel.
- She exchanged her skates for wings.
- He received his angel wings after 99 years of living life to the fullest; he took flight to his heavenly home.
- Heaven has a spicy, spunky, new angel.

> **"He heard the voice of God whisper in his ear to come home and take his rest."**
>
> — *Kenneth's obituary*

Wording suggests that life on earth is over, and the future will be in heaven, a pain-free permanent abode.

- He entered heaven's gates without pain, sadness, or his addictions.
- She changed her residence to a mansion in heaven.
- He departed this earthly home in Florida for his permanent home with God.
- She peacefully closed her eyes for rest from this earthly scene, and went to be with her Savior.
- He is finally free of the chains that bound him and is at peace in the halls of heaven.

Obituaries speak of the comfort found in returning to God.

- He accepted the hand of our Lord after facing many challenges.
- She bid this earthly home adieu as her eternal spirit soared heavenward to rest with Jesus and await her reunion with those she left behind.

- She left an old, sickly body of clay, her spirit straightway returned to God who gave it, and her eternal soul began its never-ending rest in the presence of the Lord Jesus Christ.
- Dad left on Easter day and returned to his heavenly Father on the completion of a 63-year mission serving others and exploring the mysteries of life.

"He was cleared for departure and flew west."

— Jacques' obituary

Some of the deceased are not necessarily going to heaven, but are called to another adventure or journey.

- He graduated to his final retirement home.
- She left this world to become a part of the larger universe of beauty and art she loved so well.
- She left to rest with artists in the garden of dreams.
- He went on to the next great adventure; travel safely.
- Her spirit is now free to roam at will.
- He left for the Sky World.
- He decided it was time to go flying with the eagles.
- He quit dying and started to live.
- He departed on his last and longest trip to that undiscovered country from whose bourn no traveler returns.
- He was called home to a happy hunting ground where the sun always shines and there is no pain.

This obituary painted a picture of a spirited woman: "She died in her sleep, in a house that she built as single-handedly as possible. That was her way, in more ways than one. Her truck had a full tank of gas, a full bed of dirt, three water bottles, a rake, and a shovel. She was ready for her next adventure."

> **"Her spirit has joined her husband in an existence free of confusion and full of wonder."**
>
> — *Eva's obituary*

These richly detailed obituaries offer deep insights into the life that ended.

- A golden heart stopped beating and hardworking hands are at rest.
- After shoveling the snow off his front walkway, his heart finally could not keep up with him.
- It turns out cancer is more stubborn than even he was.
- He died due to a heart that couldn't quite keep up with his adventurous spirit.
- The prettiest girl on the beach is now the prettiest girl in heaven.
- Through all her projects she never really embraced the concept of a schedule. Life itself was the only project she ever finished early—the timing uncharacteristically out of her control.
- We lost an outdoorsman, a great protector of public lands, and consummate fly fisher; he was on the river guiding when his heart decided it was tired.
- House lights down, she has left the theater of life and is now sharing ideas, deep conversation, and world-changing creativity with her favorite authors and playwrights.

> **"Clouds parted and the heavens rumbled as the '74 Caprice made its final journey through the pearly gates carrying him into the comfort of God's arms."**
>
> — *Ron's obituary*

Some death announcements make us smile and tell us much, in just a few words, about the departed.

- He has finished telling stories.
- St. Peter stood by the pearly gates awaiting his new arrival and Dan made his way to the gate with a big smile and his arms spread out ready to meet everyone.

- Always an Elvis fan, he is now singing "Hound Dog" with him and making angels smile. Rock on.
- He passed away at home surrounded by his beloved family with a full head of hair and all of his own teeth.
- Waffle House lost a loyal customer.
- He made his last wildly inappropriate and probably sarcastic comment.
- She took off for that pool party in the sky.
- He was killed when he rushed into a burning orphanage to save a group of adorable children. Or maybe not. We all know how he liked to tell stories.
- Montana's fish and elk can rest easy knowing the greatest threat to their longevity is now recreating in heaven.
- She marched through the pearly gates of heaven twirling her batons, sat down at the piano, and played Malagueña.
- The kindest, most selfless person we know is now looking down on us with her new set of wings and a Black Russian in her hands.

"Killed in the line of duty; hold us tight in your arms."

—Jason's obituary

These tributes are touching in their directness.

- Taken away too early, her jarring absence is a devastating insult to our collective sense of fair play—56 years young, tanned in Anguilla in February, stolen in March by a disastrous finger surgery that left MRSA in her system.
- She was fatally injured during a catastrophic airplane crash while performing her duties as a flight nurse.
- He tragically and unexpectedly was lost at sea on or around June 10.
- A Marine has landed at the Pearly Gates. All is well, and Sarge is ready to stand guard.

Some writers are especially eloquent in creatively conveying news of a death.

- His stitch in the rich fabric of human solidarity joins in the warp and weft of the long struggle toward a richer and more interesting humanity.
- He left this earthly home to go tell jokes and seek free meals on God's celestial plane. He was greeted by his son in his tomfoolery of death.
- Oh, by the way—cause of death—his heart stopped.
- Platt's gone. Suddenly. Full moon Sunday morning. Heart….

My interest in the different ways obituary writers find to avoid using "died," led me to write them down in a notepad on my kitchen table as I read the morning newspaper. That list became the seed of this book. So many interesting life stories are captured in obituaries, each one tender in its own way. They make us think about the life of that person, as well as our own. That's why I am sharing them with you. Obituaries such as this one have the power to touch our heart: "He beat the heck out of stage four pancreatic cancer for more than five years and fulfilled his lifelong dream of doing stand-up comedy in the midst of chemo treatment. Even after being diagnosed and being told he had three months to live, he kept practicing medicine, took classes, painted, and wrote music. He also decided he had enough once Alex Trebek died and then he went peacefully."

Celebrating a Life

"His parting leaves a large void; please fill it with remembered joys."

— A. J.'s obituary

Traditional memorial services have long been the expected way to formally and publicly bid farewell to a loved one. Services are usually held in a house of worship or funeral home with scripted prayers. Attendees are invited to the burial or entombment where additional ceremonies are then held. There are numerous options for memorial services, depending on nationality, ethnicity, religion, and local customs.

- There will be a memorial service held at the Housing Authority Recreation room.
- The family will receive friends in the Ladies' Parlor of the church following the memorial service.
- Following the graveside service, there will be a continuation of his going-away party at the public school gym.
- Following interment, the family will receive friends with a meal of consolation back at the synagogue.
- His service will include military honors, a big rig convoy, and a potluck.
- A funeral Mass will be celebrated, and the family invites those who knew her to the golf course after Mass.

> **"There will be a Celebration of Life so just drop by anytime, because there will be no structured service. He would want us to kick back, share some drinks, laughs, and good times that we've all had with him, and celebrate that he's no longer hurting."**
>
> *— Dave's obituary*

Formal memorial services were common before the restrictions brought on by the pandemic. They are increasingly being replaced by other approaches. Obituaries invite mourners to a Celebration of Life, a popular way to memorialize a loved one. What comprises a Celebration of Life is at the discretion of the family. No two are alike.

- There will be a Pig Roast Celebration on the Ranch, BYOB.
- The family will host an End-of-Life Celebration at the barn on the mountain. There will be no mediocre cookies.
- A Celebration of Life will be held, and like all her parties, it will be epic.

> **"We see him in the trees and hear him in the music of our lives."**
>
> *— George's obituary*

Some Celebrations of Life are held in a natural environment, perhaps chosen for its serenity.

- We will meet near the confluence of the Gallatin and Missouri Rivers at her favorite place in the Superstition Mountains.
- Her ashes will be put into Resurrection Bay near the Gulf of Alaska where the puffins that she loved so much roost.
- The family will meet in the spring when the flowers bloom and the blossoms can bid her farewell.
- We will gather under the large tree on the right-hand side of the lane just as it climbs the rise.

Attendees are sometimes asked to wear particular colors.

- Join the family in wearing a touch of Carolina Blue!
- She loved color, so with that in mind, we encourage you to "dress happy" for this occasion.

- Dress comfortably with a splash of pink if you have it.
- Wear an accent of the color red, please no pink. If you knew her, you will understand.

> **"He believed a Hawaiian shirt, shorts, white socks, and Keens were proper attire for any occasion. Please feel free to follow his lead while attending his service."**
>
> — *Alan's obituary*

Families even specify what articles of clothing to wear.

- He was a man of elegance, and the family requests men wear a collar shirt and tie to his Life Celebration.
- Please feel free to dress casually; he hated a suit and tie.
- All attendees of her memorial are encouraged to wear Sunday hats or Fascinators.
- You are encouraged to wear a silly, pop culture T-shirt, as T-shirts were his favorite attire.
- Guests are encouraged to wear their fanciest shoes to her memorial service in honor of her incurable fixation and incomparable passion for footwear.
- He was a cowboy and a sports fan; feel free to dress as he knew you. Boots and jeans, Ducks and Seahawks gear are welcome.

Directives are also provided on what not to wear: "Anyone wearing black will not be admitted to the memorial."

Some color requests serve as small acts of activism that have special significance to the family.

- A memorial service will be held, and the family requests that everyone wear orange in support of ending gun violence.
- Please wear purple in honor and support of all who have suffered from domestic violence. She was shot and killed by her boyfriend.
- Children and children-at-heart are encouraged to wear pink. She was passionate about helping people cope with the effects of domestic violence and addiction issues that touched her life as well.

Families suggest that unusual items to brought to the Celebration of Life.

- A Celebration of Life will be a potluck, and family requests that everyone brings a dish to share and a flashlight or two for something the family has planned.
- Donations of canned goods or school supplies will be accepted at her Celebration of Life.
- There will be a celebration service on his farm with fellowship and conversation. Bring a chair and a dessert to share. The Holy Spirit will already be there.

An unconventional approach was offered by this family: "A Celebration of Life will be held at your own convenient location on Oct. 20, 2019, at noon. She would hope that you will do an unexpected and unsolicited act of kindness in her honor."

Private services are a compromise between full services and no services. Private funeral services range from some type of formal memorial service with invited guests, to only the family remembering the person in a home or restaurant.

- The family will host a private party to toast his newfound freedom.
- A small private viewing was held where her father gave a memorable prayer and blessing for his first daughter.
- In keeping with his expressed wishes, funeral services and burial will be private. Visiting hours are respectfully omitted. Kindly omit flowers.

The family may prefer privacy for a number of reasons. Perhaps it is an untimely death or tragic circumstances: "Services will be by invitation only as the family requests privacy during this difficult time."

> **"She wished for no service and wanted to be cremated and returned to nature."**
>
> — *Tina's obituary*

Not having any service seems to be an increasingly common option, particularly in certain areas of the country including Alaska and the Western states. People may not want the expense of a formal funeral with an expensive casket. Or the deceased may not have belonged to a church and considered religious services unnecessary or even hypocritical.

- In lieu of a service, she asks that you remember her the next time you see a dog running, or hear a small airplane flying overhead, or walk on the beach, or watch a beautiful sunset over the ocean.
- It was her wish not to have a funeral service. She will be cremated and have her ashes scattered at places that had significance in her life. She wanted no tears, and her family encourages everyone who knew her to find their own favorite memory and spend a moment remembering her life with a smile.
- Although there will be no public services, taking some of your time to say a prayer for her or thinking a kind thought about her would be wonderful.

This woman shows consideration for her mourners: "At her very specific instructions, there will be no visitation or funeral service. What she wanted was a Celebration of Life scheduled not to conflict with anybody's football game."

Here's a unique reason: "There will be no services since his wife refused to honor his request to have him standing in the corner of the room with a vodka tonic in his hand so that he would appear natural to visitors."

> **"A traditional New Orleans Second Line will start at the Moon Walk in the French Quarter riverfront and end at the Boondock Saint."**
>
> — *Andrew's obituary*

Deeply personal, often unique, tributes to the deceased honor their wishes or reflect their interests.

- His Celebration of Life will start with a ski day at the resort. Participants are asked to meet at the bottom of the Six Pack Trail.
- Her ashes will be placed next to those of her husband near their former home. She asked that a bagpiper play at the ceremony.
- There will be a four-day viewing on the Reservation.
- The family and close friends will parade at noon from his residence through the community with a horse-drawn cortege.
- A Tlingit 40-Day Party will be held and a Tlingit Potlatch with an exact date to be determined. *(The potlatch is a culmination of funeral rituals and ceremonies, practiced among indigenous groups of the Northwest, with the finale being a feast.)*
- There will be a memorial service/art show reception in his honor. There, showing of his art will include a silent auction of some of his works to benefit his son.

Here's a one-of-a-kind service: "His ashes will be scattered over the grave of James Tiberius Kirk on Viridion 3." *(In the Star Trek series, Kirk is a fictional starship captain and Viridion 3 is an uninhabited planet.)*

This obituary told of a practice both old and new. It is the natural process of birth, growth, death, and rebirth, returning a body to the land to nourish new life: "She will be buried in a natural burial cemetery overlooking a river, and a tree will be planted at her resting place."

This might be the most morbid and direct request I've seen, as written by the deceased: "I was sent as life's gift to death with my first and final hug from the Grim Reaper. At the ripe age of 75, I refuse a funeral and the flood of tears. Rather, I request an informal gathering so you can feed me to the fish at 3 p.m. If you're late, too bad. Once I'm with the fishes, I start my new adventures with my mom and my dad. I will also be joining my brothers in causing havoc around the world. I love you all and will see you on the other side."

Finally, this family covered it all with loving humor: "A celebration of his life, with Joe laid out in all his glory, will be held. A light dinner will be served as Joe felt no get-together was complete without food. None of his leftovers or kitchen concoctions will be pawned off on any unsuspecting guests. Feel free to be as late as you'd like as Joe was never on time for anything because of his napping habits. Joe despised formality and stuffiness and would really be ticked off if you showed up in a suit. Dress comfortably. The family encourages you to don the most inappropriate T-shirt that you are comfortable being seen in public with, as Joe often did. Joe faced his death and his mortality, as he did his life, face on, often telling us that when he dropped dead to dig a hole in the back yard and just roll him in. Much to his disappointment, he will be properly interred with full military honors next to his wife. Sorry, Mom, we did the best we could to take care of him and keep him out of your hair as long as we could. Back in your court now."

Memorial Tributes

> **"She would want us to be moved by the glory of nature and remarkable sunsets, listen to Motown and beach music, embrace moments of calm and peace, love each other with all our hearts, and never take ourselves too seriously."**
>
> — *Beverly's obituary*

When a person dies, it is customary for mourners to honor them in some manner. The family has unlimited freedom to decide how to memorialize their loved one, and usually include their preferences in the obituary.

Floral arrangements are the most traditional way to show respect. They are sent for display to the funeral home or church. This family shared the appropriateness of floral bouquets: "Send flowers. It would make her happy." Other families had specific requests: "If you would like to send flowers, she loves orchids and lilies. Calla lily is her favorite." These thrifty or pragmatic loved ones wanted more permanence than soon-to-wilt flowers: "In lieu of flowers, we ask instead for living plants." One obituary offered a generous option: "She loved flowers, so get some in her honor for someone you love."

Recently I have read more requests like these: "Flowers are gratefully declined," and "For religious reasons, the family respectfully requests that no flowers be sent."

Some obituaries share a need for financial assistance and ask that money be sent to the family.

- A memorial fund has been established for Joe's grandchildren.
- She had planned on passing down her life savings to her grandchildren; however, her savings were depleted due to her medical expenses and care. The family suggests making donations to the bank to benefit her grandkids.

Donations may also be requested to help with expenses.

- Friends and family are asked to extend the gratitude of monetary gifts to offset the cost of laying him to rest.
- Memorials are suggested to the family for a future designation.
- A small donation in her memory would be appreciated in order to help with the funeral arrangements. Envelopes will be available at the funeral home.

> **"In her honor, loved ones are asked for donations to benefit migrant youth."**
>
> — *Phyllis's obituary*

Requests for charitable donations to specific causes are selected because the work of these organizations held special meaning to the deceased or their family.

- Because he loved dogs so much, contributions can be made in his name to any organization that benefits dogs.
- Her family asks that you consider a contribution in her memory to an organization committed to promoting social and economic justice.
- As a testament to his fearless defense of civil rights for 50 years, contributions may be made to the American Civil Liberties Union.
- The family requests that donations be made to a social cause close to his heart—American Veterans for Equal Rights, focused on equal rights for current and former LGBT military personnel.

> **"The family asks that you make a donation to the Animal Humane Society, as he always liked animals best (except, perhaps, his foul-mouthed parrot with whom he had a love/hate relationship for 40 years."**
>
> —*Albert's obituary*

Contributions to more unusual organizations reflect particular passions: The National Fragile X Foundation, Girls in Tech, Wild Salmon Defenders Alliance, Reel Recovery, Defenders of Wildlife, and The National Fallen Firefighters Foundation.

- Please donate to his foundation to provide tennis lessons and supplies to underprivileged children.
- Please donate money to help her daughter sew dresses for little girls in third-world countries.
- Send donations to help exploited street children in India.
- She requested that backpacks, filled with school supplies, be donated to local schools.
- Donations may be made in her fur baby's name to Kitty Connection.
- Please donate to the ACLU to support its ongoing fight for an open society and opportunities for new immigrants.
- To honor her, money is requested to repair the church in Corfu.

Families increasingly request non-monetary tributes: donating blood, becoming an organ donor, showing love to your family, writing a great postcard to your loved ones, spending some time creating memories, toasting the preciousness of your friends, hugging your children every chance you get, extending grace to someone in your life, and performing an unexpected and unsolicited act of kindness for some unfortunate soul.

> **"He would like you to go plant some flowers and put up a bird feeder in your yard."**
>
> — *David's obituary*

The healing power of nature probably prompts these tributes to the deceased: plant a garden, enjoy the beauty in nature, watch the sun set, and dance in the rain.

- Plant a tree to commemorate all the ones he cut down during his 80 years, since his favorite toy was his chainsaw.
- On the occasion a beautiful and vibrant flower catches your eye may you think of her. Picture her admiring its beauty, smiling, picking it to pin in her hair. She'd love that.
- Take a walk on the beach with a litter bag, an activity she enjoyed all her life.

Some families want mourners to be inspired to find their own rewards: playing your favorite jazz record; hoisting a pint; reading an engaging yet obscure anthropological history; enjoying your life as you receive it each day; sleeping in your recliner; working a jigsaw puzzle; and jumping up, getting outside, stretching to the sky, and enjoying your life.

One obituary included this reminder: "Oysters and champagne or guacamole and margaritas should be part of any celebration."

> **"We ask that you honor him by smiling and laughing through the pain, make amends, be tolerant, and be a better friend. All the things he possessed."**
>
> — *Tim's obituary*

Obituaries suggest ways to honor the deceased by doing something to better the world: consider doing an act of kindness for another person and let them know how much they are loved, pick up garbage without judgment, thank a veteran for their service, give someone a book, use a re-usable cup, adopt a pet and shower it with love, and perform an unexpected act of kindness on a beautiful, sunshiny day.

Some families ask that the bereaved honor their loved ones by bettering themselves: pray for compassion and try to understand those suffering from mental illness and addiction, read a good book and share it, volunteer your time, just lose 10 pounds because she knew life was better lived thin.

This request covers a lot of righteous ground: "If you'd like to honor his good life, just live your values, grow as you age, listen more than you speak, consider all sides, love your people unconditionally, show up, pave the way, come to the table with a plan, and do good for those who need it most."

> **"His family honors his memory with an award given at his college for the 'Most Talented Undergrad with the Worst GPA.'"**
>
> — *Alexander's obituary*

Some final requests are unique.

- Go buy a couple of flashlights.
- In lieu of flowers, the family prefers that you play the Mass State Lottery (MegaBucks Doubler was his favorite; his birthday was 8-18-28) and split any winnings with his grandchildren's college fund.
- The family requests donations be made to her memorial fund; proceeds will assist her mom as she travels back to Laos after the funeral.

This family's request probably captures, in the end, what we all wish for: "Mom didn't want any flowers, or cards, or gifts. She just wanted assurance that people knew her, loved her, and cared that she lived."

Expressions of Appreciation

In an obituary families often express their appreciation for those who helped care for their loved one.

- The family thanks the many wonderful people who guaranteed her comfort, dignity, perspective, shopping, coffee, and desserts.
- Special thanks go out to his wife for adding care and spark to his later years. Phone calls and many breakfast visits by his friends were all a cheer to his heart during his last weeks.
- We wish to thank all of you who have reached out to us with visits, food, calls, and flowers. Your love, hugs, and words have been needed and greatly appreciated.

Often the deceased has been in the care of medical professionals.

- All the staff at the cancer center really helped make this unfortunate, #$^%#& illness more tolerable, and the support made all the difference to the family.
- The loving healthcare providers made the seemingly unbearable conquerable.
- Her family is extremely grateful to the hospital staff for helping

them cope with this sad outcome.

- The family thanks the amazing staff and chaplain for their attentive care for both our mother and our family.
- We wish to express our overwhelming gratitude to our hospital family. Without you we never would have made it this far.
- Special thanks to her doctor for always making her laugh. She called him "Mi doctor bonito."

Church members offer comfort when it is needed most.

- Our gratitude is beyond words for the people of her church. The life-giving love they shared with her and her family for decades was the foundation of her work in the world. Their full inclusion of her and recognition of her at all times as a child of God is a witness to what and who matters.
- His family is grateful to his church family, which were dear to his heart. They were faithful and tireless in the care of his family while navigating through years of agony in cancer's devastation.

> **"The family extends special thanks to her extraordinary team of caregivers. Those remarkable women made it possible for her to remain in her own home and face the challenges of aging, illness, and dying with comfort and dignity."**
>
> — *Sunny's obituary*

Caregivers help ease the burden of illness and provide comfort near a journey's end.

- Thank you to the caregivers of "Miss Fancy Pants," who made sure she never came to dinner without her lipstick on.
- The family wishes to thank hospice for their care, their continuing compassion, and their amazing ability to make this grievous event manageable.
- A special thanks to his nurse for her loving kindness and care for our dad. Here's to unsung angels such as you.
- Many thanks to volunteers at Meals on Wheels who took the time to have a chat when they delivered her dinner.

- We are deeply grateful to the dedicated and kind staff and also the angels at hospice for their sweet care of her and their valiant efforts to ease the distress and anxiety Alzheimer's disease caused her and her family.

> **"The family thanks the many members of the staff who for over five years gave her the best of their skills, care, love, and affection. Their professionalism and outstanding attention to her will always be remembered."**
>
> — *Consie's obituary*

People may live in care facilities near the end.

- Her family wants to thank and express their profound gratitude to the incredible nursing staff for their compassionate care during her final days. Considering her 40 years of nursing care for others, it is good to see that some things in life do come full circle.
- The family would like to thank the staff for their extraordinary care and unwavering commitment to her grace and dignity.

> **"Please consider a donation to the Rescue Squad. Every time Esther had fallen and couldn't get up by herself they very graciously picked her up with a welcome combination of professionalism and compassion."**
>
> — *Esther's obituary*

Often help comes from personnel in various community agencies.

- Her family extends a special thank you to the police department, whose officers went above and beyond the call to comfort her, even during their off-duty hours.
- Our profound thanks go out to the paramedics and firefighters that worked so valiantly to revive her.
- His family wants to thank the kind, diligent, and hard-working police department, Marine unit, and fire department for the search for and recovery of his body from the lake.

Some words of appreciation are unusual, but especially meaningful to the family.

- The family would like to extend a special thank you to all who worked so tirelessly to prepare the burial site.
- We would like to thank the coroner's office for positively identifying his body, as this gave us the closure we needed to move forward. And finally, we would like to thank the cremation center for their kind and respectful handling of his remains.

> **"Our mother felt the love and kindness you all shared with her, her dog, and her 100 incredible hats. We, her 10 children, thank you for the smiles, hugs, laughter, tears, rodeos, ball games, music shows, compassion, and understanding you extended to her. Our wish is that all our journeys in life be as rich and full as hers."**
>
> — *Trilby's Obituary*

Some families are just plain grateful.

- We were the recipients of many miracles and tender mercies, and recognize they came about from the righteous desires of your hearts.
- Thank you to everyone who touched his life; he believed that it is the people we know who make the lives we live so meaningful.
- We would like to thank the nurses, hospice home care team, and our friends and our family for taking part in his journey and allowing him to experience dying with stateliness and grace.
- In her last days she was surrounded by her family, loving caregivers, and a motley crew of beloved characters only she could assemble.

In the end, solace may be found in the most unusual ways: "The ones closest to her during the past year were a pair of ravens who visited her on her third story apartment deck on a daily basis. They gave her great pleasure and reflected the sanctity of her connection to nature and all of its creatures."

Reading these notes of thanks was comforting. The dying are treated with respect and compassion on the final leg of their journey. This expression of gratitude sums it up: "After his stroke, although he could not verbally communicate, he kissed the hands of his caregivers as a way to show his love and appreciation (or perhaps to persuade them to remove the many tubes so he could climb out of bed and escape!)."

A Closing Thought

There are innumerable stories between birth and death, the bookends of our lives. It is these stories that inspired me to write this book, for each one leaves us lessons. Obituaries are the ideal medium to make them known and remembered.

For me, reading obituaries is a treasure hunt. You never know what you will find. Who could invent the astonishing things one learns about another person in their obituary? These slices of life remind us of the humor, unexpectedness, and wisdom to be appreciated in every person. Reading them is cathartic. Compiling these "treasures" has been my privilege.

It became apparent to me that each person's specific story has a universal component that speaks to us. Obituaries reveal our shared need for love, our delight in others, our passion for work, the pleasures we enjoy, and our struggle with inevitable trials. How we uniquely find our way to embrace life's opportunities and manage its challenges is the story and legacy of our life.

A lesson I learned from this research is to make the most of each day. The words "unexpectedly" and "suddenly" describe the death in an uncomfortable number of obituaries. Avoid the mistake made by this man who wrote an online condolence note filled with regret: "I drove by Wayne's house every day on the way to my house. We were neighbors, but never got a chance to really know each other. After reading his beautiful obituary, I am sad that it never happened. I will feel the loss as I continue to drive by his home." Don't wait to reach out to a friend, relative, or even a stranger.

Another lesson I learned is that there is an urgency in celebrating life just because it is so finite: "Our daughter was sunshine. Quite honestly, we do not know how we will go on without her long hugs, her bright smile, and her boundless compassion. We only know that we must try, like her, to live life consciously. To hike and ski and dance and notice the beauty around us while doing it. To say 'yes' to every opportunity to enjoy this precious life. To take the time to enjoy the sunrises and sunsets that are offered each day, to look for the best in people, and truly love each other deeply with joy and not dwell on our faults. She would want us to linger in the mountains, at the beach, in the woods, by the campfire, and on the dance floor. To honor her and her life, we will." Remember you are alive, and it is your daily gift to delight in this experience.

While writing this book, I noted a personal change in my outlook on death. I received medical news that could have had dire consequences. Instead of panicking and thinking, "Why me?" I remembered the thousands of obituaries I had read. Thinking of those people, I asked, "Why was it them?" This perspective truly lessened my anxiety. When I received good news, of course I was relieved. A reprieve. But I think the truth of mortality, including mine, was made more real to me during this project. It had been their turn. Someday it will be my turn.

Death is an inevitable ending, an inescapable fate, and the price of a life. We are gone. But our stories endure.

Appendix A

Describing Your Loved One

Most obituaries share some of the personality traits that defined the deceased. This is the longest list I came across in one obituary.

> "He was a complex man and, depending on who was describing him, one might hear any of the following: young-at-heart, cantankerous, witty, informative, challenging, kind, bawdy, strong-willed, savvy, prankster, political wonk, raconteur, provocative, empowering, observant, dynamic, larger-than-life, impatient, handsome, powerful, engaging, supportive, loving, magnetic, passionate, interesting, full of life, smart, blunt, and an awesome sense of humor."
>
> *— Jerome's obituary*

This appendix is intended to help obituary writers. This list is compiled from the thousands of obituaries I read for this project. I hope reading these traits prompts the writer to remember the fullness and complexity of their loved one's personality.

Most traits in the women's or men's columns can be used for either sex. Interestingly though, some traits do seem more applicable to one sex. I don't think a man would be described as feisty, tiny, beautiful, captivating, dazzling, exquisite, mischievous, or innocent. Women might not be portrayed as dashing, goofy, stern, ornery, or a natty dresser. But it's up to you!

Women

accepting	effervescent	indomitable
advocate	energetic	innocent
ageless	ethical	intellectual
ahead of her time	exquisite	intense
altruistic	fashionable	intentional
amazing	feisty	iron willed
amusing	ferocious	irrepressible
articulate	fierce	irreverent
artistic	force of nature	joie de vivre
astute	forgiving	joyful
authentic	formidable	magnetic
beautiful	forward thinker	million-dollar smile
beloved	free spirited	mischievous
brave	genial	multifaceted
bright	genteel	noble
candid	gift of gab	open minded
captivating	giving	openness to all
clarity of purpose	good natured	opinionated
classic	good sense	passion for life
competent	good spirit	passionate
critical insights	green thumb	patience
dance loving	gullible	penny pinching
dazzling	happy spirit	perseverance
delightful	headstrong	persistent
devout	health conscious	playful
dignified	high expectations	plucky
disarming	honest	poised
direct	impetuous	positive
disciplined	incisive	practical
dynamic	indispensable	prim

Women (cont'd)

protective

proud

radiant

refined

regal

relentless

remarkable

resilient

ribald

sarcastic

sassy

self-deprecating

self-reliant

shy

social

solid

smart-mouthed

socially conscious

sophisticated

spirited

spry wit

spunky

statuesque

stubborn

stylish

subtle

sweet

talented

tall

tenacious

tender

tiny

tough

tough as nails

treasured

true

unassuming

unconditional love

understanding

unique

unmistakable spark

unstoppable spirit

vibrant

virtuous

vivacious

voracious reader

welcoming

willful

wry sense of humor

zest for life

Men

accomplished
affable nature
athletic
benevolent
bon vivant
brusque
cheerful
colorful
commanding
committed
common sense
concerned
congenial
cranky
cynical
daring
dashing
decent
discerning
distinguished
doting
driven
ebullient
eccentric
enormous stature
erudite
exacting
exhausting
faithful

firm handshake
fortitude
free thinking
friendly
genuine
goofy
great spirit for life
gregarious
handsome
iconic
immense strength
inclusive
infectious smile
inspiring
integrity
intrepid
light hearted
marvelous
meticulous
moral
natty dresser
objective
opinionated
original
ornery
outspoken
precise
prescient
principled

private
profound
prominent
rock of the family
romantic
scholarly
sentimental
short tempered
singular
sly wit
soft spoken
steadfast
stern
stoic
storyteller
strategist
strength
supportive
sympathetic
taste for adventure
trusted
unassuming
unbridled curiosity
uncompromising
unflappable
unpretentious
visionary
wanderer
wily

Both Women and Men

active	funny	quiet
adored	generous	radiant
adventurous	gentle	reserved
affectionate	graceful	respectful
beautiful blue eyes	gracious	selfless
big hearted	gritty	sense of humor
brilliant	hardworking	sharp intellect
caring	humble	sincere
charismatic	humorous	singular
charitable	independent	smart
charming	infectious laugh	social grace
classy	insightful	sparkling
compassionate	intellectual	strong
competitive	intelligent	strong-willed
complex	interesting	thoughtful
confident	irreplaceable	tolerant
courageous	irreverent	twinkling eyes
creative	keen mind	upbeat
curious	kind	warm
dependable	loving	wise
determined	loyal	witty
devoted	magical	wonderful
elegant	modest	worldly
empathetic	optimistic	
engaging	outrageous	
enthusiastic	patient	
exuberant	polite	
fearless	polymath	
fun	quick-witted	

Each person is a unique blend of many traits. To do justice to your loved one, be as precise as possible in your choice of words. Capture those specific qualities that made them who they were. This eloquent obituary showed a woman who was more than funny and thoughtful: "She was riotously funny, deeply thoughtful, and steadfastly authentic. She was a born entertainer who delighted friends with her impeccable imitations." A well loved daughter, a well written tribute.

Appendix B

Nicknames

> **"He was a gregarious mixologist and literally and proudly wore his nickname 'The Vest.' Receiving over 300 vests from bar patrons, he would choose a different one to wear each night, delighting his customers with the choice."**
>
> — *Nicholas' obituary*

While reading thousands of obituaries, I spotted many unusual nicknames and started a list. The list became longer and longer. This is the result.

Nicknames can cleverly capture some aspect of a person.

- He was known as "Bam-Bam" by many because he was the guy that would break just about anything placed in front of him.
- He was known as "Talk-a-Lot" because of his long entertaining stories which he loved to repeat often.
- "Icehouse" was always willing to impart his knowledge about some little known historical fact about an icehouse, which earned him the nickname.
- He made lifelong friends in college who bestowed upon him the nickname "Doc" in tribute to his knowledge of all things, true or not.
- He was affectionately known as "Tom the Toter" since he was always toting something around for someone else.

Some people are anointed with an enduring nickname early in life.

- He entered the world as a mere "Speck," a nickname given to him by the nurses at the hospital. He was only four-and-a-half pounds.
- She weighed only five pounds at birth and remained tiny, earning the nickname "Peanut."
- Her father nicknamed her "Cricket" while listening to her first vocal sounds, and that was her name for the rest of her life.
- He weighed 11 pounds, 13 ounces at birth, and was quickly nicknamed "Chubby Cheeks."
- She earned her nickname "Chatty Natty" because no matter who you were, she could find something to talk about and she would find a way to make you see it from a different perspective, even if you were reluctant to do so!

- He was coined "Peace Punk" in his school days.
- Her nickname "Pinky" was created when a neighbor viewed her in an outfit in pink made by her mother.
- His nickname "Moose" came about during his high school sports days.
- "Hawky," originally "Hawkeye," was a nickname given to him in grammar school. It was bestowed upon him because he was known to challenge a situation and to never be fooled. Later in life the nickname appropriated itself to his athletic prowess.
- He was so avid a reader as a child that his nickname was "Dictionary."
- Even though he was six feet tall, everyone called him "Pee Wee," which he hated. That was his nickname since he was a little tyke and it just stuck.
- He earned the nickname "Chick" in high school because of the family's chicken business.
- He came into the world during a tornado earning him the nickname "Twister," and he definitely lived his life like a tornado—wild and free.

> "When she was a child, her father often sang the song "Little Sally Walker" to her. She loved the song so her family began calling her "Sally," and she was known by that nickname her entire life."
>
> — *Mary's obituary*

Many family members have nicknames for each other: "His greatest treasures were his six wonderful children. He gave each one their own special nickname."

- She earned the nickname "Sarge" for teaching her children a strong work ethic through a long list of chores.
- His grandchildren will always remember him lovingly as "Trebor"—his name spelled backwards.
- Her protective dedication to her children earned her the nickname "Mamma Bear."
- She was given the nickname "Honey" by her grandson, because she was as sweet as honey.

- She received her nickname when she was born. Her Great Aunt looked at her and said, "Oh what an itsy, bitsy baby." "Bitsy" stuck.
- She was a fighter and earned the nickname "Ol' Stubborn" from her family.
- She was lovingly nicknamed "Loafer" years ago by her husband.
- Many have characterized him as an angel, which is not surprising since his family nickname has been "Star Child" for many years.
- Her greatest joy was spending time with her husband, whom she nicknamed "Daddy."
- He enjoyed cooking for friends and family and created his own recipe for hotcakes and homemade syrup. This is how he gained the nickname "Hotcake."

> **"If you didn't know "Rowdy" when you walked in a bar, you certainly did by the time you left. He awarded everyone a nickname. Just ask "Sniffer," "Sappo," "Ronny 2-Motors," "Bird," "Weenie," "Stud," or "Tramp." You know who you are."**
>
> — *Roger's obituary*

Some people have a knack for making up nicknames.

- If you were around him, you could not save yourself from having a nickname, which he had a habit of christening you, whether you knew it or not.
- He found humor in giving each of his family and friends a special nickname. It was a sign of dear affection.
- He fondly gave each grandchild a unique nickname that made them feel especially close to their grandpa.

> **"He was especially fond of organic gardening,
> earning himself the nickname "Mulch King."**
>
> — *Carey's obituary*

A person's interests or abilities can lead to an appropriate nickname.

- He was nicknamed "Go-To" for his ability to fix virtually anything.
- In her younger years, she was infamous for spending summers processing fruits and vegetables, earning her the nickname of the "Pickle Queen."
- His love of fishing earned him the name "Catfish."
- His skills at basketball and bocce ball earned him the nickname "Magic Hands" among the Special Olympics community.
- His legendary ability to catch salmon earned him the nickname "Sure Shot."

> **"He was given the nickname "Ajax" by his co-workers so
> he would not be confused with another driver with the
> same first name, and it stuck for the rest of his life."**
>
> —*Jack's obituary*

Sometimes a workplace reputation leads to a nickname: "While on the job, he was a hard worker and a jokester who provided all of his co-workers and friends with a nickname—perhaps for something stupid they had done."

- He had a legal career befitting his nickname "Legal Eagle."
- He was nicknamed "Big Al the Kiddies' Pal" by his co-workers due to his gentle nature.
- He was lovingly nicknamed "Grizz" at work because he was as big and ornery as a grizzly bear when people didn't do their jobs!
- His years of influence as a federal marshal resulted in his fellow marshals giving him the nickname "M.O.U." or "Marshal of the Universe."
- He received his nickname "Peaches" because he was a forklift driver in Mexico and always eating a peach.

- Although his nickname at the firehouse was "Grumpy," he always had a smile on his face and a joke on his lips.
- He worked as a delivery boy and eventually wound up behind the meat counter, where he was promptly nicknamed "Butch."

> **"He was a Mafia captain whose work as an FBI informant helped the organization take down three mob bosses, and earned him the nickname "Fat Rat."**
>
> — *Ronald's obituary*

Other nicknames have unusual beginnings.

- She loved to tell people she was a beauty queen, earning her the nickname "Queenie."
- His nickname "Chocolate" came about when a girl thought he was the Cuban boxer Kid Chocolate. He was married eight times and had nine children.
- He invented a tomato-planting machine that earned him the nickname "Tomato King" and made him a fortune.

> **"One of his nicknames was "High Pockets" due to his 6 foot 6 inches height and slender build."**
>
> — *Bill's obituary*

Physical attributes can prompt a nickname.

- In 1977, the local newspaper chose him as one of the best-dressed men and even earned him the nickname "The Silver Fox," as he would be recognized strolling down the street.
- He was very good looking, earning him the nickname "Gorgeous George." His wife was his "Precious Plum."

Nicknames cleverly capture the traits of the unusual cast of characters who make the world an interesting place. These are some of the nicknames gleaned from thousands of obituaries.

Abbott	Brown Buns	Dinky
Ace	Bubbles	Dreadnaughts
Aristotle	Bubby	Duck
Backslider	Buck	Duke
Bahroo	Buddy	Dynamite
Bam Bam	Buggy	El Rey (The King)
Bammer	Bull	Fat Rat
Barney	Bum	Firecracker
Barney Rubble	Bunky	Flathead
Beanpole	Bus	The Flounder
Beefy	Butch	Flower Man
Beezer	Catfish	Fly
Beto	Chainsaw	Foxy
Bibbs	Chatty Natty	Gerdie
Bibby	Chick	Gino
Big	Chicken	Glamour Girl
Big Al	Chickie	Goose
Big Daddy	Chilly	Grouchy
Biggin	Cookie	Guppy
Bing	Cookie Crumb	Hammer
Bird	Cool	Hard
Bock	Crash	Hawky
Boo Boo	Cupcake	Honey
Boodee	Dali	Hootie
Bookie	Dancing Bear	Hotts
Boots	Deter	Hut
Bootsie	Dime Bag	Iron Man
Boxer	Dink	Jiggs

Jolly
Juggy
Kitty
Kraze
Lala
Lean Dog
Legal Eagle
Little Reb
Little Ruby
Loafer
Lurid Lee
Macho
Mama Bear
Mims
Mocha
Money
Moo Moo
Moon Shooter
Moondi
Mudder
Nek-Bone Blues
Oats Ole Buddy
Ol' Stubborn
Ornery
Oyster
Papa Smurf
Peaches
Peanut
Peewee
Pep
Pinky
Pistol

Pocket
Pooh
Poor Tiny
Poss
Pow Wow
Punkin
Rabbit
Rawhide
Rebel
Red
Regal
River Jim
Rosebud
Santa
Sarge
Scooter
Shorty
Shotsie
Silver Fox
Skeeter
Skip
Smoke
Snarky
Sonny
Sparky
Speck
Sport
Spud
Squeaky
Star Child
Stringbean
Stub

Stumpy
Sunshine
Taurus the Bull
Teddy Bear
Tib
Toad
Tootie
Toots
Tutti-frutti
Wild Bill
Wildcat
Woody

Made in the USA
Middletown, DE
13 November 2021